Big Things Start Small

Big Things Start Small

How Small Groups Helped Ignite Christianity's Greatest Spiritual Awakenings

Joe M. Easterling

WIPF & STOCK · Eugene, Oregon

BIG THINGS START SMALL
How Small Groups Helped Ignite Christianity's Greatest Spiritual Awakenings

Copyright © 2021 Joe M. Easterling. All rights reserved. Except for brief quotations in critical publications or reviews, no part of this book may be reproduced in any manner without prior written permission from the publisher. Write: Permissions, Wipf and Stock Publishers, 199 W. 8th Ave., Suite 3, Eugene, OR 97401.

Wipf & Stock
An Imprint of Wipf and Stock Publishers
199 W. 8th Ave., Suite 3
Eugene, OR 97401

www.wipfandstock.com

PAPERBACK ISBN: 978-1-6667-1285-8
HARDCOVER ISBN: 978-1-6667-1286-5
EBOOK ISBN: 978-1-6667-1287-2

11/23/21

Scripture taken from the New King James Version®. Copyright © 1982 by Thomas Nelson. Used by permission. All rights reserved.

I dedicate this, my first book, to my first and greatest love, the Lord Jesus Christ.

Soli Deo Gloria!

Contents

List of Tables | viii
Acknowledgments | ix
Abbreviations | xi

Introduction | 1

Chapter 1: Small Groups in Scripture and Early Christianity | 7

Chapter 2: Small Groups during the Rumblings of Reformation | 31

Chapter 3: Small Groups in the First Great Awakening (1726–1791) | 44

Chapter 4: Small Groups in the Second Great Awakening (1780–1850) | 68

Chapter 5: Small Groups in the Layman's, Welsh, and Korean Revivals (1857–1910) | 100

Chapter 6: Small Groups in the Mid-Century Revival (1949–1979) | 136

Epilogue: How Small Groups Can Help Ignite the Flames of Revival Again | 163

Bibliography | 175

List of Tables

Table 1: Key Observations of the Catalytic Small Groups during the First Great Awakening (1726–91) | 67

Table 2: Key Observations of the Catalytic Small Groups during the Second Great Awakening (1780–1850) | 99

Table 3: Key Observations of the Catalytic Small Groups during the Layman's, Welsh, and Korean Revivals (1857–1910) | 135

Table 4: Key Observations of the Catalytic Small Groups during the Mid-Century Revival (1949–79) | 162

Table 5: A Summary of the Key Observations of the Catalytic Small Groups during Christianity's Four Major Awakenings | 171

Acknowledgments

THE PUBLICATION OF MY first book is a dream come true—a dream not limited to just one person. Anybody who has ever had a book published knows full well that they did not run this race alone. With the completion of this book and the conclusion of a second doctorate from which this study derived, I am all too aware of the many who sacrificed greatly to help me along the journey. To them all, I offer my most humble and heartfelt gratitude.

Above all, I wish to give thanks to my Lord and Savior Jesus Christ. His grace has flowed over me for the past thirty-seven years, without which I would still be lost, in my sins, and bound for an endless hell. It is this same unending grace that has called and equipped me to fervently serve him, even leading to this joyful accomplishment. Considering all he has done for me, I only ask that he take whatever I have and use it to advance his kingdom and glorify his holy name.

To my amazing bride, Anne, who deserves as much credit as myself, thank you for going the distance with me—putting up with the late nights, the added expenses, and the weeks away from home. Without you by my side, I would never have left the starting line. You are and will always be my ACE! To my two sweet girls, Noelle and Moriah, who have spent almost their entire childhood with me in school, thank you for encouraging me and especially for tolerating me when I was not always easy to live with. Know that I am far prouder of being your dad than I could ever be of writing any book! To my wonderful parents, words can never express how proud I am to be your son. Especially to Dad, who passed about a year before this book was released, I only wish you could have been here for this.

To my church, Northside, and my pastor, Kenny Chinn, thank you for your undying support and incredible sacrifice on my behalf during this long

ACKNOWLEDGMENTS

journey. There is no way I can ever repay you for all you have given over the years to make this happen—the months of time granted for me to work on this project, the encouragement to keep going when things got incredibly busy at church, and even the light-spirited jesting to keep me humble. I only hope to make you as proud of me as I am of you!

To my colleagues at Liberty University, thank you for making my time with you unforgettable. I not only gained an immense amount of invaluable training among the world's greatest Christian scholars, I also gained lifelong friendships with some truly brilliant brothers and sisters in Christ.

Abbreviations

ANF   *Ante-Nicene Fathers*
OED   *Oxford English Dictionary*
DCA   *Dictionary of Christianity in America*

Introduction

WE NEED A REVIVAL. While this statement has been declared so often over the years many dismiss it as a quintessential example of a cliché, the statement is true nonetheless—and no more relevant than now. As I am writing these words, our world is writhing in the grip of a pandemic that has killed millions and left the rest of us suffocating under face masks, separated from each other, and simmering under quarantine. Our nation is being ripped apart by assaults coming from an array of deceptive and divisive "causes." Our churches are no longer in a decline but a deep dive, hemorrhaging nearly 4 percent of American adults from membership records each year over the past two decades. So severe is this tumble, Gallup reports that, while American church membership had remained generally steady at 70 percent from the 1930s through the 1990s, this number has dropped precipitously since 2000 and fell to 47 percent in 2020, dropping below 50 percent for the first time since Gallup began measuring the data eight decades earlier.[1] As cliché as it may seem, these chronic symptoms of spiritual and societal deterioration are the reasons for the rising and desperate plea for revival.

But there is good news. History suggests that worldwide spiritual awakenings usually come in the midst of such dark times as these. Revivals seem to accompany a global crisis, be it war, economic depression, or a pandemic. They often emerge out of deep societal division, such as periods leading up to the American Revolution, the Civil War, or the Vietnam protests. Plus, major spiritual awakenings almost always rise out of a time of deep spiritual apathy and a distaste for the things of God. In short, while

---

1. Jones, "U.S. Church Membership."

we need revival today, it was during times much like today that God's Spirit brought such a greatly needed awakening.

In truth, spiritual awakenings have been one of the most mysterious, profound, and studied phenomena in human history. After generations of researchers producing scores of works on revivals, they still remain enigmatic in many ways. One of the most elusive elements of Christianity's spiritual awakenings is how these revivals erupted in the first place. From the beginning, we must admit that true spiritual awakenings cannot be manufactured, and certainly not by any human-made external agent. They are first and foremost initiated by God alone and embraced by his children in repentance from sin and a renewed dependence upon the Holy Spirit. Nevertheless, history suggests that spiritual awakenings consistently emerged when, at the time, certain conditions were met both in the hearts of individual Christians and in the dynamics of the church as a whole. Based upon the historical data, a number of theories as to what may have prompted these revivals have been proposed—a charismatic leader, a repentant parish, and societal circumstances to name a few. What appears not to have been emphasized as a major catalyst for revival is the role of small groups in these awakenings.

To be sure, small groups have played an indispensable role in the Christian church, starting with its formation, continuing with its preservation, and ultimately its permeation to "the end of the earth" (Acts 1:8). Even since the days of Moses, different types of small groups have been employed to govern God's people and convey God's message. Further, while in Christ's earthly ministry he often engaged large crowds, the lion's share of Jesus' work was done with a small group of disciples who became the direct beneficiaries of his teaching and example. As a result, the first-century Christian church was typically comprised not of a large congregation but of small clusters of believers meeting in private homes for teaching, fellowship, and ministry. Even after the church became more established and moved to larger venues, the small group concept was never abandoned, but became the model for monasticism used for the development of future clergy. Thus, throughout the history of the Christian faith, some type of small group strategy has always been present and has played an integral part in the discipling of believers and the growth of the church.

Small groups have been well-chronicled in historical records concerning Christianity's spiritual awakenings as well, especially those that spread globally and across decades of time. Yet despite their notice, small groups do not appear to have been given the credit they deserve in the study of these major revivals. This is not to say that small groups have been deprived of notoriety altogether, for they certainly have not. Even in recent years, a litany of excellent works have been made available to offer reasons for, and strategies on, how to employ small groups within current Christian communities. Nor is this to say that small groups have been completely ignored in the study of these major revivals. Indeed, many credible studies of the details surrounding these awakenings have found that small groups were a part of the revival's story. However, few if any such studies have seriously considered the possibility that small groups may have been a catalyst for these revivals. Instead, the small group dynamic is usually sidelined as a mere characteristic or even an outcome of the awakenings rather than actual contributors to them. In light of this oversight, it seems necessary to throw the small group element into the mix as a major player in these revivals.

To this end, this book's purpose is to answer the following question: *In what way and to what degree did small groups serve as a catalyst for the emergence of spiritual renewal during the four major spiritual awakenings in Christian history?* With this purpose in mind, it may be prudent to emphasize what will be addressed and what will not. First, I will restrict the focus to what are believed by most scholars to be the most significant spiritual awakenings in Christian history. What is meant by a "significant spiritual awakening" will be discussed a little later. Second, I will focus on the direct events and impact of the spiritual awakening itself. History suggests that each major spiritual awakening had deep and long-lasting effects on the societies it permeated, even to the point of altering the course of some societies' trajectory.[2] While this is significant for the specific societies and for the history of Christianity as a whole, attention will be limited to the role of small groups in the emergence, impact, and longevity of the awakening itself. Third, I will confine our discussion regarding each awakening to the role and influence of their respective small groups. There are certainly several features within each awakening that fueled the revival flames, and many of these features are likely held in common with the other awakenings. However, since small groups have been too often overlooked as a

2. Some examples that have been offered regarding the course-altering impact spiritual awakenings have had on a society include the First Great Awakening aiding in the rise of the American Revolution and the Second Great Awakening spurring demands for the end of slavery. Some resources regarding these connections include Lanyi, "Great Awakening" and Taylor, "Social Effects."

factor for these revivals, this study is intentionally narrowing its focus to that dynamic. Finally, this work is specifically trying to determine if there was a clear presence and pivotal influence of small groups on each major spiritual awakening. True, small groups have enjoyed a long and rich history in the Christian church, and a brief overview of this history is appropriately provided to understand their role in the overall historical context. However, this study is not designed to detail the impact of small groups throughout the whole history of the faith, but to highlight their part in the rise of each major spiritual awakening.

It is also important to bring clarity to what I mean when I use certain terms. For example, debate continues to rage regarding how to define a *great spiritual awakening*. Some emphasize its evangelistic effects while others the spiritual renewal of believers. Some suggest it can be either regional or global, while others insist on limiting it to an international phenomenon. Because of these varying perspectives, many studies have explored nearly a dozen different periods of historic spiritual revival which they consider awakenings. However, this book is built on the premise that the *great* awakenings in Christian history consisted of a series of regional revivals initiated primarily as spiritual repentance and renewal among current believers, but then, secondarily, yielded remarkable evangelistic outcomes. Moreover, the reach of these awakenings expanded across national or international lines as well as decades of time. From these criteria, historians generally agree that Christianity has experienced at least four periods of spiritual awakening: the First Great Awakening in North America (1726–91); the Second Great Awakening in North America (1780–1850); the Layman, Welsh, and Korean Revivals (1857–1910); and the Mid-Century Revival in North America (1949–79).[3]

Another term in need of definition is *small groups*. Throughout much of church history, small groups have been called by several different names, such as conventicles, conferences, class meetings, collegia, societies, Sunday school, and bands. For our purposes here, I have adopted the classical definition of small groups as "a more or less cohesive collection of individuals who relate to each other personally and at intervals in more or less patterned ways because they share certain beliefs, values, affections,

---

3. While the First and Second Great Awakenings and the Mid-Century Revival were predominantly manifested in North America, it is important to emphasize that these awakenings were international occurrences, either in origin or in impact.

motives, norms, and roles and have a common goal."[4] Such small groups can comprise a variety of dynamics: the age range of a group's constituents, the typical topic of discussion within the small group, the general format of the group's meetings, as well as the venue, method, time, and frequency of these gatherings. While the diversity of these details among small groups may demonstrate the expanse and depth of their impact, all of the small groups in question share certain commonalities: (1) the participants typically enjoy a personal connection or relationship with one another, (2) the participants have a basic, common goal of spiritual formation, and (3) the small group's activities are largely designed and focused on fulfilling this goal of discipleship.

These considerations determine the shape of the book. As promised earlier, chapter 1 sets the stage for the role of small groups throughout Christian history by examining key roles they have played in the earliest biblical and historical contexts. The chapter begins by exploring how the small group dynamic has been used in various ways throughout the Old Testament and intertestamental period, then investigates how Jesus used small groups, both with his disciples and in private homes, to establish his gospel and plant the seeds of the New Testament church. Then, in the final pages of the chapter, we learn how small groups were initially used in the form of house churches during the first century but adapted to the major transitions of the Christian church while remaining true to its original purpose and key qualities. Chapter 2 explores how small groups were often the context from which calls to reform the established church emerged, beginning with the Waldensians, Lollards, and Hussites, and moving on to many of the Reformers, such as Martin Luther and the Anabaptists. Then, beginning with chapter 3, we move into the crux of the study, discovering the critical role small groups played prior to and during the First Great Awakening (1726–91), as they were championed by Christian influencers like Jonathan Edwards and Charles Wesley. Picking up from there, chapter 4 addresses the influence of small groups during the Second Great Awakening (1780–1850), beginning with its rise among colleges and reaching its zenith with camp revivals, the Sunday School movement, and the ministry of Charles Finney. Chapter 5 surveys a cluster of awakenings that occurred roughly at the same time (1857–1910): the Layman's Prayer Revival, the Welsh Revival, and the Korean Revivals. As each of these revivals is unpacked, we will see the intricate influence of small groups on

---

4. Hare, *Small Group Research*, 1.

display in a variety of forms, including in the ministry of D. L. Moody. Chapter 6 narrates the final spiritual awakening, the Mid-Century Revival (1949–79), where it reveals how small groups were used in the form of coffeehouses during the Jesus People Movement, as well as how they were instrumental in the formative years of the ministries of Bill Bright, Chuck Smith, and Billy Graham. By way of summary, chapters 3 through 6 offer important principles regarding the role and characteristics of the catalytic small groups during their respective revival, as well as a table that summarizes key observations of these small groups. Finally, a short epilogue concludes the study with an overview of the principal features that these historic small groups had in common and how they may be emulated in today's context. Through these chapters, it is my prayer that this book will benefit everyone from the Christian scholar, in the continued pursuit of understanding these incredible awakenings, to the local church pastor and the small group leader, as they seek ways to minister to their congregation effectively and enliven them toward revival.

This book seeks to answer the call to demonstrate how small groups have influenced the rise and sustainability of Christianity's most significant spiritual awakenings. In the following pages, we will discover there is a clear and powerful link between the presence and use of a small group strategy and the emergence of Christianity's significant spiritual awakenings. At its heart is the conviction that small groups have been present prior to or near the beginning of at least each major spiritual awakening as one of its most indispensable contributors. But we need not only to give a historical look at small groups during revivals, but also a practical one. As the book brings to light the critical and dynamic role of small groups for these spiritual awakenings, it will also highlight the common features of each of these groups that helped launch their respective revival. By bringing attention to these common features, the Christian church today may be able to emulate these features in the modern context in hopes that, if God wills, we may be gripped with spiritual revival once again.

1

Small Groups in Scripture and Early Christianity

THE USE OF SMALL groups of one kind or another appears to be a common element in all major movements of the Holy Spirit throughout Christian history. Still, even beyond these moments of significant spiritual renewal many have enthusiastically embraced small groups as a prominent means for churches to organize for ministry and believers to grow in their faith. The use of small groups, however, is far from a recent invention. It is important, then, to set small groups in their proper biblical and historical context to understand how God may have used—and continues to use—this strategy to fulfill his purposes. To that end, this chapter has four main purposes: (1) to explore how the small group dynamic was used in various ways throughout the Old Testament and intertestamental period, (2) discover how Jesus used small groups, both with his disciples and in private homes, to establish his gospel and plant the seeds of the New Testament church, (3) to learn how the first-century church effectively used the small group strategy in the form of house churches, and (4) to briefly examine up through the Reformation period how small groups adapted to the major transitions of the Christian church while remaining true to its original purpose and key qualities.

Small Groups in the Old Testament

Biblical accounts suggest that small groups had their beginning soon after creation. Indeed, the Old Testament indicates that God worked through family groupings and other forms of small groups to establish his covenant purposes. Perhaps the most consistent form of small group discipleship that can be seen in the Hebrew Scriptures is the family unit. Indeed, one need only to read the first eleven chapters of Genesis to find small groups in the form of the family, such as Adam and Eve in Eden, and Noah's family in the ark. But such evidence extends well beyond the opening pages of the Old Testament. Time after time, the people of God are referred to as "the children of Israel," and family-oriented metaphors are peppered throughout the Old Testament to describe God's relationship with his people (1 Chron 29:10; Pss 68:5, 89:26; Prov 18:24; Isa 9:6; Mal 2:10). Additionally, the home was the center of religious instruction, emphasizing this familial relationship with God (Deut 6:1–9). The Passover and other Jewish feasts were held in households, either one large household or several smaller homes together (Lev 23). This intimate setting fostered the opportunity for children to ask the meaning of the feast (cf. Josh 4:6, 21); thus, it had both essential educational and symbolic implications.[5]

Old Testament examples of the use of small groups can also be found outside of the immediate family structure. For instance, God used Noah's family of eight more broadly, not only to demonstrate to all of creation his desire for a righteous humanity (Gen 7:1), but also to establish his covenant of renewal (Gen 9:8–9). Furthermore, when God delivered his chosen people from slavery in Egypt, he began forming them into a new nation structured around small groups. Exodus 18 records how God, through the advice of Moses' father-in-law, Jethro, instructed Moses to organize the Hebrew people into groups of tens, fifties, hundreds, and thousands. This division into larger and smaller groups enabled Moses and the other leaders to care for the needs of the people more efficiently.

Other parts of the Old Testament show a similar pattern of God working through small groups to meet the needs of the people and equip them for his purposes. The Hebrews were organized according to their tribes when camping in the wilderness (Num 2), and Moses commissioned a small group of spies for a reconnaissance report of Canaan (Num 13). Even during the dark years of exile, God used a small group of faithful followers to infiltrate and influence the pagan king for his divine will (Dan 1:3–7). Moreover, Nehemiah 3 documents how post-exilic Jews were organized in groups to rebuild the ruined wall of Jerusalem.

Nehemiah 8 describes what seems to be a combination of a large assembly worship and small group teaching. On this occasion, Ezra the priest read the Law of Moses to the Hebrew congregation, and the Levites helped

---

5. Plueddemann and Plueddemann, *Pilgrims in Progress*, 2.

the people understand its meaning. This account is particularly relevant, for it details what many have viewed as a significant spiritual awakening among the Old Testament Jews. Malcolm McDow and Alvin Reid write that several key Jewish institutions were impacted in some way by the revival, including temple worship, synagogues, scribes, Pharisees, and Judaic traditions. They continue, "Out of this awakening, patriotism intensified; moral corrections were implemented; ethical standards were altered; domestic patterns were established; and religious reforms were achieved."[6] C. E. Autrey agrees, adding, "The post-captivity revival was, in many respects, the most far-reaching revival recorded in the Old Testament. It abolished idolatry forever among the Jews. We have no record that as a people they ever lapsed into idolatry after the post-captivity revival."[7]

Throughout the Old Testament, then, God used a variety of large and small group settings—and sometimes a combination of both—to meet the needs of his people and equip them to fulfill his purposes. Moreover, at least in the occasion of Nehemiah 8, the use of a small group strategy contributed to a significant spiritual revival among God's people.

Small Groups in the Intertestamental Period

Despite the occasional occurrence of small groups, most of Jewish worship described in the Old Testament was highly organized and complex, led by priests and Levites, and centered around the tabernacle or temple. However, beginning sometime during the exilic years—perhaps during the Babylonian Captivity (ca. 600 BC)—a seismic change came upon Jewish worship and the emergence of the synagogue took place. This shift to the synagogue solidified during the period between the Old and New Testaments. Although the history of its origin is wrapped in obscurity, the synagogue has played a key role in the preservation of the essence of Judaism.[8] The word *synagogue* is a transliteration from the Greek and means "gathering place" or "place of assembly." As such, the synagogue became the fulcrum of each Jewish community, much like the temple in Jerusalem had been for the entire nation. Indeed, the Jewish Targum interprets Ezekiel 11:16 ("Yet I shall be a little sanctuary for them in the countries where they have gone.") to mean that in its dispersion Israel would keep

6. McDow and Reid, *Firefall*, 65.
7. Autrey, *Renewals before Pentecost*, 138.
8. Bacher and Dembitz, "Synagogue."

the synagogue as a miniature sanctuary in lieu of the temple. In practice, wherever twelve Jewish families lived in any area, they were required to build a synagogue and come together for worship on the Sabbath day.[9] Typically consisting of small groups of Jews in a community, worship in the synagogue was a time of teaching from the Hebrew Scriptures, fellowship, and prayer. It usually consisted of a rabbi and a group of laypersons who often participated in the readings, prayers, and open discussions. Reflecting on the nature of synagogue worship during the intertestamental periods, Elmer Towns and Vernon Whaley write:

> Of primary importance to synagogue worship was the teaching of the Word of God. During those years when there were no prophets, the faith of Israel became increasingly institutionalized. Whereas during the Old Testament period the Jews were mostly illiterate, during the intertestamental period they became a reading people. This helped preserve the Jewish identity while other cultures disappeared.[10]

The synagogue, then, provided an ongoing presence of the small group dynamic among the Jewish people. It is this system of assemblies that Jesus and his disciples would often utilize as they spread the gospel message during New Testament times.

Small Groups in Jesus' Earthly Ministry

The employment of a small group becomes even more pronounced in the New Testament, beginning with Christ. The Gospels offer at least two different ways in which Jesus employed a small group strategy during his earthly ministry: his mentoring of the twelve disciples and his use of homes as a venue for ministry and teaching. Regarding the first, all four Gospel accounts detail how Jesus brought together a small group of twelve men and spent three years living with them, teaching them the Scriptures, ministering with them, and demonstrating the message of grace before them. Within this group of twelve, Jesus appears to invest even more training into three disciples: the two brothers, James and John, and Simon Peter (Matt. 16:16–19; 17:1–13; 26:36–38). Jim and Carol Plueddemann summarize the significance of Jesus' small group ministry

---

9. Towns and Whaley, *Worship through the Ages*, 39–41.
10. Towns and Whaley, *Worship through the Ages*, 40.

with his disciples: "Jesus needed a small group. He allowed others to minister to Him, however faltering and imperfect their ministry was. And Jesus made optimum use of the small group as an effective educational setting to help His disciples learn and grow."[11]

Additionally, Joel Comiskey describes what the "effective educational setting" of this Christ-led small group may have looked like:

> Jesus didn't simply gather them once a week for a 'discipleship class.' He lived with them, shared financial resources, and taught them about kingdom values. He didn't only instruct his disciples about how to pray, but asked them to accompany him to prayer meetings, so they could see him praying. When the disciples finally asked him what he was doing, he seized upon the opportunity to teach them about prayer (Luke 11:1–4). The disciples learned while doing, but they were also guided to carefully reflect on what they did.[12]

The importance of this small group of disciples can be surmised by the fact that his ministry with them was bookended by Jesus' prayers for them. Jesus spent an evening in prayer before choosing his disciples (Luke 6:12–16). Likewise, John 17:6–19 records Jesus's prayer for them on the evening of his betrayal, where Jesus states, "As you sent me into the world, I also have sent them into the world" (John 17:18). Thus, in light of Jesus's prayer, the major purposes of Jesus's small group ministry with these twelve men were to teach them God's Word, reveal to them his gospel mission, and to call them to be in the world as his ambassadors. As Jesus's mission was to glorify God by his life, so this community of Christ-followers are commissioned to glorify God by its words and deeds.

The Gospels also record that Jesus's public ministry was primarily found in the small group setting of an individual's house. Nearly a dozen examples of Jesus ministering in people's homes can be cited, including: Peter (Matt. 8:14), Matthew (Matt. 9:10), Zacchaeus (Luke 19:1–10), Lazarus and his sisters (Luke 10:38–42), Jairus (Mark 5:35–38), two blind people (Matt. 9:28–30), Simon the Leper (Matt. 26:6), a paralyzed person (Luke 5:19), and a Pharisee (Luke 14:1). Beyond these examples, the Gospels record that Jesus taught his disciples in a house (Mark 7:17–18; 9:33; 10:10), instituted the Lord's Supper in a house (Matt. 26:18), and sent out

---

11. Plueddemann and Plueddemann, *Pilgrims in Progress*, 3.
12. Comiskey, *2000 Years of Small Groups*, 19.

His disciples to minister and teach from village to village in the homes of the people (Luke 9:1–6; 10:1–11).

In his seminal work, *House Church and Mission*, Roger Gehring suggests that at least three important factors may have played into why Jesus used houses for teaching and ministry. First, in the first-century world, a private home was a common meeting place for religious and intellectual instruction and dialogue. Second, the *oikos* (a house or home) in the ancient world, especially in Palestine and Galilee, wielded a high level of economic and social significance. Third, synagogues were likely widespread in the first century, especially prior to AD 70, and primarily found in private homes that served as a place of assembly for the Jewish community. In light of these factors, Gehring concludes, "Jews of the first century were accustomed to meeting for worship in private homes. . . . Therefore, it appears reasonable to assume that Jesus would have used houses at least for his teaching ministry and possibly for other activities as well."[13] Furthermore, Luke 4:38–40 reports that Jesus used the home of Simon Peter as a base for ministry. Reflecting on the implications of such a home-based ministry, Gehring further suggests that the house of Simon Peter may serve as a kind of prototype of the house church, a small group model that would become a prominent feature among the first Christians. "The house of Peter before Easter was a place where the first core group of disciples gathered around Jesus in a house community that can be described as a kind of house church in embryonic form, the 'cradle of the ecclesia in its early formation.'"[14] At the very least, Christ's use of small groups, and his house church strategy in particular, became the starting point for the apostles' ministry after his resurrection.

Small Groups as House Churches during the First Three Centuries

Since the time of Christ, the first Christians gathered in existing buildings, such as the Temple in Jerusalem and Jewish synagogues (typically for evangelism and apologetic purposes), as well as the homes of individual believers. As the gospel spread, Christianity grew explosively—from 120 people (Acts 1:15) to over 3,000 (Acts 2:41) in one day at Pentecost—and the church expanded to other parts of the world. With this growth came

13. Gehring, *House Church and Mission*, 29–30.
14. Gehring, *House Church and Mission*, 46–47.

the challenge of accommodating the gatherings of believers within these communities. As an answer to this challenge arose the house church, for no other venue met the needs of these local gatherings better.[15] The house-church model was so successful during the New Testament time that virtually every instance in the book of Acts of a local church meeting refers to the gathering being in someone's home. Observing this fact, Harley Atkinson and Joel Comiskey declare, "House churches played an essential role in the rapid growth and ultimate triumph of Christianity, and it would be safe to say that the first three centuries belonged to the house church movement."[16] Indeed, throughout the Roman Empire and even into its North African regions, Christian churches began by gathering in homes. The impact of house churches was so significant that J. Patout Burns and Robin Jensen note, "References to buildings dedicated exclusively to Christian worship begin in the fourth century, and even then, especially during persecutions, Christians still worshipped in houses."[17]

Apart from the urgent need for gathering places and the effectiveness and versatility of homes to meet that need, at least three other reasons can be given for the emergence of house churches in early Christian life. One reason for house churches was to provide a haven for Christians from hostility and persecution. During the first three centuries, Christians suffered recurring periods of official and unofficial persecution at the hands of the Romans. Even though the surrounding community may have generally known about local Christian gatherings, they were moderately inconspicuous. Richard Krautheimer explains this rationale: "Inconspicuousness was both prudent and ideologically desirable for Christianity, and could be best achieved behind the façade of domestic middle-class architecture."[18]

In addition to protection, house fellowships provided a sense of community for believers. Reaching back to its Old Testament roots, the early Christians believed the family is a primary institution created by God to foster security, identity, and a sense of belonging to its members. Robert and Julia Banks suggest that, for some, "the [house] church family replaced the original family that they had lost upon conversion," while for others "relationships in their churches restored or deepened the family

---

15. Filson, "The Significance of the Early House Churches," 106.
16. Atkinson and Comiskey, "Lessons from the Early House Church," 76.
17. Burns and Jensen, *Christianity in Roman Africa*, 43.
18. Krautheimer, *Early Christian and Byzantine Architecture*, 27.

bonds that already existed."[19] Noting the relatively small number of people that made up an individual house church, along with its relational atmosphere, John Paul Vandenakker affirms how such an environment would have "promoted a more personally focused experience of catechesis and discipleship." He adds, "It would not have been difficult for the Christians of these house churches to get to know and support one another in a very direct and personal manner."[20]

A third reason for the success of the house church in early Christianity is its strategic value for evangelism. Despite many immoral elements that characterized Roman society at the time, pagan culture did have a key trait in common with both its Jewish and Christian counterparts: the home as the foundational unit to society. This commonality which Christians shared with their otherwise adverse neighbors proved to be instrumental in the spread of the gospel. Michael Green emphasizes the importance of this commonality, declaring, "Sociologically speaking, the early Christians could not have hit on a sounder basis."[21] Consequently, the apostles Paul and Peter and other early Christian witnesses went "house to house" (Acts 20:20) sharing the gospel, endeavoring to lead entire households to Christ.[22] These and other reasons are why the house church was so instrumental in helping the Christian faith turn the "world upside down" with the message of Christ.

House churches in early Christianity did more than provide a place of security and community for Christians during the turbulent times of persecution. Since they were the initial means by which Christians gathered for worship and fellowship, with Christ as the central focus, these home gatherings also provided a list of additional features by which future Christian small groups could be patterned.

First, initial house-church gatherings commonly met for meals. Andrew B. McGowan notes that this distinctive meal tradition was neither something Christians did in addition to worship nor even a practical attempt to generate fellowship, "but the regular form of Christian gathering."[23] Every participant took part in these meals both by bringing and eating the food

---

19. Banks and Banks, *The Church Comes Home*, 32.

20. Vandenakker, *Small Christian Communities and the Parish*, 12.

21. Vandenakker, *Small Christian Communities and the Parish*, 208–9.

22. Vandenakker, *Small Christian Communities and the Parish*, 210. See also Acts 11:14; 16:15, 31; 18:8.

23. McGowan, *Ancient Christian Worship*, 19.

for the banquet. These meal gatherings, ostensibly where bread was broken, the cup blessed, and various forms of fellowship fostered, are clearly seen as the forerunners of what would become the church's perennial celebration of the Lord's Supper. Describing how it originally began as a meal with family or friends in a private home, William Barclay writes, "It was there that the Lord's Supper was born in the church. It was like the Jewish Passover which is a family festival at which the father at the head of the household is the celebrant."[24] Although fellowship meals were common, the Lord's Supper eventually became the centerpiece of these meetings.

A second distinction of house churches was the spirit of love, joy, and excitement that permeated these gatherings. As noted earlier, the early Christians saw the church as their new family. This filial atmosphere doubtlessly translated into an intense love shared among its members. Observing the high spirit of fellowship hinted in the church, Banks and Banks record, "We find no suggestion that these meetings were conducted with the kind of solemnity and formality that surrounds most weekly Christian gatherings today."[25] Instead, its participants seem to have enjoyed each other's company, as they laughed, sang, ate, learned, and generally drew closer to Jesus together.

A third feature of the early Christian house churches is the basic elements of these meetings. While they maintained an organic nature characterized by flexibility, the gatherings generally consisted of several important components. Recorded in the Book of Acts, a multiplicity of practices is already found in these early church gatherings, including prayer (2:42; 12:12), fellowship (2:42), meals (2:42, 46), doctrinal teaching (2:42; 5:42), and evangelism (2:47).[26] Similarly, in his important work, *Ancient Christian Worship*, McGowan traces seven common worship practices that emerged in these early house gatherings: meals (including the Lord's Supper), Scripture teaching, singing and dancing, initiatory rites (for example, baptism, anointing, and foot washing), prayer, and special feasts and fasts.[27] While these components would have certainly varied from church to church and according to the occasion, historians have generally agreed with McGowan's list, only perhaps adding fellowship to the mix.[28]

24. Barclay, *The Lord's Supper*, 101.
25. Banks and Banks, *The Church Comes Home*, 39.
26. Atkinson and Comiskey, "Lessons from the Early House Church," 80.
27. McGowan, *Ancient Christian Worship*, 19–20.
28. Gehring, *House Church and Mission*, 27. In light of such an active itinerary, it

A fourth distinction of the early house church is the emphasis that each person in the church had a contribution to make. The Apostle Paul taught that every member had an essential part in the church according to his or her spiritual giftedness and calling (1 Cor 12–14; Rom 12; Eph 4). Furthermore, when Paul wrote to a specific church, he addressed the letter to all its members, because they were all ministers. As another example, Paul writes to the Corinthian church, "How is it then, brethren? Whenever you come together, *each of you* has a psalm, has a teaching, has a tongue, has a revelation, has an interpretation. Let all things be done for edification" (1 Cor. 14:26, emphasis mine). Clearly, each person was expected to participate in the church, for each person in the church had a special contribution for the benefit of all.[29]

A final feature worth noting about these early house churches is their communal networking with the other churches. Individual house churches did not consider themselves independent of each other. Rather, early Christians recognized that they were part of a larger worldwide family—the universal church. Evidence indicates that this realization manifested itself by churches in a common locale recognizing and functioning as part of a greater citywide Christian community. One important sample of such evidence is the communication that occurred among these early house churches. Sending news from visitors, sharing correspondences, warning of persecutions, and even reporting accounts of persecutions were all

---

is especially interesting that archaeologists have discovered many Roman houses to be well-suited for the practices of early house churches. Also known as *domus ecclesiae* ("house assembly"), remains of some of these structures can be found as early as the third century. Among the findings, archaeologists observe that these houses closely resemble the domestic Roman architecture of this period, especially the peristyle house, in which the rooms were arranged around a central courtyard. In these instances, the houses in which these churches generally met had a central courtyard surrounded on three sides by several rooms. Some of the rooms were often connected to create a larger gathering space that could hold small crowds of around fifty people. Other rooms were used for different purposes including discipleship, private prayer and counsel, celebration of the Lord's Supper, baptism of Christian converts, and even storage of charitable items. What is believed to be the earliest house church of which traces remain is the *Dura Europos*, a typical courtyard house in Syria. Constructed by the early third century, the house was adapted and used as a Christian church at some point between AD 240 and 250. Two rooms were combined for the celebration of Communion, while another room served as the place for baptism, and another may have been used for Christian instruction. See "Dura Europos and the Early Christian 'House Church,'" and Sefton, "Buildings and Beliefs," 38–39.

29. Atkinson and Comiskey, "Lessons from the Early House Church" 81.

different types of information that was passed from assembly to assembly.[30] Evidence also indicates that individual house churches were also linked by leadership, even occasionally gathering together for a larger meeting, such as the Jerusalem Council in Acts 15. Commenting about the leadership of the New Testament house churches (Acts 20:17, 28; 1 Pet. 5:1–5), Gehring writes that these were overseers of the churches that met in their homes. "In other words," he explains, "they were leaders of individual house churches. Together as a group such overseers could have formed the leadership team or council for the whole local church in that city."[31]

The rise of the house church to accommodate the birth and growth of the Christian faith is by the account of many a God-ordained phenomenon. During the first centuries of the church's life, to open one's home for such an assembly of imperial outlaws and social outcasts could result in arrest, imprisonment, and even death. Yet it appears that many did, which attests to the transforming power of the gospel in the personal lives of these homeowners. As a result, Christians grew in their faith and many more were added to their ranks so that, by the end of the first century alone, estimates of the Christian population reach as high as five hundred thousand.[32] Nevertheless, starting subtly in the second century and significantly by the fourth, the Christian faith would find itself changing in profound ways, including its worship, evangelism, discipleship, and ministry. Along with these changes came a gradual adaptation of the church's small group strategy.

Congregational Consolidation and the Shift to Small Group Agape Feasts

House church gatherings had characterized Christian worship and community for the first two decades in the life of the faith. However, as congregations grew, the practices of Christian worship and discipleship began to change. Instead of smaller gatherings in the intimate venue of people's homes, these growing Christian communities began to consolidate the smaller assemblies into larger congregations. To accommodate these more populous and diverse assemblies, buildings that had primarily been homes of individual families began to be renovated into larger structures for the

---

30. Osiek et al., *A Woman's Place*, 14.
31. Gehring, *House Church and Mission*, 206.
32. Comiskey, *2000 Years of Small Groups*, 30.

primary use of Christian congregations—in essence, house churches began to change to church houses.[33] Consequently, these larger number of Christians began to encumber what was once a versatile Christian gathering. Therefore, in the first half of the second century, between the time of the church leaders Tertullian and Cyprian, the eucharistic meals of house church gatherings began to be consolidated to morning gatherings for these larger assemblies of believers, limiting the scope of the small group gatherings to evening fellowship meals.

Though aware of both practices, Tertullian of Carthage (ca. AD 160–220) continued to maintain the evening meal gatherings as the primary assembly. Tertullian observed that the morning eucharistic service was an innovation of the church in his time with no biblical precedent. Rejecting the idea that the Lord's Supper was only limited to the full assembly of the congregation, he rather explained that the Lord himself had commanded that the Communion celebration should be observed at meal times and by whomever was present.[34] In addition, against the growing notion that ordained clergy was necessary for the service, Tertullian indicates in his writings that private observances in households, where any believer could serve as the leader, were appropriate.[35] The particular form of Christian celebration which Tertullian seems to especially endorse is what he calls the *agape*, or "love feast."[36] As Tertullian describes it, the feast involves a full meal in a reclined position.[37] These meetings, it seems, would have been most commonly held in private homes and would not have included the whole Christian community.

According to his writings, Tertullian's desire to retain some aspects of the small group model in the church seems to come from the combination of an intense intolerance of personal sin and his belief in the power of the body of Christ to aid in the individual's repentance and eventual victory over it. Using images such as society, body, and threefold witness,

---

33. Gehring, *House Church and Mission*, 12–15.

34. Tertullian, *On Prayer* 19.1–4, in Schaff, *Latin Christianity*, 687; Tertullian, *On the Soldier's Crown* 3.3 in Schaff, *Latin Christianity*, 94.

35. Tertullian, *To His Wife* 2.8; in Schaff, *Fathers of the Third Century*, 39–40; Tertullian, *Exhortation to Chastity* 7.3, in Schaff, *Fathers of the Third Century*, 54.

36. Burns and Jensen, *Christianity in Roman Africa*, 234. Tertullian uses other names for the meal as well, including love feast (*dilectio*, in *Apology* 39.16–18, in Schaff, *Latin Christianity*, 46–47) and the Lord's Banquet (*Conuiuium Dominicum*, in *To His Wife* 2.4, in Schaff, *Fathers of the Third Century*, 39–40).

37. Tertullian, *Apology* 39.16–17, in Schaff, *Latin Christianity*, 46–47.

Tertullian teaches that as the spiritual body of the church, other members share in the suffering of any member who is afflicted.[38] Tertullian similarly relates the church to the forgiving power of Christ. He writes that someone who is truly repentant of his sin will demonstrate his remorse with personal indignity and self-mortification. Moreover, the extravagant humiliation should be done in the presence of the church, which is Christ's body.[39] These are profound responsibilities of the church in the life of individual believers, far too important to be executed in the impersonal forum of a corporate liturgical gathering. Such a weighty role in a believer's life must be done in a more intimate setting of believers. Thus, the smaller gatherings in a home for the evening *agape* meal was essential to the church in the eyes of Tertullian.

Although the nature of the household celebration of the *agape* feast is not completely clear, a few key characteristics can be noted. One important feature is their diverse and organic nature. Some of the worship gatherings took the form of a more formal eucharistic service, complete with its own bread and wine. Others were simpler celebrations, some of which may have even used bread left over from a previous ceremony in the community. Some gatherings may have included a complete meal, brought in by everyone and shared by everyone. Still other gatherings may have only been prayer services, without any food, and occurring at different times of the day. The point seems that these gatherings were less about formalities and rituals and more about Christian fellowship.[40]

On the other hand, a second feature of these *agape* feasts is the typical format which these gatherings should take. Tertullian instructs that participants are to first pray, and then share a modest meal while comfortably reclined at the table. Once the meal is completed, participants are to wash their hands, bring in lights, and then lead the group in praising God through expounding a scriptural passage or singing a song. Finally, the feast closes with a communal prayer. Though he did not require this format to be followed at every feast, Tertullian felt that the quiet, worshipful attitude of these celebrations would distinguish it from the larger gatherings of the whole church.[41]

---

38. Tertullian, *On Repentance* 10.5, in Schaff, *Latin Christianity*, 664. See also Osborn, *Tertullian, First Theologian of the West*, 172.

39. Tertullian, *On Repentance* 10.6, in Schaff, *Latin Christianity*, 664.

40. Burns and Jensen, *Christianity in Roman Africa*, 246.

41. Burns and Jensen, *Christianity in Roman Africa*, 240.

A third feature of the *agape* feasts is that almost any Christian could conduct these household gatherings. Although he recognized the clergy as the normal overseers of the community worship, Tertullian was more anti-clerical in his approach to church governance than many of his colleagues. As a result, he argued that, at least in the case of necessity, any male Christian could perform the function of leading the group of believers in prayer and worship.[42] Even more, any Christian could preside at a Communion celebration should clergy not be present. In such cases, the head of a household would function as the leader of these meals.[43]

A fourth feature of these worshipful gatherings of small groups is their benevolent welcome of all believers. These assemblies were small, intimate gatherings that did not include the entire congregation, but they were not limited to household or friendship groups either. Rather, participants of the love feasts were generally a cross-section of the community, incorporating people from all social classes.[44] McGowan notes that when these feasts were held in more domestic settings, participants would often invite leaders along with the needy, such as widows, to dine with them.[45] More broadly, these gatherings characteristically provided food for those in need. In fact, such special deference for the poor may have been the reason of the meal's name.[46]

Having his life split between the second and third centuries, Tertullian sought to hold on to many elements of the initial church while embracing other elements of the emerging church. He was a staunch advocate of the priesthood of the believer and suspicious of the growing tendency toward hierarchical authority.[47] Above all, Tertullian saw the continuing need for relational intimacy among believers, especially for the purposes

---

42. Tertullian, *On Baptism* 7.1, in Schaff, *Latin Christianity*, 672.

43. Tertullian, *On the Soldier's Crown* 3.3, in Schaff, Latin Christianity, 94. It has been suggested (Osiek, et al., *A Woman's Place*, 157–62) that a widow who managed her own home might have functioned in some leadership capacity in or for her household. Tertullian, however, objected to the woman serving as minister of emergency baptism (*On Baptism* 17.4–5). For further discussion on this matter, see Burns and Jensen, *Christianity in Roman Africa*, 242–43, n.76.

44. Tertullian, *Apology* 39.16, in Schaff, *Latin Christianity*, 46-47. Tertullian did require all participants to be baptized members of the community. He also indicated that Christians guilty of grave sin were excluded from sharing the Communion meal (Tertullian, *To the Martyrs* 1.6, in Schaff, *Latin Christianity*, 693.

45. McGowan, *Ancient Christian Worship*, 50.

46. Burns and Jensen, *Christianity in Roman Africa*, 240.

47. Williams, et al., *Continuity and Discontinuity*, 59–60.

of restoring suffering or repentant members to the body. To this ancient Christian thinker, the answer for incorporating small group gatherings in the corporate church came in the form of *agape* feasts.

Full Congregational Worship and the Rise of Basilicas

While *agape* feasts in smaller settings enjoyed much popularity and practice, eventually the voice of Tertullian was drowned out and the banquets set aside. This shift was very gradual, with hints of its causes seen as early as the end of the second century. Moreover, it was not without reason, one of the most significant reasons being calls for unity in response to emerging heretical challenges. Gnosticism and various other pseudo-Christian cults had threatened the unity of the Christian church and the clarity of the gospel message. In the fog of their convoluted teachings, Christians began clamoring for an authoritative Christian voice. That authoritative voice became defined in the teacher's evidence of apostolic authority. Irenaeus (130–202) was one of the first church fathers to advocate what came to be known as the apostolic succession of Christian leaders.[48] Accompanying this call for apostolic authority among the church leaders was also a move toward the full assembly of congregations to assure the singular doctrine of the apostles was taught.

One of the most influential proponents for unity through the consolidation of worship assemblies was the bishop of Carthage, Cyprian (210–58). While the evening agape feasts continued for a time, Cyprian led a shift toward the morning assemblies as the preferred form of Christian gatherings for worship and celebrating the Lord's Supper. Besides the ongoing heretical threats, fallout from the Decian persecution during Cyprian's bishopric had resulted in divisions within the Carthagian church. It has been noted by some that the smaller Christian assemblies may have been the platform used by the schismatic groups to break off from Cyprian's leadership.[49]

---

48. "[Irenaeus] was emphatic that the apostles had appointed as successors bishops to whom they had committed the churches.... These bishops had been followed by others in unbroken line who were also guardians and guarantors of the apostolic teaching. He hints that he could, if there were space, give the lists of the bishops of all the churches, but he singles out that of the Church of Rome." Latourette, *A History of Christianity*, 131.

49. Burns and Jensen, *Christianity in Roman Africa*, 247n100.

In response, Cyprian began to emphasize the Lord's Supper as a sacrament of unity for the local church, which all of its members were expected to attend. While the bishop seems to have continued to recognize the evening feasts, he subordinated it from the church's primary eucharistic service, the daily morning liturgy.[50] The call for a full assembly to celebrate the Eucharist was questioned by some during his time as contrary to the practice taught in the Scriptures and exemplified by Christ. Cyprian responded by explaining that it had become necessary to assure all of the church's members understood the meaning and significance of the Communion celebration. He also insisted that the entire congregation needed to be together to realize the true meaning of the sacrament, and an evening feast could not accommodate such a large crowd.[51]

Some had further retorted to Cyprian's call for a full assembly by reminding of Jesus' promise that "where two or three are gathered together in My name, I am there in the midst of them" (Matt. 18:20). Cyprian agreed, but reminded them that such a gathering had to also be in a spirit of peace and unity, as Jesus stated one verse earlier: "If two of you agree on earth concerning anything that they ask, it will be done for them by My Father in heaven" (Matt. 18:19). Thus, Cyprian asserts, there is a clear order to Christ's promise: "He placed agreement first; He has made the concord of peace a prerequisite."[52] He then asks:

> But how can he agree with anyone who does not agree with the body of the Church itself, and with the universal brotherhood? How can two or three be assembled together in Christ's name, who, it is evident, are separated from Christ and from His Gospel? For we have not withdrawn from them, but they from us.[53]

To Cyprian, while the small group gatherings had proven beneficial to the church in the past, they had in most cases become a rallying point for division.[54] As a result, the bishop ordered the abandonment of the practice.

---

50. Burns and Jensen, *Christianity in Roman Africa*, 246–47. See also Cyprian, *To Donatus* 16, in Schaff, *Fathers of the Third Century*, 280; and *Letters* 63.16.1 in Schaff, *Fathers of the Third Century*, 364-65.

51. Cyprian, *Letters* 63.6.1–17.1 in Schaff, *Fathers of the Third Century*, 364-66. See also Burns and Jensen, *Christianity in Roman Africa*, 251.

52. Cyprian, *On the Unity of the Church* 12 in Schaff, *Fathers of the Third Century*, 425.

53. Cyprian, *On the Unity of the Church* 12 in Schaff, *Fathers of the Third Century*, 425.

54. Hall, *Learning Theology*, 239–40.

Indeed, Cyprian's writings provide no evidence of endorsing private or household celebrations; the Eucharist was celebrated by the whole Christian community.[55] To Cyprian and the majority of his contemporaries, "the morning service became a symbol of the unity of the church and the authority of the presiding bishop; the household meal services became instruments of division and rebellion."[56]

In 312, Constantine rose to power over the Roman Empire. With his imperial ascent came the legalization of Christianity, a faith which before him had endured seemingly endless periods of fiery persecution since its birth three centuries earlier. However, the tide had turned, and what had once been the whipping boy of an otherwise religiously pluralistic society had suddenly been established as the state religion. Constantine's ascent and official endorsement of Christianity brought with it the commissioned construction of public basilicas. These buildings—modeled after and often used as Roman community centers—began to emerge as a replacement to the intimate meetings of Christians in private homes. However, as it was from small groups to larger congregational worship gatherings, the evolution from houses to basilicas was equally gradual. A correlation between the growth of worship crowds and the structures needed to house them are necessarily found. As the size of the churches grew so did their worship needs, including a building to facilitate their worship. Robert Wilken explains, "Christian worship required a large interior space where people could gather, a podium, called an "ambo," at which the Scriptures could be read, a table or altar, where the vessels holding the bread and wine could be placed, and ample space for movement of clergy and the people." In contrast to the reclining position common in the evening agape feasts held in private homes, Wilken continues, "There were no seats in the early churches, and people stood during worship."[57] While recalling that early Christians opted for home meetings during times of conflict, Ed Smither writes, "Once peace was accorded to the church . . . [Christians] chose the basilica—a multi-purpose building already common in Roman society." He goes on to explain the reason for their choice. "Such a structure facilitated

---

55. Burns and Jensen, *Christianity in Roman Africa*, 251.

56. Burns and Jensen, *Christianity in Roman Africa*, 252. Agape meals did continue in Cyprian's time, however, and it is likely that there were still eucharistic celebrations attached to them in some places. Nevertheless, it appears that such gatherings were viewed more as the preserve of subgroups than assemblies of the Christian community. See McGowan, *Ancient Christian Worship*, 50.

57. Wilken, *The First Thousand Years*, 137.

the needs of the congregation—including worship, fellowship, and even mission to the community."[58] Although there were occasions when congregations would temporarily return to smaller assemblies in private homes (particularly during times of persecution), the change from the simple house gatherings to formal large congregations in basilicas had gained such momentum that house churches eventually disappeared.

The Adaptation of Small Groups for Catechism and Clerical Training

The use of small groups, on the other hand, continued to play an important part in the growth of the church and its members by adapting to the new template of large congregations in basilicas. Small groups shifted from being a place of worship and fellowship in homes to a means of discipleship and training by becoming a platform both for preparing catechumens for baptism and for training clergy in the context of the monastery.

One of the most common uses of small groups since the rise of the congregational worship in basilicas was the catechumenate. Deriving from the Greek term *catechumen*—meaning "one receiving instruction"—the early church organized a process of discipling individuals ("catechumens") in preparation for baptism.[59] While there is no way of knowing when catechetical instruction began in the church, the earliest existing non-biblical writing on baptism is the *Didache*, which states, "Now about baptism: this is how to baptize. Give public instruction on all these points, and then 'baptize' in running water, 'in the name of the Father and of the Son and of the Holy Spirit.'"[60] From this template (and perhaps along with others), a process of education and spiritual transformation was developed for baptismal candidates, a process that lasted for years. By the fourth century, church leaders began inviting non-believers to submit themselves for baptism. Then, after being evaluated and approved by the church leadership, these baptismal candidates became catechumens and began a forty-day period of preparation which culminated at Easter. During this period, the small group of catechumens were privately instructed

---

58. Smither, *Mission in the Early Church*, 156.

59. McGowan, *Ancient Christian Worship*, 150. McGowan goes on to explain that the term was used in *Passion of Perpetua and Felicitas* 2. See also Smither, *Mission in the Early Church*, 159 n.59.

60. *Didache* 7.1, in *Apostolic Fathers*, 151–52.

in the Scriptures. Some church leaders, such as Irenaeus and Augustine, included a historical survey of the Bible and the doctrine of salvation in their instruction. In addition, during this Lenten season, they were exorcised and compelled to renounce their former lives. In the case of catechumens under Augustine's tutelage, this aspect was especially rigorous, prompting patristics historian William Harmless to label the process a "bootcamp" for baptismal candidates. He explains:

> During Lent, *competentes* embraced a strict ascetical regimen. According to Augustine they were expected to fast each day until the "ninth hour" (around 3 p.m.). They also sustained from all meat and wine and kept their diet bland and simple. On Sundays and on Holy Thursday the fast was lifted, while on Holy Saturday it was tightened so that they, together with all the faithful, would take neither food nor drink. The *competentes*, if married, were strictly enjoined to fast from sex. They also distributed alms to the poor and, on occasion, spent all night praying.[61]

Finally, the focal point of the catechetical instruction became the Nicene Creed, from which the catechumens received a line-by-line explanation and were required to "hand it back" (*traditio*), that is, recite it as a public declaration of faith. During the week following baptism, the new church members were given further teaching on the meaning of baptism, the anointing of oil, and the Lord's Supper.[62] The process of baptismal preparation was serious and rigorous, which explains why the small group setting became the ideal platform for its execution.

Small groups also adapted to become a common feature of monastic life. Because of Constantine's endorsement, Christianity had suddenly become fashionable, bringing droves clamoring for admission. With such a flurry of newcomers, the meaning and sacredness of Christian baptism and life under the cross began to be diluted. In response, many sought a new way to develop and express their faith, and monastic life emerged as an appealing alternative. Even though traces of monasticism can be found as early as the third century, its popularity exploded by the time of Constantine. Justo González notes, "Monasticism was not the invention of an individual, but rather a mass exodus, a contagion, which seems to have suddenly affected

---

61. Harmless, *Augustine and the Catechumenate*, 214–15. Harmless's work provides an extraordinary summary of the preparatory process for baptism, especially for candidates under Augustine's purview.

62. Smither, *Mission in the Early Church*, 160–61.

thousands of people."⁶³ Derived from the Greek word *monachos* ("alone, solitary"), monks essentially sought a life apart from others. Although it is impossible to know who the first monk was, what is known is that the initial monks pursued holy seclusion in the desert to seek God alone through the practice of asceticism. These were mostly known as "anchorites" ("hermit, withdrawn, fugitive"), one of the first and most famous being St. Antony (ca. AD 254–356).⁶⁴ Although extreme to some, this complete seclusion became quite common by the end of the third century, so that "those who fled society for the withdrawn life of a hermit were legion."⁶⁵ However, not everyone seeking solitude wanted complete isolation. Some aspiring monks desired a solitary life, but what they meant by this was not to live completely alone but in a community separated from the world. This gave rise to a new form of monastic life called "cenobitic," meaning "communal life."⁶⁶ One of the reasons for the emergence of these monastic communities was perhaps for protection from hostile attacks by pagan forces. Judith Herrin writes that some of these monasteries even built defenses to keep out such intruders.⁶⁷ Another reason for these communities was spiritual in nature, as monks began to connect their relationship with God with the need to connect with other believers.⁶⁸ Indeed, most monks wanted to learn from an experienced teacher further along in the faith.⁶⁹

As monastic communities developed, so did their living quarters. Monastic housing often included dining rooms, reception areas, libraries, and bathing facilities to serve their daily needs.⁷⁰ The typical day for cenobitic monasteries included both work and devotion. Devotional life generally consisted of regular periods of communal and private prayer, spiritual reading, and meditation. More specifically, McGowan notes

63. González, *The Story of Christianity* 1: 139.

64. Harmless, *Desert Christians*, 18.

65. González, *The Story of Christianity* 1:142.

66. González, *The Story of Christianity* 1:143–44. Like its anchoritic counterpart, it is unclear who the first cenobitic monk was. However, Pachomius (ca. AD 292–346) certainly deserves credit as its most significant contributor, giving organization to these monastic communities.

67. Herrin, *The Formation of Christendom*, 59. González states that these monasteries were commonly encircled by a wall with a single entrance. González, *The Story of Christianity 1*, 145.

68. McGuire, *Friendship and Community*, 38–60.

69. González, *The Story of Christianity* 1:143.

70. Burns and Jensen, *Christianity in Roman Africa*, 92.

particular elements of worship among the monks. One such element is singing, especially the Old Testament psalms. Although they considered this as a means of reading the Scripture or a form of daily prayer, it was nonetheless a distinctive and musical form of worship.[71] Another worship practice noted was foot washing, mainly as an act of hospitality to guests. In this, the monks understood themselves to be imitating and obeying Jesus, thus an act of worship.[72] Of course, prayer was an intricate dynamic of monastic worship, but what is especially interesting is their discipline to pray in community at fixed times during the day, and and this involved orienting their body and posture in a demonstration of humility. McGowan states that prayer for these monks, like the early Christians, involved far more than speaking: "It was profoundly communal as well as highly personal, and a matter of body as well as the mind."[73]

Their work life, however, was not separated from their devotional life. Indeed, under the model of the apostle Paul's admonition to "pray without ceasing" (1 Thess. 5:17), all elements of their worship practices were incorporated in their daily chores. Thus, while bakers kneaded bread or cobblers made shoes, all of them sang psalms, recited the Scripture, prayed out loud or in silence, meditated on a biblical passage, and so on.[74] As the centuries passed, scholastic work and teaching often replaced the manual labors of farming, crafts, and the like.[75] What did not seem to change, however, was the integration of worship into the group's work. As a result of this atmosphere of spiritual comradery and integration of worship in other aspects of life, the small group of the monastic community became the prime place to develop clergy for serving the increasing demands of the large churches of the time.

Although no record exists of small group structures being established to care for the spiritual and social needs of the general church populace, small groups were still used quite commonly among the clergy in monastic communities. Indeed, it appears that several early church fathers saw tremendous benefit in small-community interaction. Surprisingly, one example is Cyprian of Carthage. Even though he passionately advocated for

---

71. McGowan, *Ancient Christian Worship*, 125.

72. McGowan, *Ancient Christian Worship*, 178.

73. McGowan, *Ancient Christian Worship*, 184. For a more thorough description of the practice of prayer among the fourth-century monastics, see 203–8.

74. González, *The Story of Christianity* 1:145.

75. Comiskey, *2000 Years of Small Groups*, 49–51.

replacing small group celebrations of communion with the full assembly in liturgical services, Cyprian did not dismiss the value of the small group strategy for spiritual development and ministry training. Indeed, Smither lists five pieces of evidence that demonstrate Cyprian's use of small groups for training the clergy.[76] First is the mere fact that Cyprian mentored approximately forty clergy who served in his church in Carthage, and he did so in a group context. A second indication of his value of small-group discipleship is that his clerical communications as bishop were typically addressed to several clergy serving together, suggesting that his discipling of these correspondents were intended to be as a group. Similarly, Cyprian's personal letters often contained ministry instruction or assignments to groups of clergy, suggesting that he anticipated each group's support and accountability toward one another for completion of the task. Fourth, the bishop had been known to set apart church leaders together, intending that they would support each other as they advanced through the ranks of the clergy. Fifth and more broadly, Cyprian had an ongoing mentoring influence on other African bishops, as was often demonstrated in the church councils he attended, believing that important church issues were best settled by a body of clergy.[77]

Ambrose (AD 339–97), the bishop of Milan, is another church father who seems to have employed small groups to train clergy. History suggests that Ambrose's pastoral appeal was quite compelling. Neil McLynn records that the bishop's influence even caused three African foreigners (Augustine, Alypius, and Evodius) under his tutelage for a time to abandon their illustrious employment by the Roman Empire for Christian baptism and ministry in the church.[78] What is particularly remarkable about Ambrose's pastoral appeal was his distinctive desire to study and meditate alone. While he allowed free access to visitors into his study, he rarely acknowledged their presence but immersed himself into reading quietly, leaving his puzzled spectators to ponder his behavior.[79] Despite this odd conduct, Ambrose is shown to be personally involved in the development of his small group of clergy. Through his direct involvement, Ambrose

---

76. Smither, *Augustine as Mentor*, 36.

77. Jan Joncas suggests that Cyprian may have coined the term *collegium* to refer to the group of bishops. Joncas, "Clergy, North African," 213. See also Cyprian, *Letters* 55, in Schaff, *Fathers of the Third Century*, X–X.

78. McLynn, *Ambrose of Milan*, 220–21.

79. McLynn, *Ambrose of Milan*, 239. See also Augustine, *Confessions*, 137–38.

developed a loyal and productive community of ministers molded in the bishop's own image. He imposed strict discipline on his subordinates, assuring that unity prevailed over the dangers of individualism.[80] Moreover, when Ambrose was not directly involved, he appointed an able presbyter to teach, lead, and exhort the Milanese clergy on his behalf. To use as a guide for how ministers are to conduct themselves and serve the church, Ambrose wrote *On the Duties of Ministers*, which he addressed to his ecclesiastical "sons," the clergy under his authority. Ambrose was so effective in his use of the small group context for training his Milanese ministers that "nowhere, perhaps, was Christian life supervised as comprehensively—and effectively—as in Ambrose's Milan."[81]

A third example is the bishop of Hippo, Augustine (AD 354-430) who was himself influenced by the small group mentorship of Ambrose. From his earliest years even before conversion, Augustine was drawn toward a community with others. "It is no surprise," Smither writes, "that once Augustine became a Christian he would also want to pursue his faith in the context of friends."[82] This "context of friends" was most often found in a monastic setting, first in Cassiciacum, then Thagaste, and finally in Hippo. As bishop of Hippo, Augustine organized his clergy into a monastic community adjacent to the basilica. Drawing from his previous experiences with Christian community, Augustine developed a few key features for his monastic group in Hippo.[83] One feature was that his approach to discipleship was personal, involved, and direct. Leading from a position of clear spiritual authority, the bishop drew others to himself. He then began to disciple them by training them on how to understand and teach the Scriptures, modeling before them a life of holiness and transparency, and dialoguing with them regularly during common meals. Second, Augustine was intentional in equipping and empowering his monastic group for ministry, particularly for the purpose of serving the needs of the church. Smither writes, "The daily disciplines of prayer, scriptural study, and reading, as well as regular interaction with Augustine's teaching, prepared many monks for a possible future in church ministry."[84] A third key feature was its ongoing culture of personal denial and spiritual discipline.

---

80. McLynn, *Ambrose of Milan*, 253.

81. McLynn, *Ambrose of Milan*, 237.

82. Smither, *Augustine as Mentor*, 134.

83. Smither, *Augustine as Mentor*, 146-53.

84. Smither, *Augustine as Mentor*, 146-47.

Drawn from Acts 4:32–35, he guided his subordinates against both marriage and the retention of private property. All lived by a common fund, and all ate at a common table.[85]

Along with these three examples, other church leaders who trained clergy in small group monastic settings could be added, including Basil and Gregory the Great. Indeed, as Herbert Mayer concludes, "This was the common pattern for centuries: the real strength and vitality of the church lay in the small groups of clergy gathered around a cathedral and the bishop or in a small group of monks gathered around a strong and influential leader."[86] Akin to its original practice in biblical times, the monastic version of small groups served well for gathering both men and women into purposeful communities for spiritual growth and ministry integration. Having adapted to meet a legitimate need for the church in the context of clerical training and the catechumenate, small groups would flourish and serve the church for generations ahead as viable component of the Christian community.[87]

Conclusion

Throughout the Old Testament, some version of a small group has been used to care for God's people to prepare them for God's purposes; since the time of Christ and his first-century followers, small groups have also played a vital role in the formation and spread of the Christian church. It has experienced many ebbs and flows, times of triumphs and times of turbulence. Nevertheless, small groups have been able to adapt to the major changes the Christian faith has undergone, while remaining true to its key identity—a place of community through which people can grow closer to Christ together. This tenacity, along with its adaptability to meet the demands of the Christian faith under various circumstances, is certainly a significant reason why small groups can be found in churches today.

---

85. Burns and Jensen, *Christianity in Roman Africa*, 415.
86. Mayer, "Pastoral Roles and Mission Goals," 298.
87. Plueddemann and Plueddemann, *Pilgrims in Progress*, 6.

2

Small Groups during the Rumblings of Reformation

RELIGIOUS HISTORIANS AGREE THAT a reinstitution of the use of small groups has accompanied virtually every revival on record. Hints of evidence for this notion can be seen during the few centuries that preceded the Protestant Reformation. These clues become so clear that the renowned revivalist J. Edwin Orr observes, "Just before the fifteenth century something started to change the church. It resulted in a progression of spiritual awakenings in which small groups either spearheaded, became strong catalysts of, or followed as nurturing environments to revivals."[1] This engagement of small groups that accompanied spiritual awakenings can be seen as early as the twelfth century, when a groundswell of disenchantment with Roman Catholicism was growing, as indicated by the rise of three particular movements: the Waldensians, the Lollards, and the Hussites.

The Waldensians

The first of the pre-Reformation movements occurred during the twelfth century, led by Peter Waldo. History's first record of Waldo is in 1170, where he is seen as a wealthy merchant of Lyons, France, who, about this time, had a spiritual encounter with Christ that brought about his conversion. In response to what he believed to be Christ's call to preach the gospel, Waldo decided to sell his substantial possessions and serve Christ through a life of poverty.[2] Out of this passion for spiritual knowledge, Waldo persuaded

---

1. Quoted in Hurston, "Home Groups: Channels for Growth," 67.
2. Tourn et al., *Waldensians*, 5. See also Comba, *History of the Waldenses*, 20–21.

and paid two sympathetic monks to translate large sections of the Scriptures from Latin into French. McDow and Reid describe what happened next: "As he absorbed the truths of God's Word, he began to share verses with other people. He became a walking Bible. The admonition of the Lord, 'Go and preach the gospel to every creature,' was indelibly engraved upon his soul."[3] As a result of his preaching, Waldo quickly attracted a band of followers who became known as the "Poor Men of Lyons." Patterning themselves after Jesus's disciples, this group joined Waldo in going out in pairs and preaching the gospel. However, Waldo and his band ran into one important problem: the Roman Catholic Church had officially forbidden people to preach the gospel unless they received explicit permission from Rome. He and another follower sought an audience with the Third Lateran Council of 1179 to request permission to preach, but they were unequivocally prohibited. In reply to the diocese's decision, Waldo declared, "Judge ye whether it be lawful before God to obey you rather than God: for we cannot refuse to obey him who hath said, 'Go ye into all the world and preach the Gospel to every creature.'"[4] Thus, with this biblical command as the motto of the Waldensians, they continued to preach the gospel, believing they had authority from heaven.

At first, the Waldensians engaged in a combination of large public venues and small private groups to share their message.[5] However, due to their anti-Catholic teachings, they were excommunicated from Lyons, declared schismatics by Pope Lucius III in 1184, and condemned as heretics by the Fourth Lateran Council of 1215. Consequently, their efforts were confined to house-to-house preaching. During this time, Waldo and his cohort developed a system by which they would enter a town and secretly meet with small groups of Waldensians, usually in a local's home. At times, these small groups would meet in poor outskirts of the town, which they called *scholas* ("schools"). Regardless, these meetings usually consisted of a meal, prayer, and participation in the Lord's Supper. The gatherings also served as an opportunity for the locals to minister to the traveling preachers with hospitality, and for the itinerants to make further plans for their house-to-house campaign.[6] Reflecting on the Waldensian small group gatherings, Alan Kreider writes:

3. McDow and Reid, *Firefall*, 114.
4. Comba, *History of the Waldenses of Italy*, 28.
5. Tourn et al., *You Are My Witnesses*, 16.
6. Comiskey, *2000 Years of Small Groups*.

These Waldensian cells, meeting generally at night, in houses and barns, were marked by intense activity. Those present were laypeople, often "persons of basest occupations" such as tailors, shoemakers and smiths. Women were there in disproportionate strength. Largely excluded from using their gifts in the church, they were finding among the "heretics" liberty to teach and preach. Everyone participated: "Old and young, men and women, by day and by night, they do not stop their learning and teaching others."[7]

As a result of their persistent memorization, recitation, and application of the Bible during these meetings, Kreider goes on to report that illiterates were learning to read, and in Austria one critic even met "an unlearned rustic who could recite the Book of Job word for word, and many others who know the entire New Testament perfectly."[8] Sadly, centuries of severe persecution would follow the Waldensians. Nevertheless, their home-based movement continued to spread across the continent, as Rad Zdero notes, "They expanded their work all over Europe, so much so that it was believed by the canon of Notre Dame that a third of all Christendom had attended the Waldensian meetings."[9]

The Lollards

Just over a century later a second movement emerged that served as a precursor to the Protestant Reformation. This movement can be traced back to the "Morning Star of the Reformation," John Wycliffe.[10] Born of noble heritage around 1324 in Yorkshire, England, Wycliffe graduated from Oxford with his master's degree in 1361 and his doctorate in 1372. Appointed warden of Canterbury Hall in 1365, he found himself in the middle of a dispute between the monks and the secular priests over distinctions the Catholic Church placed on the two offices. Since both parties had been residents of Canterbury Hall, Wycliffe felt compelled to appeal to Pope Urban V for a resolution, only to see the pope uncaringly dismiss it. It was this event along with later disappointing experiences with the pope that sparked the fires for reform in Wycliffe's heart.[11]

---

7. Kreider, "Protest and Renewal," 21.
8. Kreider, "Protest and Renewal," 21.
9. Zdero, *Global House Church Movement*, 63.
10. Wiersbe and Perry, *Wycliffe Handbook*, 174.
11. McDow and Reid, *Firefall*, 124.

John Wycliffe had a unique reverence for the Bible in contrast to the growing philosophical pursuits of his academic surroundings. His knowledge and passion for the Scriptures would provide the foundation for his ministry of reform. McDow and Reid note Wycliffe's peculiarity, commenting, "In this spiritually depraved culture, Wycliffe demonstrated the courage to be the voice of God, a translator of the Bible, and an expositor of Scripture."[12] Indeed, while his theological views and his calculation that Scripture was the highest authority and not the papacy prodded the antagonism of others, it was Wycliffe's translation of the Bible into English that brought him into direct conflict with the Church of Rome. "Wycliffe's Bible," as it was called, was widely distributed throughout England and had an enormous influence over the populace, further undermining the pull of the papacy in the nation. Thus, as expected, the translation was denounced by the Catholic Church as unauthorized and inaccurate. As for Wycliffe, he was condemned as a heretic by the faculty at Oxford and then by the Archbishop of Canterbury in 1382.[13] On December 28, 1384, while observing mass at his parish church in Lutterworth, Wycliffe suffered a massive stroke, dying three days later.[14] Ultimately, in protest to Wycliff's influence on the emergence of the Lollards, his remains were exhumed from St. Mary's Church cemetery, burned, and scattered on the Swift River.[15]

Before his death in 1382, Wycliffe organized a small group of his followers called Lollards or "Poor Priests." It would be through this group that Wycliffe's work toward reform would persist. The Lollards believed the Catholic Church was corrupt and, among other doctrines, refuted its claim to be the true church as not biblically justified. Championing a lay priesthood, the Lollards denied that the Catholic Church had the divine authority to determine who was called to be a priest. In addition, they rejected the Catholic teaching that a priest had the authority to forgive sins, the practice of clerical celibacy, and that priests can hold government positions. Most importantly, they embraced the doctrine of priesthood of all believers. It is this doctrine, much like the Waldensians, that prompted the Lollards toward a culture of mutual accountability fostered in home meetings. However, it was not only this doctrine that led them to return to

---

12. McDow and Reid, *Firefall*, 124.
13. Estep, *Renaissance and Reformation*, 64.
14. Dyson, *Life and Work of John Wyclif*, 121.
15. Hall, *Perilous Vision of John Wyclif*, 261.

the early church practice of house church gatherings, but fierce persecution they were facing also made it necessary.

What is particularly notable about the Lollard small group system is that they tended to gather according to homogeneity. Examining the legal evidence against the Lollards, Shannon McSheffrey observes, "These loose groups can be discerned from the court book evidence: groups of men, groups of married couples, and groups of women. While these categories were by no means hard and fast, it is natural that the general tendencies of social interactions in medieval society would be duplicated within the Lollard communities."[16] In addition to this dynamic, Robert Lutton noticed that the Lollards were often connected to one another through family relations, which allowed their small groups to be networked together via the extended family. "Everyday or occasional relationships helped to hold the geographically disparate Kentish Lollard groups together into the more closed circles of conventicle or household meetings."[17] Within these meetings, the agenda was clear: to read, understand, and memorize the Scriptures. Alan Kreider explains:

> The central activity of these cells was reading the English Bible . . . These Scriptures were of course available only in manuscript, and so expensive to buy; like other English books, they were also dangerous to possess. So, although some people had good collections ("book of Luke and one of Paul, and a gloss of the Apocalypse"), many others could possess the Bible only by memorizing it. Groups of believers stayed up all night to do this. Some of them took private instruction to commit the Beatitudes to heart.[18]

These small group gatherings served as a key element for the spread of the movement as well. Indeed, the movement relied as much on house-to-house visits as it did on evangelizing in pubs and preaching in markets. Lollards conversed over meals in homes and passed out tracts and invitations to reading circles. Its leaders moved from place to place, encouraging and instructing existing cells and establishing new ones.[19] As a result of their concerted and persistent efforts, one observer claimed that the Lollards

---

16. McSheffrey, *Lollards of Conventry*, 37.

17. Lutton, *Lollardy and Orthodox Religion*, 182. Lutton goes on to illustrate that Lollard teachings would spread through natural conversations in ordinary affairs, such as a carpenter sharing his beliefs while working on someone's house.

18. Kreider, "Protest and Renewal," 1.

19. Comiskey, *2000 Years of Small Groups*, 73.

grew with such "amazing vitality that it became a proverb that every second man you met in England was a Lollard."[20] Perhaps more accurately, historians believe that about a fourth of the nation was at least sympathetic to Wycliffe.[21] By 1395 under the rule of King Richard II (1377–99), the Lollards were represented in Parliament and some of their propositions were presented for legislative enactment.

However, with the ascent of King Henry IV (1399–1413) to the English throne came the passage of *De haeretico comburendo* (*On the Burning of a Heretic*) in 1401, whereby the Lollards became the focal targets of persecution and martyrdom.[22] Nevertheless, the reformational ideas of Wycliffe and the Lollards had made their mark in England; moreover, by virtue of King Richard II's marriage to the daughter of the Bohemian King in 1382,[23] these same notions would spread to Bohemia and into the heart of the eventual leader of a third pre-Reformation movement, John Huss.

The Hussites

A third pre-Reformation movement in which small groups were significantly engaged came through a group of believers under the name of their leader, John Huss. Huss was born in Husinec, Bohemia around 1372. Although nothing is known about his parents or early childhood, he apparently was raised in a godly but poor home. To escape poverty, Huss trained for the priesthood, stating, "I had thought to become a priest quickly in order to secure a good livelihood and dress and to be held in esteem by men."[24] In 1390, he enrolled in the University of Prague, where he received his master's degree in 1396 and another in theology in 1404. In 1401, Huss became the dean of the university, and a year later he was appointed the preacher at the Church of the Holy Innocents of Bethlehem in Prague.

During these years, Huss had been influenced by Wycliffe's ideas through Czech students who studied at Oxford and carried Wycliffe's teachings back to Prague. After reading Wycliffe's writings, Huss found himself embracing them as his own, and he began teaching them to his congregation and classes. Huss was widely popular, and his preaching attracted

20. Carrick, *Wycliffe and the Lollards*, 190.
21. McDow and Reid, *Firefall*, 126.
22. Lucas, *Renaissance and the Reformation*, 119–22.
23. Estep, *Renaissance and Reformation*, 69.
24. Quoted in Comiskey, *2000 Years of Small Groups*, 74–5.

large crowds to his church, including some Bohemian rulers. Using his platform as the most popular preacher in the country, Huss attempted to reform the church through his sermons by attacking the immorality of the clergy, bishops, and even the papacy. Some of the Bohemian rulers joined his cause, and the archbishop of Prague even seemed to quietly endorse Huss, making him preacher to the clergy's synod.

Unfortunately, political infighting between the university's German and Czech alliances was growing, and Huss's invocation of Wycliffe's teachings only made matters worse. On May 15, 1408, charges were filed against Huss by the German members of the university faculty, claiming his views on reform were heretical. However, the king of Bohemia sided with Huss, giving the Czechs the upper hand, and leaving the Germans no choice but to flee to other universities. Still, the archbishop had had enough, and he excommunicated Huss from the Roman Church in 1411. Not wanting to cause problems for the people of Prague, Huss left his post in 1412 to begin an itinerant ministry. In that same year, a papal bull was issued against Huss and his followers. Erwin Weber reports, "Anyone could kill the Czech reformer on sight, and those who gave him food or shelter would suffer the same fate."[25] Weber goes on to describe that when three of Huss's followers spoke publicly against the selling of indulgences, they were arrested and beheaded. In 1414, the Bohemian king's brother, King Sigismund (who would eventually become the Roman emperor) convened the Council of Constance. In December, at the urging of Sigismund and the promise of safe conduct, Huss appeared before the council to present his case. However, when he arrived, Huss was immediately arrested and his safe conduct denied. He was kept in chains and relentlessly tortured for three months until March 1415. Finally, on July 6, 1415, Huss was condemned as a heretic on thirty different counts, and subsequently sentenced to death.[26] He, along with his books, was burned at the stake the same day.

Even though Huss did not establish a system of small groups himself, his biblical preaching and teaching forged a path to what has been called the "Hussite Reformation" or "Czech Reformation."[27] In 1457, more than forty years after Huss's death, these Hussites would form the *Unitas Fratrum* (Unity of Brethren), and its movement would grow primarily through house-to-house ministry. As a result, the Unity of Brethren would swell to

25. Weber, "Luther the Swan," 10.
26. McDow and Reid, *Firefall*, 127–28.
27. Atwood, *Theology of the Czech Brethren*, 5.

a membership of over two hundred thousand people throughout the nations of Bohemia and Moravia.[28] However, fierce persecution raged against the Hussites, especially during the Thirty Years' War (1618–48), forcing the group to meet in underground house churches. Still, they persisted, and the Hussite cell groups continued to meet until they relocated—nearly two hundred years later—to the estate of Count Ludwig Von Zinzendorf, where they changed their name to the United Brethren and became an essential element of the Moravian Church.[29]

Martin Luther

Just before John Huss was burned at the stake in 1415, one tradition records that one of his accusers gloated, "Your goose is cooked," a derisive play on the name Huss, which means "goose" in Czech. In response, Huss declared, "Today, you are burning a goose; however, a hundred years from now, you will be able to hear a swan sing, you will not burn it, you will have to listen to him."[30] Just over one hundred years later, on October 31, 1517, Martin Luther presented his Ninety-Five Theses. Luther later came to believe that he was the fulfillment of Huss's prophecy, writing in 1531, "John Huss prophesied of me when he wrote from his prison in Bohemia: They will now roast a goose (for Hus means a goose), but after a hundred years they will hear a swan sing; him they will have to tolerate. And so it shall continue, if it please God."[31] Thus with the rise of Martin Luther, the early work of Waldo, Wycliffe, and Huss had begun to come to fruition.

Like these three early Reformers, probably the greatest contribution of Martin Luther was his proclamation of the truths that justification came by faith alone and that Scripture was the final authority. Beyond these, Luther also championed other positions that deviated from the Catholic Church. He argued that salvation did not come by the sacraments but through faith in Christ. He rejected that faith consisted of obedience to the teachings of the church, insisting that it rather came through trusting in the promises of God and merits of Christ as declared in the Scriptures. Luther further believed that the church was not the institution defined by apostolic succession but a community of faith. Finally, Luther taught the doctrine of the

28. Butalia and Small, *Religion in Ohio*, 193.
29. Comiskey, *2000 Years of Small Groups*, 76–77.
30. Weber, "Luther the Swan," 10.
31. Plass, *What Luther Says*, 1175.

priesthood of every believer. He was convinced that each individual believer is capable of reading the Bible and understanding its plain meaning, can pray directly to God, and should be actively involved as a minister of the gospel. It is especially out of these last two teachings—the community of faith and the priesthood of the believer—that Luther saw the benefit of small groups among Christian congregations.

Looking for ways to implement these doctrines led Luther to entertain the idea of using small groups as part of the church's reformation. Moreover, with his new translation of the Bible into the common German language and the advent of the printing press, Scripture had quickly become available for personal and group study. Thus, Luther envisioned the possible use of home meetings as a venue for believers to learn the Scriptures, grow in a community of believers, and personally express their faith—all of which they did not experience within the institutional church. He expressed his vision for these house gatherings in his preface to the *German Mass and Order of Service*:

> The third kind of service should be a truly evangelical order and should not be held in a public place for all sorts of people. But those who want to be Christians in earnest and who profess the gospel with the hand and mouth should sign their names and meet alone in a house somewhere to pray, to read, to baptize, to receive the sacrament, and to do other Christian works.... Here one could set up a brief and neat order for baptism and the sacrament and center everything on the Word, prayer and love.[32]

However, even from the outset, Luther had his doubts, "because I have not yet the people or persons for it, nor do I see many who want it."[33]

Later, in light of several troubling circumstances that had emerged as a result of the Reformation, Luther felt compelled to "change his mind" about the implementation of a small group strategy. Indeed, in a personal letter written on April 14, 1529, to a priest named Karl Weiss, Luther shared that he no longer believed that "earnest Christians" should meet together privately in homes "to pray, to read, to baptize, to receive sacraments, and to do other Christian works."[34] He gave at least three reasons for his change of mind. First, Luther was concerned that some would errantly consider themselves earnest Christians, thereby be in danger of falling into devil-devised

---

32. Luther, "German Mass," 63–64.
33. Luther, "German Mass" 63–64.
34. White, "Concerning Earnest Christians," 274.

pride. "He [Satan] would be able to get us to isolate all the strongest Christians, and keep them from the weak. Then the strong would grow proud, the weak would give up, and all would go to hell in a handbasket."[35] Luther also was worried that "such self-styled 'earnest Christians' will start to think of themselves as the one, pure church," and he believed that "if we allow small groups of Christians to separate from the rest, to read the Word, to baptize, and to receive sacraments, we will have established a new church."[36] This suspicion led him to express a third reason for his rejection of small groups—his fear of a rising movement among those called Anabaptists and the damaging division their movement may cause. He writes,

> All the elements would be there in these small groups and, as sure as Satan seeks to destroy our souls, some Pharisaical spirit will conclude that his little group is the church, and that everyone outside is damned. Indeed, it has already happened, if I am to believe the rumor I hear. Certain false brethren rebaptize themselves and then sneak away from God's church to meet with other misled fools in various holes and corners. They claim that they are the only true Christians, and teach that they must separate from all inquiry.[37]

As a result of his opposition to the rise of the Anabaptists, Luther finally concluded in 1529 that the Scriptures did not warrant the use of small groups.[38] Thus, although at first Luther saw great potential in the spread of reform and the discipleship of believers through the venue of small groups, he ultimately did not see them through because of cultural implications. Reflecting on this missed opportunity for Luther's legacy, Joel Comiskey summarizes, "Meeting in home groups was Luther's unwritten thesis which he believed, but failed to implement because of a spirit of caution, political considerations, and fear of losing the movement to the Anabaptists."[39]

The Anabaptists

While Luther and other Reformers flirted with the use of home meetings, it was the Reformation's more radical factions, especially the Anabaptists, who fully embraced a small group strategy. In general the Anabaptists,

35. White, "Concerning Earnest Christians," 278.
36. White, "Concerning Earnest Christians," 275.
37. White, "Concerning Earnest Christians," 275.
38. White, "Concerning Earnest Christians," 276–77.
39. Comiskey, *2000 Years of Small Groups*, 85.

or Radical Reformers, had much in common with the other Reformers. They agreed with the Reformers on the doctrines of justification by faith and the authority of the Bible, and they were likewise fierce defenders of the priesthood of all believers. However, there were differences as well. In terms of focus, for example, while the Reformers concentrated on altering doctrines and church practices, the Anabaptists (while still stressing these same issues) majored on spiritual conversions. As a result, at the same time that followers of the Reformation merely switched their allegiances from Catholicism to their chosen Reformer's position regardless of spiritual change (or lack thereof), followers of the Anabaptists joined the movement *because* of their spiritual conversion.[40]

The most significant difference between the Anabaptists and the other Reformers centered on the doctrine of baptism. The Anabaptists rejected the long-standing church tradition of infant baptism as a blasphemous formality. Instead, they believed that a public confession of their faith in Christ after their conversion, confirmed by baptism as an adult, was the only biblical baptismal practice. Moreover, they held that infants and small children are not held accountable for sin until they become cognizant of good and evil and can receive Christ out of their own free will. Only then, upon their conversion, should they be baptized. This doctrine of baptism became their signature characteristic among other believers and the primary source of their derision. Joel Comiskey explains the reason for such animosity by so many against the group:

> The fierce resistance to this practice had more to do with culture than Christianity. In other words, to be baptized was a civil issue, and those who refused to be baptized as an infant tore at the seams of a Christian society. When Luther, Zwingli, and others led their movements away from Catholicism, many practices were changed. But infant baptism, the accepted baptismal mode for most of Christian history, was not. Baptizing only adults tore at the heart of both church and state.[41]

Consequently, both Catholics and mainline Reformers alike rejected and even persecuted the Anabaptists. Luther called them "swarms of raving fanatics—'too many bees chasing too many bonnets.'"[42] They were labeled *Anabaptists* ("rebaptizers") as a means of scorn and insult. More

40. McDow and Reid, *Firefall*, 154.
41. Comiskey, *2000 Years of Small Groups*, 96.
42. Lindberg, *European Reformations*, 169.

importantly, under the legal codes of the time, rebaptism was a crime punishable by death.

In 1522, the Anabaptists gathered as small groups in private homes for worship, discipleship, and fellowship. These meetings grew into a large number of lay reading groups, concentrated mainly in and around the city of Zürich. These home-based cell groups became so popular that at one point even the Zürich Reformer Ulrich Zwingli promoted them, observing that the group members appeared more knowledgeable of the Scriptures than some priests.[43] However, when the Anabaptist leaders Conrad Grebel and Simon Stumpf proposed to separate the movement from the rest of society so to establish it as consisting only of true Christians, this was too much for Zwingli, causing him to join his fellow Reformers in opposing the faction.[44]

The history of the Anabaptists is a turbulent one. They endured the combined persecution of both Catholics and Reformers. It is largely due to this hostility that small groups played such an important role in the Anabaptist movement. In her study of the Anabaptists' use of small groups, Jane Latham concludes:

> As well as being used as an effective means of evangelism and cultivation of the Anabaptist faith, the small group was also employed out of necessity. Anabaptists met in small groups because all Anabaptist activity was illegal. The Anabaptist concept of church as a gathered community combined together to produce the small group meeting as the movement's main mode of existence.[45]

On the other hand, while small groups may have originally been used by them to avoid hostility, history suggests that the Anabaptists found its benefits extended beyond protection from persecution. Indeed, Donald Durnbaugh points out that even after persecution subsided, they continued to meet in homes, believing it was more faithful to the Scriptures and the practice of the early church.[46]

---

43. Latham, "In Search of the True Church," 15.
44. Latham, "In Search of the True Church," 17.
45. Latham, "In Search of the True Church," 110–11.
46. Durnbaugh, "Intentional Community," 18.

Conclusion

The aim of the first two chapters has been to paint a picture of the biblical and historic background of the presence, adaptation, and significant influence of a small group dynamic throughout Christian history leading up to the time of the first major spiritual awakening. Chapter 1 addressed the biblical precedent and early use of small groups during the time preceding and during the early church era. The focus of this chapter, on the other hand, was to carry the historical baton through the centuries leading up to and throughout the Protestant Reformation. In this conclusion, it seems necessary to note that, much like the Waldensians, Lollards, and Hussites of the preceding centuries, Martin Luther and the other Reformers were not revivalists in the conventional sense nor in the way this book has defined it. On the contrary, their desire appears to be for the doctrinal and institutional change in Christianity rather than its revival. While similarities do exist between them, spiritual awakening is not the same as reform. Spiritual awakening is immediate, rejuvenates the believer, and usually produces unusual evangelistic outcomes. Reform, on the other hand, is a gradual change to the church's doctrine and practice. Despite their differences, both can be directed by God, and both often receive strong opposition. As was seen with the pre-Reformation movements, both have also contained some aspect of small groups as a key element. Although the small group dynamic was not as widely welcomed among the Reformers as with their predecessors, it nonetheless found its place in Reformation. Thus, while the employment of small groups ebbed and flowed throughout these turbulent centuries, they nonetheless found favor among enough of the factions to weather these storms of Christian conflict. Perhaps more importantly, this continuation of the small group dynamic helped set the stage for the first major Christian revival, the First Great Awakening.

3

Small Groups in the First Great Awakening (1726–1791)

DURING THE EARLY YEARS of the United States, French philosopher and political scientist Alexis de Tocqueville toured the infant nation to understand the secret to its unexpected success. Although a great deal of dispute rages over the quote's authenticity, the Frenchman's observation is often summarized by the simple quip, "America is great because America is good." De Tocqueville recognized that the strength of America was found in its churches, as they deposited moral aptitude and a steady sense of dependence upon Almighty God. Indeed, the First Great Awakening (1726-91), arguably Christianity's first historic revival, wielded significant influence on the moral character of the new nation.[1]

The First Great Awakening of Europe and North America arose out of a tide of dead formalism in the church and humanistic rationalism in the world, taking place predominantly in Britain (where it was known as the Evangelical or Methodist Revival) and the North American colonies (where it was called the Great Awakening). As powerful and vast as this renewal was, research indicates that much of it was rooted in small group gatherings.

---

1. Towns and Whaley, *Worship through the Ages*, 114. For a full reading of de Tocqueville's observations during his nine-month tour of America, see de Tocqueville, *Democracy in America*.

Early Evidence of Small Groups: The Pietists, Puritans, and Moravians

While this famous era of Christian prominence is typically known by its champions like Jonathan Edwards, George Whitefield, and John and Charles Wesley, the background of the First Great Awakening can be traced several years earlier with the spiritual renewal in other movements throughout Europe during this time, namely Pietism, Puritanism, and the rise of Moravians. These three movements shared at least two common characteristics: an emphasis on spiritual transformation that results in personal holiness, and the use of small groups to accomplish this spiritual objective.

The Conference of Puritanism

The modern caricature of Puritans is plagued with visions of sour, legalistic, killjoy Christians in black steeple-hats who were bent on preventing people from doing what they wanted. In truth, Puritans were sold-out Christians who were excited about biblical truth and convinced that spiritual transformation was possible to experience in a believer's life. Seeing something quite different in the teaching and lifestyle propagated by the Anglican Church, they sought to "purify" their motherland's doctrine, ecclesiology, and culture. Puritans believed this purification would be accomplished by the combined approach of biblical preaching and small groups, sometimes called *conference, conventicles,* or *prophecy meeting*. While the terms varied at different times for different reasons, they all shared the common description of a small group of believers gathering together to discuss spiritual matters. The *Oxford English Dictionary* defines the sixteenth-century usage of the term *conference* as "the action of conferring or taking counsel, not always on an important or serious subject," noting that it formerly had the general sense of "a meeting or rendezvous for conversation."[2] Joel Comiskey explains that *conventicle* referred to an "unlawful or secret religious gathering" during the time of the Puritans. He goes on to explain that during the period of 1570–1620, the term *prophecy meetings* was used based on 1 Corinthians 14 and implied a discussion about prophesy in house groups.[3] It was from this frame of reference that sixteenth- and seventeenth-century Puritans frequently gathered for the purpose of prayer, Scripture reading,

2. "Conference," *OED*.
3. Comiskey, *2000 Years of Small Groups*, 107.

Bible memorization, and discussion of a recent sermon for the purpose of practical application. John Eliot (ca. 1604–90) wrote that in the gathering he was a part of, "We pray, and sing, and repeat sermons, and confer together about the things of God."[4] A particularly common activity in these conventicles was the discussion of the latest sermon, as John Udall (ca. 1560–92) in his *Certaine Sermons* explained:

> After that sermon is done, we ought at our coming home to meet together, and say one to another: "come, we have all been where we have heard God's word taught; let us confer about it, that we may not only call to remembrance [sic] those things that every one of us have carried away, but also that one may have the benefit of the labours of others."[5]

The importance of these small group gatherings as a means of spiritual transformation (called "a means of grace") cannot be understated. Puritans believed that spiritual transformation was not complete until a person was committed to fellowship with other believers. For this reason, Puritans gathered together both at a place of worship and in homes, as well as at various times—some monthly, some weekly, and some even twice per week. What also cannot be understated is the effect the Puritan small group strategy had both on their adherents and at large. Joanne Jung summarizes this significance:

> Adding to the ubiquitous sounds of the Bible in this Puritan era, conference served to weave a believing community together. Conference was a means of grace that was promoted and exercised by both clergy and laity. From parish to household, whether academic or popular, clergy present or not, conference was a widely accepted means of grace among the godly: a form of enabling that was encouraged and enjoyed.[6]

Moreover, Frances Couvares expresses the significance of Puritan small groups for future generations of Christians:

> From these private meetings, which perhaps more than any institution or idea provided Puritans with a group identity, sprang not only the likes of John Winthrop, Thomas Hooker, Thomas

---

4. Mather, *The Life and Death of the Renoun'd Mr. J. Eliot*, 19–21, cited by Hambrick-Stowe, *Practice of Piety*, xv.

5. Udall, *Certaine Sermons, Taken Out of Several Places of Scripture*, cited by Tiller, *Puritan*, 10.

6. Jung, *Godly Conversation*, 89.

Shepard, and others who became staunch supporters of non-separating congregationalism, but also those individuals who by the mid-1640s had helped to generate a myriad of radical Puritan sects that threatened to fulfill the prophecy of Acts 17:6 and turn the known world upside down.[7]

The Pietist Conventicles

At the beginning of the seventeenth century, much of Christianity found itself in the mire of spiritual stagnation, ecclesiastical corruption, and denominational conflict. In response, a movement of Christian renewal emerged in the form of what is historically called Pietism, with Philip Jakob Spener (1635–1705) as one of its chief leaders. Peter Bunton explains that the Pietists viewed themselves as completing what the Reformers started, stating, "To them [the Reformation] had largely been a reformation of doctrine rather than of life. Such a reformation of life would require direct application of biblical insights to everyday living involving the laity's using the Scriptures for themselves."[8] Spener was perplexed by the spiritual shallowness and theological ineptness becoming prevalent in the church in his day. In 1670, he began to hold religious meetings in his home, which he called *collegia pietatis*, or "schools of godliness;" and in 1675, Spener published the seminal *Pia Desideria* ("Godly Desires"). In *Pia Desideria*, Spener highlighted several pieces of evidence regarding spiritual decline, exposing sins among the political authorities and laity, and particularly calling out the clergy for their insatiable appetite for controversial nit-picking and theoretical preaching. He then called for a six-point plan for church reform.[9]

The very first proposal Spener offered was an earnest and thorough study of the Scriptures employed in various ways, including private meetings. Spener argued that small groups were needful because the people were not learning the Scriptures through the conventional practice of preaching. He explained that the congregation did not hear much of the sermon at all, or they heard only a few sayings or directives which are mentioned. Even then, they are not able to understand their significance even though there is something important in them. Therefore, citing 1 Corinthians 14, Spener suggests:

7. Couvares, *Interpretations of American History*, 54.
8. Bunton, "300 Years of Small Groups," 92.
9. Comiskey, *2000 Years of Small Groups*, 116–19.

> It would perhaps not be inexpedient (and I set this down for further and more mature reflection) to reintroduce the ancient and apostolic kind of church meetings. . . . Anybody who is not satisfied with his understanding of a matter should be permitted to express his doubts and seek further explanation. On the other hand, those (including the ministers) who have made more progress should be allowed the freedom to state how they understand each passage. Then all that has been contributed, insofar as it accords with the sense of the Holy Spirit in the Scriptures, should be carefully considered by the rest, especially by the ordained ministers, and applied to the edification of the whole meeting.[10]

Spener believed that these small group church meetings were the most effective way for people to experience spiritual transformation. If left to the sermon alone, Spener was concerned that most would easily forget the Scripture's message instead of applying it for spiritual transformation. Spener recognized that without the Scripture's immediate and personal application, its impact would be lost in the busyness of life. Donald F. Durnbaugh observes a key distinctive of Pietism:

> The congregation was understood not so much as a vehicle for administering grace and the deposit of faith but rather as an association of the regenerate who came together to strengthen each other in the Christian walk. For this reason, a hallmark of Pietism came to be conventicles, small groups of earnest Christians who met privately for mutual edification and encouragement, the so-called *ecclesiola in ecclesia* (the little church within the church).[11]

While *Pia Desideria* was embraced by many parts of European Christendom, Spener's idea of *collegia pietatis* was severely criticized. One of the main causes for this opposition was due to some who participated in small group meetings, using it as a replacement for corporate worship.[12] Despite Spener's forceful rebuke of such practices as a distortion of its design, the opposition toward Pietism nonetheless severely hindered its small group movement as well as Spener's general reforms. In fact, Spener's hometown of Frankfort, Germany ordered that these small group meetings be shut down.[13] Nevertheless, despite all its setbacks, Pietism and its conventicles

---

10. Spener, *Pia Desideria*, 88.
11. Quoted in Schneider, *German Radical Pietism*, vii.
12. Latourette, *History of Christianity*, 895.
13. Young, *New Life for Your Church*, 109.

continued its effectiveness under the leadership of August Herman Francke (1663–1727), becoming the forerunner of the Moravian small group model and certainly playing a role in influencing the idea of small groups in the ministries of Jonathan Edwards and John Wesley.

The Moravian Bands

Count Nicolaus Ludwig von Zinzendorf (1700–1760) was an aristocrat who was raised by a Pietist grandmother. While attending school in Halle, he came under the influence of A. H. Francke. In 1722, Zinzendorf became aware of the persecution of the Bohemian Brethren (spiritual descendants of John Huss) and, having inherited an estate at Berthelsdorf, he began offering asylum to the persecuted believers in Bohemia and Moravia. This community was eventually named Herrnhut, meaning "the Lord's watch," and became the headquarters for Moravian Christians. In 1727, the community experienced a revival that would change the course of their lives. Alvin Reid describes a pivotal moment at the beginning of this revival, when Zinzendorf is in prayer with a small group of believers.

> On August 5, 1727, Zinzendorf spent the whole night in prayer with about a dozen others. Powerful revival came on August 13 in conjunction with the celebration of the Lord's Supper. On that day the Moravian Church was born.... Forty-eight adults committed to cover the twenty-four hours of each day in prayer, while the children held their own meetings for prayer and praise. This practice continued for a century; thus, the reference by some to the One Hundred Year Prayer Movement of the Moravians.[14]

Like the Pietists, the Moravians cultivated a grassroots and communal culture among its believers, stressing unity, holiness, and intimate fellowship. Even before arriving in Herrnhut, the Bohemian Brethren had already begun holding small group meetings for prayer and Bible study.[15] It was natural, then, for the Moravians to codify small groups as part of their culture. In July 1727, Zinzendorf began developing three types of communal structures: choirs, diaspora societies, and bands. Choirs were essentially the structure designed for how the believers would live together. Diaspora societies were geographically diverse groups of believers

---

14. McDow and Reid, *Firefall*, 180.
15. Hamilton and Hamilton, *History of the Moravian Church*, 32.

from the same general region that met together, usually in homes, for prayer, singing, reading, and discussion of sermons. For the purpose of evangelism, these societies spread throughout many European nations, so that by 1746 they had expanded to nearly 700 societies.[16] The most direct application of small groups, however, came in the form of bands (*banden* in German, later called *kleine Gesellschaften* ["little societies"]).[17] The bands were formed by grouping people of the same sex and marital status. People could join whichever band was most suitable to them, and the band's activities were generally controlled by its members. Bands met for one to three hours, depending on the group's desire, and they could meet virtually anywhere except a church building. Bands were encouraged to use their meeting as a safe place for confession of sin, spiritual growth, community discipline, and character building.

Zinzendorf was the Moravian small group strategy's greatest champion, defending them from biblical, theological, and practical perspectives. As justification for the practice, he and his cohorts would cite Mary's visit to Elizabeth (Luke 1:39), the biblical call for mutual confession (Gal 6:1–2; Jas 5:16), and Jesus' use and teaching of small group fellowship, including Matthew 18:20, "For where two or three are gathered together in My name, I am there in the midst of them."[18] John Weinlick reports Zinzendorf as stating, "I believe without such an institution, the church would never have become what it is now."[19]

The British Revivals and Wesleyan Methodism

The eighteenth-century revivals in Britain continue to hold great significance for the nation's history and heritage. Indeed, historian Earle Cairns ranks the Methodist movement alongside the French Revolution and the Industrial Revolution as "one of the great historical phenomena of the century."[20] Accordingly, few individuals stand more significant in the history of British Christianity than the founder of Methodism, "the apostle of England," John Wesley (1703–91). Clearly, Wesley's work was a key spark that erupted the fires of revival. His contributions to the eighteenth-century

16. Bunton, "300 Years of Small Groups," 95.
17. Bunton, "300 Years of Small Groups," 95.
18. Bunton, "300 Years of Small Groups, 96–97.
19. Weinlick, *Count Zinzendorf*, 84.
20. Cairns, *Christianity through the Centuries*, 416.

spiritual revivals in Britain and America—indeed to Christianity itself—are both legion and legendary. Yet Wesley did not work alone, nor did his influence on the British revivals derive out of nothing. Rather, it was the product of equally powerful partners and, indeed, influencers on Wesley himself, starting with his mother, Susanna.

The Early Influence of Small Groups on John Wesley

John Wesley was born in 1703 in Epworth, England, the fifteenth of nineteen children of Samuel and Susanna Wesley. His father was a graduate of Oxford and an Anglican minister, but both Samuel and Susanna were products of a strong Puritan heritage and staunch advocates of what was known at the time as "primitive Christianity." At its core, this ideal emphasized "imitation of the faith and life of early believers, ascetic practice for the self, godly discipline for society and regular participation in the church's celebration of the Eucharist."[21] Along with these high moral standards also came a strong engagement in voluntary religious societies designed to promote personal piety and doing good among people in general.[22] Out of these convictions Susanna raised her children through a "homeschool" approach, emphasizing conscientious efforts of personal holiness and frequent celebrations of communion. Academically, the children began learning to read by the time they could walk and talk. As they developed, they were expected to become proficient in both Greek and Latin as well as learn large portions of the New Testament. Aside from their academics, the family followed a disciplined schedule which included gathering together for morning and evening devotions. Susanna examined each child before lunch and prior to evening prayers, and each child spent an extended time with their mother one evening each week for intensive instruction on spiritual matters.[23] This rigid upbringing had an enormous impact on Wesley's spiritual and doctrinal development, eventually manifesting in some definitive elements of Methodism, namely the methodical practices of personal and corporate worship and the doctrine of holiness (the attainability of Christian perfection). Moreover, Susanna's strategy of discipleship also influenced her son and laid the groundwork

21. See Duffy, "Primitive Christianity Revived," 287–300.
22. Noll, *Rise of Evangelicalism*, 66–67.
23. McDow and Reid, *Firefall*, 186. See also Comiskey, *2000 Years of Small Groups*, 153.

for another characteristic of Methodism: small group discipleship. Jim and Carol Plueddemann describe the development of this phenomenon:

> His own mother, Susanna, had initiated home meetings in the parsonage years before. These began with devotional times which Susanna led for her children. A few neighbors asked to attend, and eventually the group grew to over 200 people . . . the vision for home groups would become an important dynamic in the ministry of her sons, John and Charles.[24]

The "Holy Club" at Oxford and the Conversion of George Whitefield

In June 1720, John Wesley entered Christ Church in Oxford, graduating with a bachelor of arts degree in 1724 and then a master of arts degree in 1727. Sensing a call to the ministry, Wesley returned to Epworth to assist his father in pastoring a neighboring church in Wroote, but then returned to Oxford in November 1729. While John was absent, his younger brother Charles (1707–88) had begun his studies at Christ Church. During this time, Charles was becoming serious about his faith in Christ, and he began a small group with two other like-minded students, Robert Kirkham and William Morgan. Casually organized, the three began to meet each day for prayer, spiritual reading, and self-examination. When John returned to Oxford he joined the group, firmed up its organization, began recruiting more participants (including George Whitefield 1714–70), and eventually became its leader. The small group began to practice strict discipline in their spiritual practices. Besides Bible study, prayer, and self-examination, the group took communion weekly and fasted on Wednesdays and Fridays. In addition, they began to minister to the poor, develop schools for children of the less fortunate, and proclaim the gospel wherever they went. Alvin Reid reports that after one of its members met a prisoner, he beckoned the group to begin ministering to the inmates. Upon gaining approval from Oxford's chaplain, the group began an evangelism ministry in the prison.[25]

Given the climate of low spirituality in Oxford at the time, however, this small group was met with derision. They were considered religious fanatics. Scoffers coined their group a "Holy Club," and its members

---

24. Plueddemann and Plueddemann, *Pilgrims in Progress*, 8.
25. McDow and Reid, *Firefall*, 186–87.

"Bible-Moths," "Enthusiasts," "Supererogation-Men," and "Methodists."[26] J. Edwin Orr records that on December 9, 1732, a local journal published a letter criticizing this "Holy Club," a copy of which was sent to William Law, a respected and pious writer at the time. After investigating, Law could find no one with a good word to say about the group. Rather, they were described as "gloomy," "melancholic," "zealous," and "miserable." Law then sought the group out himself and, after discovering their true nature, published an anonymous pamphlet in its defense. Summarizing Law's observation, Orr writes, "True, they took the communion once a week in the Cathedral, but they found that 'religion is a cheerful thing.' They were observing church fasts and prayers, but they also visited the sick and poor and prisoners."[27] Ultimately, the group embraced its "Holy Club" label, and declared that its "Methodist" description was a welcomed compliment. Moreover, this derided small group became in many respects the launching pad for the spiritual awakening that exploded in England, and eventually extended to America during the mid-1700s.

A. Skevington Wood claims that it is in this "Holy Club" small group that Charles Wesley guided George Whitefield through devotional reading before Whitefield's conversion during the spring of 1735.[28] Of his experience, Whitefield journals, "About this time God was pleased to enlighten my soul, and bring me into knowledge of His free grace, and the necessity of being justified in his sight by *faith only*."[29] With this particular event the fires of revival that eventually engulfed England had begun. After graduating from Oxford, Whitefield began an evangelistic campaign that would spiritually shake England to its core. In that same year, John and Charles Wesley and other members of the "Holy Club" deployed to Georgia as Christian missionaries.[30] In early 1737, while preparing to join his comrades in America, Whitefield began preaching in the cities of Bristol, Bath, Gloucester, and London. By the mid-point of that same year, unprecedented throngs began to crowd the churches where Whitefield was preaching. Mark Noll reports that between August and the end of December of that year, the twenty-two-year-old Whitefield preached over one hundred times—averaging six to

---

26. Noll, *Rise of Evangelicalism*, 68. For more discussion on these names, see Heitzenrater, *Wesley and the People Called Methodists*, 41; and Rack, *Reasonable Enthusiasts*, 84.

27. Orr, *Campus Aflame*, 24.

28. Wood, "John and Charles Wesley," 447.

29. Whitefield, *Journals of George Whitefield*, 43.

30. McDow and Reid, *Firefall*, 187.

seven times per week.³¹ Noll goes on to share that when Whitefield returned to England from his American voyage, he began to fuel the flames of revival even higher. Whitefield had become a national sensation and the English awakening was in full force. Indeed, Whitefield is an iconic figure of the First Great Awakening to many students of Christian history. Yet Whitefield's own personal revival, resulting in his conversion, began among a small group of friends in the Holy Club at Oxford.

John Wesley's Encounter with the Moravians

On their voyage to the colony of Georgia, John and Charles Wesley encountered the Moravians for the first time. John was deeply impressed by their faith, spirituality, and love, and this is seen no more clearly than during their voyage to America. On that trip, this small group of Moravian shipmates—twenty-six in all—began leading John Wesley down a spiritual journey that would ultimately change his life. While on the trip, he was taught German by one of them, and he eagerly participated in their worship services. More significantly, Wesley was profoundly moved by their spiritual peace in the midst of hopeless circumstances.

Halfway across the ocean, three storms had assaulted the ship, and a fourth storm was brewing to be even larger than the others. While hearing the liquid thunder of the waves crashing in erratic rhythm, Wesley wondered what eternity would be for him—for he was surely going to die. Terrified, Wesley wrote in his journal, "Storm greater: afraid!" But his Moravian shipmates had a different demeanor. John Wesley described in his own words this seminal moment:

> There was now an opportunity of trying whether they were delivered from the spirit of fear, as well as from that of pride, anger, and revenge. In the midst of the psalm wherewith their service began, the sea broke over, split the main-sail in pieces, covered the ship, and poured in between the decks, as if the great deep had already swallowed us up. A terrible screaming began among the English; The Germans calmly sung on. I asked one of them afterwards, "Was you not afraid?" He answered, "I thank God, no." I asked, "But were not your women and children afraid?" He replied, mildly, "No; our women and children are not afraid to die."³²

31. Noll, *Rise of Evangelicalism*, 87–89.
32. Wesley, Jan. 25, 1736; in Wesley, *Works*, 8.1.

Wesley marveled at the peace of the Moravians, especially during this time of imminent danger. More importantly, he realized that he did not share that same peace. The source of this peace became clear during another discussion with the Moravian leader on February 7, one day after setting foot on land:

> [The Moravian leader] said, "My brother, I must first ask you one or two questions. Have you the witness within yourself? Does the Spirit of God bear witness with your spirit that you are a child of God?" I was surprised and knew not what to answer. He observed it, and asked, "Do you know Jesus Christ?" I paused, and said, "I know he is the Saviour of the world." "True," he replied, "but do you know he has saved you?" I answered, "I hope he has died to save me." He only added, "Do you know yourself?" I said, "I do." But I fear they were vain words.[33]

Although he was on mission to share Christ with the Native Americans, Wesley realized he did not personally know Christ for himself. Reflecting on this dark time in his life a couple of years later, Wesley wrote in his journal, "I left my native country in order to teach the Georgian Indians the nature of Christianity. But what have I learned myself in the meantime? Why . . . that I who went to America to convert others was never myself converted to God."[34] Indeed, Wesley was on a turbulent spiritual journey, but one that yielded life-changing results. Orr summarizes, "Alas, Wesley's venture overseas was a qualified failure; but upon his return, he experienced in heart what he had preached from his mind, the grace of God."[35] That moment of experience came on May 24, 1738. Wesley was in attendance at a small Moravian meeting on Aldersgate Street, London. In some of his most famous words, he testifies about that experience:

> In the evening I went very unwillingly to a society in Aldersgate Street, where one was reading Luther's *Preface to the Epistle to the Romans*. About a quarter before nine, while he was describing the change which God works in the heart through faith in Christ, I felt my heart strangely warmed. I felt I did trust in Christ, Christ alone for salvation, and an assurance was given me that

---

33. Wesley, Feb. 7, 1736; in Wesley, *Works*, 8:1.
34. Wesley, Feb. 1, 1738; in Wesley, *Works*, 8:1.
35. Orr, *Campus Aflame*, 27.

he had taken away my sins, even mine, and saved me from the law of sin and death.[36]

Wesley's conversion experience at Aldersgate Street was so impactful that he travelled to Germany to meet with the revered Moravian leader, Count Nikolaus Ludwig von Zinzendorf in the Moravian community of Herrnhut. Wesley, a keen observer and prolific chronicler, took meticulous notes while in Herrnhut, studying their practices and methodology. Kenneth Latourette notes that Wesley had "an unusual capacity to accept suggestions and to adopt and adapt methods from various quarters."[37] For three weeks, Wesley observed and scrutinized the Moravian methods, taking copious and detailed notes. He was intrigued by their music and singing, especially how they used hymn singing as a form of instruction. He deeply admired their emphasis on community, as seen in their intense fellowship and unity before biblical instruction, as well as through their special "*Agape* feast" services and "watch nights."[38] What Wesley observed the most, however, was a system broken down into smaller groups for ministry and discipleship. "Count Zinzendorf had arranged the community into compact cells, or 'bands' as he called them, for spiritual oversight and community administration."[39] Wesley observed this same small group system while with the Moravian missionaries in Georgia. He noticed there how effective these smaller bands were in promoting godliness. Similarly, Wesley mimicked their pattern by dividing the larger body of Christian converts into smaller groups that he asked to meet weekly for exhortation and discipleship.[40]

Late in 1739, partly due to differences with Moravian doctrine and practices, Wesley broke ties with his Moravian brethren. Still, he was indebted to the Moravians for their invaluable influence on him. It was through the small group ministry of the Moravians that Wesley observed the peace of God in dire circumstances; it was in a small group meeting that Wesley felt his heart "strangely warmed," resulting in his conversion; and it was the small group strategy that Wesley documented as a powerful tool for organizing ministry and discipleship. While Wesley and the Moravians ultimately parted ways, their influence would remain irrevocably

36. Wesley, May 24, 1738; in Wesley, *Works*, 8:2.
37. Latourette, *History of Christianity*, 1026.
38. Comiskey, *2000 Years of Small Groups*, 160.
39. Henderson, *Wesley's Class Meeting*, 62.
40. Watson, *Early Methodist Class Meeting*, 88.

upon him, particularly manifesting in the strategy of the Methodist ministry Wesley would construct. It is largely due to Wesley's Methodism that the fires of the British revivals and the American First Great Awakening continued to burn for decades.

The Role of Small Groups in Sustaining the Effects of Revival

In 1739, John Wesley joined Whitefield in fueling the British awakening through open-air preaching and, more importantly, developing a structure that would sustain the revival through the discipleship of these new converts. Towns and Whaley describe the impact of the Whitefield-Wesley team:

> Wesley and Whitefield forever changed England and America through their innovative methods. The Church of England was the only official religion in England and many of the colonies during this era, but the Wesleys and Whitefield established dissenter churches that emphasized preaching, small accountability groups, and prayer meetings. This new movement was called "Methodist."[41]

Borrowing heavily from the Moravian template, Wesley structured this discipleship strategy into three interlocking groups: bands, class meetings, and societies. Bands were small groups of about six people of the same age, gender, and marital status who voluntarily came together to expose sin and temptation in their lives and seek inner purity and holiness.[42] Of these three elements of the Methodist structure, class meetings became the cornerstone. In 1742, after witnessing the slow ebbing of revival and the gradual regression of many of its converts, Wesley began dividing up the Methodist societies into groups of about twelve. Once established, Wesley determined that no one would any longer be able to join a society without first being a class member, declaring, "Those who will not meet in a class cannot stay with us."[43] Class meetings were formed according to geographic location, but were otherwise heterogeneous. Group members could vary in age, gender, social standing, and even spiritual maturity. Typically, the format for these meetings consisted of singing a hymn, the leader's opening

---

41. Towns and Whaley, *Worship through the Ages*, 119.

42. Comiskey, *2000 Years of Small Groups*, 170–71; Bunton, "300 Years of Small Groups," 98. Because attendance in bands was not required, only about 20 percent of Methodists during this movement ever joined.

43. Wesley, *Works*, 2.482.

statement regarding his spiritual condition, followed by each individual member following suit. Regarding the purpose of these class meetings, Bunton comments, "Although the primary purposes of class meetings were discipleship and discipline, they also served Wesley's evangelistic vision. There were more professed conversions in class meetings than in the preaching services."[44] Finally, societies were essentially the collection of all the class meetings and bands that made up a locale, thereby consisting of all Methodists in a general area. In today's terms, societies were the equivalent to a congregation. Although societies constituted all Methodists in a geographic area, they were clearly seen as less significant than class meetings. Whereas class meetings met weekly for intense discipleship, societies generally met once per quarter for corporate worship and instruction. Moreover, allowance in a society meeting was determined by one's attendance in a class meeting. George Hunter emphasizes this important comparison, stating, "A Methodist Society was composed of the sum total of classes attached to it. As one's membership in early Christianity was primarily to a house church and somewhat secondarily to the whole church within the city, so in early Methodism one's primary membership was in the class and somewhat secondarily in the society."[45]

It is nearly impossible to undersell the impact of small groups on the British revivals of the 1700s. Small groups existed in many different forms for years prior to these revivals and can be historically cited as an essential part of their inception. Moreover, due largely to the brilliance and labors of John Wesley's class meetings, the English awakening remained strong for nearly three-quarters of a century, and it planted seeds that would eventually yield the fruit of yet another awakening. Simply put, small groups helped start and sustain a lasting spiritual renewal that powerful preaching was incapable of doing alone. Unfortunately, the necessity of a small group strategy did not burden the heart of the "Grand Itinerant," George Whitefield. While Whitefield benefitted from the small group concept both in his conversion experience and in the magnificence of his ministry, he nonetheless did not sense the urgency for these small groups as a means for sustaining the work of the revivals. This would prove to be one of his greatest failures. Adam Clarke, a Methodist preacher contemporary to Wesley and Whitefield, recounted Wesley's urging for small groups: "From long experience I know the propriety of Mr. Wesley's advice: 'Establish

---

44. Bunton, "300 Years of Small Groups," 98.
45. Hunter, *Church for the Unchurched*, 84.

class-meetings and form societies wherever you preach and have attentive hearers; for, wherever we have preached without doing so, the word has been like seed by the way-side." Clarke goes on to reminisce Whitefield's costly neglect of Wesley's advice, stating, "Mr. Whitefield, when he separated from Mr. Wesley, did not follow it. What was the consequence? The fruit of Mr. Whitefield's labor died with himself. Mr. Wesley's remains and multiplies." Then, in one of the most remarkable admissions of the necessity of small groups, Clarke writes,

> Did Mr. Whitefield see his error? He did, but not till it was too late: his people, being long unused to it, would not come under this discipline. Have I authority to say so? I have; and you shall have it. Forty years ago I travelled in the Bradford (Wilts) Circuit, with Mr. John Pool. Himself told me this. Mr. P. was well known to Mr. Whitefield, who, having met him one day, accosted him in the following manner:
>
> Whitefield: Well, John, art thou still a Wesleyan?
>
> Pool: Yes, sir. I thank God I have the privilege of being in connexion with Mr. Wesley, and one of his preachers.
>
> W.: John, thou art in thy right place. My brother Wesley acted wisely: the souls that were awakened under his ministry he joined in class, and thus preserved the fruits of his labour. This I neglected, and my people are a rope of sand.[46]

The American Awakening and Conferencing

The British Revivals spread across the nation like a mystical wave, inciting spiritual renewal among stagnant believers, bringing thousands to the Christian faith, and birthing vibrant ministries as an alternative to the established church. However, this is only half of the story regarding the first great spiritual awakening, for revival fires further raged in the new land of America with equal fortitude. Like the British Revival, the Great Awakening in America benefited immeasurably from the work of Whitefield and the Wesleys, but it also produced a few revivalists of its own in men like Theodore Frelinghuysen, Gilbert Tennent, and Jonathan Edwards. Not only that but, like Britain, the American awakening can also attribute its eruption in part to the influence of small groups.

---

46. Etheridge, *Life of Adam Clarke*, 165–66.

BIG THINGS START SMALL

Theodore Frelinghuysen and Small Group Bible Studies

The first sparks of the American Great Awakening emerged in 1726 through the leadership of Dutch Reformed pastor Theodore Frelinghuysen (1691–1747). Frelinghuysen was impacted the by the Reformed stream of Pietism located along the lower Rhine River in the Ruhr region of Germany. The pastor at the time, Theodor Undereyck (1635–93) followed the examples of his Pietist mentors, Jodocus von Lodenstein and Jean DeLabadie, by initiating weekly small group Bible studies in his home. These weekly Bible studies brought revival to the Lower Rhine Valley.[47] Frelinghuysen took part in these small group studies and he brought the strategy with him to his pastorate among the Dutch Reformed churches in the Raritan River Valley of New Jersey. Determined to bring a new vitality to his parishioners, Frelinghuysen emphasized evangelistic preaching, the necessity of conversion by faith alone, church discipline (especially pertaining to the Lord's Supper), and fervent evangelistic visits.[48] Besides these, Frelinghuysen also brought with him the practice of small groups he had learned in Germany. He organized his congregation into groups for both study and prayer, urging them to pray publicly and extemporaneously. Frelinghuysen's efforts not only began to quicken the spiritually dormant among his parishioners, but he also inspired other ministers toward his model of ministry, perhaps the most significant among them being Gilbert Tennent (1703–64). Reflecting on these initial movements in preparation for revival, Noll observes, "In a word, long before organized evangelical movements existed, significant groups . . . were already beginning to practice distinctly evangelical forms of Christian faith."[49] A small group strategy was certainly among them.

Jonathan Edwards and Conference

Like Frelinghuysen among the German Pietists, Jonathan Edwards (1703–58) found the Puritan deployment of conference an indispensable part of the Christian life. From the earliest years of his adult life, Jonathan Edwards was a fierce advocate of personal holiness and commitment to Christ. Indeed, personal holiness and commitment to Christ, in Edward's day, was understood by the popular phrase "true religion." To Edwards, true religion

---

47. Scharpff, *History of Evangelism*, 27.
48. McDow and Reid, *Firefall*, 206–7.
49. Noll, *Rise of Evangelicalism*, 73.

was impossible without the community of other believers, for community was at the heart of spirituality. No one stands under the word of God alone, but with fellow brothers and sisters in Christ. Living as the Scriptures prescribe does not happen in isolation but in community, for the believer's heart is not private property but communal property. Edwards refused to assume that someone who faithfully attended Sunday service, who kept the sabbath, and read and meditated on the Scripture and Christian literature was actually living out the gospel fully. To him, spiritual transformation that provides freedom in Christ also comes through being known deeply, not only by Christ but by a community of Christians. It consists of both acceptance and continued admonishment and guidance in the believer's life in Christ. In short, Edwards saw spiritual formation as a journey, and success in the journey requires the believer to be a good traveling companion. Kyle Strobel explains, "At the heart of the Christian life is learning to point others to Christ, to bear burdens, to encourage, to love and to be with others." He goes on to explain that this was Edwards's intended purpose for conference. "In this sense, conference is a spiritual practice designed to flourish every other spiritual practice."[50]

Not only did Edwards find conference indispensable for spiritual formation in the individual, he also saw it as a powerful adhesive for the unity of the local body of Christ as a whole. In three of his major works (*Original Sin*, *Freedom of the Will*, and *True Virtue*) Edwards directly confronts the growing ideologies of individualism and isolationism.[51] Unity in the body of Christ and the Christian community was of utmost importance to Edwards, so much so that his view of heaven was a place where "you shall be united in the same interest, and shall be of one mind and one heart and one soule forever."[52] Edwards saw conference as a means to achieve unity within the community. Therefore, to assure both unity within the body and spiritual transformation within the individual, Edwards expected everyone to have a person with which to conference. "Whether you were a minister, a farmer, a teenager or a mother of ten, you were to share life with a companion on the journey."[53]

Out of his conviction that conference was an indispensable part of the Christian life, Edwards also proved that it was equally valuable for spiritual

---

50. Strobel, *Formed for the Glory of God*, 150.
51. Jenson, *America's Theologian*, 143.
52. Quoted in Carden, *Puritan Christianity*, 142.
53. Strobel, *Formed for the Glory of God*, 149.

awakening. Upon succeeding his grandfather, Solomon Stoddard, as pastor of the church in Northampton, Massachusetts, Edwards grew increasingly convinced that some of Stoddard's dangerous theological notions were affecting the moral aptitude of many among the Connecticut River Valley. Edwards was especially concerned for the young people in the church, who had persisted for years with a disrespect for authority and questionable conduct with the opposite sex. In response, Edwards launched a two-pronged attack: an unrelenting series of sermons directly addressing these immoral practices, and a coordination of small groups among families to follow up on the matter. George Marsden describes the moment:

> During the winter of 1733–34, sensing perhaps that he might win this battle, he preached once again against "company-keeping" and urged parents to bring it to an end. The next evening he gathered at his house "men that belonged to the several parts of town." He persuaded them to organize in their several neighborhoods "meetings with heads of households" called in the name of the pastor.... The effort worked wonderfully. Persuasion had softened hearts that coercion alone would have only hardened. According to Edwards' own account, not only did the heads of households readily cooperate, but astonishingly, the parents discovered that "the young people declared themselves convinced by what they had heard, and willing of themselves to comply."[54]

Although these series of meetings in and of themselves do not generally qualify as small groups, they do present two important principles of Edwards's small group philosophy: (1) small group meetings can be an incredibly efficient way of networking and communicating throughout the congregation, and (2) the most important small group is the family. This use of a small group method alone is significant; however, it was only the beginning of Edwards's employment of the strategy that would help launch revival in Northampton and, eventually, across the colonies.

Shortly after this change of heart among the town's youth, tragedy struck in the form of the death of two well-regarded young adults. Sensing that the town's young people have suddenly been shocked by the indiscriminate reality of death, Edwards capitalized on the opportunity to bring them closer to Christ by meeting with the young people in a "private meeting" for them alone. Marsden reports that by the fall of 1734 a revival of repentance had begun to spread and transform the youth in the community. What had

---

54. Marsden, *Jonathan Edwards*, 152–53.

at one time been reserved by the young people as a favorite time of frolicking, Edwards had convinced them rather to meet for "social religion" in small groups located in homes in various parts of town. The small group strategy caught on, and soon adults began to meet in small groups of their own. "By the next spring," Marsden writes, "various groups were voluntarily meeting on Sabbath evenings as well."[55] Much like the Puritan conventicles, the Northampton small groups were divided by age and gender, in which participants met to pray, study Scriptures together, and exhort one another, all for the sake of building each other up spiritually. Besides this, Edwards introduced worship through singing in the small group meetings. During their time together, they were encouraged to sing the hymns of the English Christian composer Isaac Watts, adding even more joy and spiritual vigor to the engagements. In fostering these small groups as he did, Edwards revitalized one of the most basic components of his roots to Puritanism and Pietism. Marsden aptly connects these traditions to Edwards: "The renewal of the lay conventicals tied the Northampton awakening not only to old Puritanism but also to the British and European pietist revivals of their day. Early eighteenth-century stirrings throughout the Protestant world were marked by renewals of lay prayer meetings."[56]

After the urging from a collaboration of American and British publishers to write an account of the Northampton revival, Edwards penned his famous *Faithful Narrative*, a publication that has not gone out of print since its appearance from a London printer in October 1737. Unbeknownst to Edwards, *A Faithful Narrative* would become much more than a written account of an isolated revival. It would serve as a template for how to affect spiritual renewal and evangelistic conversions. Perhaps more importantly, it would serve as an invitation to the revivalists in Britain—namely the Wesleys and George Whitefield—to journey to America once again and join in the efforts of spreading the spiritual fires. In 1740, with the arrival and evangelistic campaigns of Whitefield and others, the Great Awakening in America reached its zenith, yielding astronomical numbers of people hearing the gospel, unbelievers being converted, and believers being quickened anew. The Great Awakening stands as one of the majestic moments in American history. Yet it, along with the British revivals, owes a great deal of overdue credit to an overlooked contributor: small groups.

---

55. Marsden, *Jonathan Edwards*, 155–56.
56. Marsden, *Jonathan Edwards*, 156.

Principles Gleaned from Small Groups in the First Great Awakening

The revivals in Britain and North America that make up the first of the four major awakenings owe a great deal of their impact to the strategic role of small groups for discipleship and renewal. For revivalists like Spener, Zinzendorf, Wesley, and Edwards, a small group was successful because it was spiritually transformational. Indeed, according to their view, if positive, spiritual life-change was not occurring, true small group discipleship did not happen. While they sought and encouraged every Christian to engage in a small group, it was for the purpose of increasing holiness, not enrollment. Thus, it was because of its focus on spiritual transformation that small groups proved to be such a powerful catalyst for this historic spiritual awakening. In light of their impact, the following are a few of the principles to be gleaned from the role of small groups during the First Great Awakening:

1. Bible study and prayer were the centerpiece of these small groups. Every small group strategy employed prior to the revivals in Britain and America were intensely engaged in Bible study and prayer. Whether it was the small group Bible study let by Wesley's mother, the "Holy Club" collection of Oxford students, the Methodist class meetings, or Edwards's gatherings of "social religion" in personal homes—all of these instances centered on an intense time of seeking God and a high regard for learning his Word.

2. Spiritual transformation required compassionate personal examination of the life of one another, which came through trusting relationships fostered in small groups. Every small group strategy employed by the revivalists in this study made a time of personal peering into the spiritual condition of its participants a priority. The Oxford "Holy Club" allotted time for personal examination, while Wesley's class meetings placed even greater emphasis on holiness by including accountability from others. Moreover, a major purpose behind Edwards's home-based groups was to foster repentance and holiness among his congregation's young people. In all of these instances, it must be noted that no evidence can be found that the spirit behind these rigors was one of legalism or self-righteous judgment. Rather, it

was out of a compassionate concern that its members begin to realize the life of blessing which God has in store for them.

3. Small groups included a time of genuine worship and contemplation. This became a strategic element of the small groups that helped prompt the British and American revivals. Beginning with the Moravians' use of hymns as a means for spiritual instruction, virtually all of the small groups during that time employed an element of singing. John and Charles Wesley, for instance, engaged singing in their class meetings and societies, becoming major contributors to Christian worship and hymnody by writing and translating over 6,500 hymns. Moreover, their style of songwriting expressed a personal encounter with God, and it was designed for the common Christian, rooted in Scripture, and full of joy and confidence.[57] To the revivalists, nothing was more important than a proper understanding of who God is and one's duty to worship him as he demands. This is why their small groups incorporated worship and contemplation into its routine. In their small groups, believers learned to speak about God with humility, which bubbled over into the rest of their life. This, in turn, made conversation about God normal, which fertilized even more the spiritual seeds of revival.[58]

4. Small groups offered opportunities for personal application leading to spiritual transformation. As important as biblical knowledge was to spiritual transformation, these revivalists believed that it alone did not guarantee that transformation would occur. The Wesleys and Whitefield's "Holy Club" in Oxford went beyond the small group time to engage in helping the poor, visiting the imprisoned, and evangelizing the lost. Edwards, too, designed his conference meetings to leave participants with points of personal contemplation that would influence their daily routines, decisions, and actions.

5. Small groups took a variety of forms while keeping its core consistent. While the purpose and driving principles of small groups did not change, the revivalists customized their small group strategies to maximize their effectiveness. Small groups were adapted to engage

---

57. Towns and Whaley, *Worship through the Ages*, 123–24.
58. Strobel, *Formed for the Glory of God*, 154–55. Strobel offers a helpful resource for modeling Jonathan Edwards's practice of conference in "Appendix 2: Practicing Conference with Jonathan Edwards," 171–72.

people where they were most comfortable and learned best. Small groups occurred with men only, or women only, or a mixture of men and women. They were sometimes age specific, while at other times they spanned all levels of adulthood. Sometimes groups met in homes, while at other times they met in public buildings, or even somewhere outside. Edwards even allowed his conference strategy to include one-on-one mentoring and letter-writing.

Conclusion

There are shelves of studies located in libraries around the world that tell the story of the eighteenth century's Great Awakening. Many of these studies offer heartwarming narratives of how God changed the lives of individual people. Others are an academic survey of the major events and possible causes of the flurry of revivals that arose during that time. Amid this mountain of research, however, very few offer insight as to the role of small groups in this spiritual phenomenon. This is unfortunate for, as Table 1 (located below) demonstrates, much of the momentous events and effects of the First Great Awakening, both in Britain and in America, began in the seemingly insignificant moments when Christians were gathered in small groups.

SMALL GROUPS IN THE FIRST GREAT AWAKENING (1726–1791)

Table 1: Key Observations of the Catalytic Small Groups during the First Great Awakening (1726–91)

Precursors to the Small Groups	• Puritan Conference • Pietist Conventicles • Moravian Bands
Emergence of the Small Groups	• Bible Studies in Raritan Valley, NJ (1726) • "Holy Club" at Oxford (1729) • Conferences in Northampton, MA (1734) • Methodist Class Meetings (1742)
Major Proponents of the Small Groups	• Philip Jakob Spener (Frankfort, Germany) • Ludwig Von Zinzendorf (Herrnhut, Germany) • Theodore Frelinghuysen (New Jersey) • John Wesley (England) • Jonathan Edwards (Northampton, Massachusetts)
Prominent Revival Leaders, Ministries, and Movements that Emerged from the Small Groups	• George Whitefield (1737) • John Wesley (1738) • Jonathan Edwards (1734) • Methodist Movement (1742)
Key Features of the Small Groups	• Open group, often mixed in terms of gender, age, social standing, and spiritual condition • Relational, casual but structured • Spiritual outputs of evangelism and missions • Emphasis on unity, discipleship, and holiness • Worship through hymns, extensive prayer, Bible study, personal inspection of one another, and peer accountability and exhortation

4

Small Groups in the Second Great Awakening (1780–1850)

REVIVALS NOT ONLY TRANSFORMED Christianity, but they were also a critical connection between the faith and society. An awakening served as a catalyst for spiritual renewal among each person; yet, as more and more people were spiritually revived, their collective renewal would inevitably have a profound impact on society at large. For instance, many historians like John Wolffe have found spiritual awakenings to be instrumental in the formation of the English working class as well as the American new market economy.[1] Indeed, the revivals in North America have been credited for leading "the dedication of entire communities to a new spirit of Christian behavior and action."[2] While such accolades may aptly describe any of the major revivals discussed in this study, they are actually in reference to the renewal generally placed between 1780 and 1850, known as the Second Great Awakening.

By the turn of the century, spiritual renewal had virtually enveloped much of the European continent and dwarfed the effects of the First Great Awakening in America. The movement of God's Spirit had such a comprehensive impact during this time that Christian historian Kenneth Latourette called the nineteenth century "the Great Century" because of the rapid spread of the faith during the period.[3] It seems that many revivalists during that century agreed. For example, Robert Baird wrote that revivals had become a fundamental part of the American religious system. He continues,

1. Wolffe, *Expansion of Evangelicalism*, 94.
2. Gauvreau, "Protestantism Transformed," 61.
3. McDow and Reid, *Firefall*, 227.

Not a year has passed with out numerous instances of their occurrence, though at some periods they have been more powerful and prevalent than at others.... All, or nearly all, agree that such a revival is an inestimable blessing: so that he who should oppose himself to revivals, *as such*, would be regarded by most of our evangelical Christians as *ipso facto* an enemy to spiritual religion itself.[4]

In light of such a testament to the awakening, the question arises as to what caused this incredible stirring of the Spirit. While, as with all revivals, a plethora of factors contributed to this massive renewal, this chapter focuses on how the element of small groups played a significant part in the rise and longevity of the revival. While parsing the details of the Second Great Awakening, Alvin Reid identifies at least three significant aspects of the spiritual movement: awakenings on college campuses, revivals in local churches, and the emergence of camp meetings.[5] This chapter will address how small groups can be found, albeit subtly at times, in each of these dynamics. However, in addition to these three factors, this chapter submits a fourth significant contributor to the awakening—the advent of Sunday schools.

Conditions Prior to the Awakening

Revivals in general do not arise in a vacuum. There are inevitably circumstances, both good and bad, that contribute to their emergence. To understand and admire the incredible events and features of any awakening requires first a recognition of the conditions that lead up to it. This is never truer than with the Second Great Awakening. The dynamic changes and diverse conditions of the international landscape during the late 1700s and deep into the 1800s is enough to make any observer of history's head spin. Yet these circumstances play a pivotal role in setting the stage for the great revival.

Social, Industrial, and Economic Conditions

One of the most significant features of this time period is the incredibly fast population growth. Between 1790 and 1851, the population in England and Wales more than doubled. While the Americas began with significantly

---

4. Baird, *Religion in the United States*, 456.
5. McDow and Reid, *Firefall*, 227–28.

fewer people, the population in the United States increased nearly sixfold and tenfold in British North America (Canada).[6] A similar factor was the mobility of this population. Between 1820 and 1850, nearly 2.5 million people migrated to the United States, most of whom were children and young adults.[7] Moreover, this period saw a major proportion of the population move to large towns, both in America and abroad.[8] These sudden shifts in population became both the fuel and the challenge for the rapid increase of evangelical Christianity that also occurred during this same time. On the one hand, those uprooted from their homeland found the Christian faith to be a powerful source of identity, encouragement, and hope. On the other hand, Christian evangelicals faced the daunting task of learning how to minister to the masses now in urban areas.[9]

Another major feature that preceded revival was the breathtaking expansion of industry and finance, primarily prompted by what historians typically call the First Industrial Revolution.[10] The revolution marked a time of development in the second half of the eighteenth century that changed largely rural, agrarian communities both in Europe and America into industrialized, urban ones. As the result of new inventions and techniques discovered in key industries such as coal mining, textiles, and iron making, many goods that had once been painstakingly unearthed or meticulously handcrafted began to be mass-produced by machines. In Britain, for instance, coal production rose from 11 million tons in 1800 to 49.4 million just fifty years later. Similarly, cotton imports grew from 28.6 million pounds in the 1790s to 550 million in the 1840s. Consequently, farms were being abandoned for factories as people by the droves left the quiet countryside for the city life. Thus, the British industrial labor force jumped from 29.7 percent in 1801 to 42.9 percent in 1851, while its agricultural counterpart fell from 35.9 percent to 21.7 percent during the same period.[11] In America, with the completion of the Erie Canal in 1825, a transportation route was created that linked the Hudson River at Albany, New York, to the Great Lakes. This

---

6. Wolffe, *Expansion of Evangelicalism*, 22–24.
7. Jones, *Limits of Liberty*, 694.
8. Mitchell, *International Historical Statistics*, 49.
9. Wolffe, *Expansion of Evangelicalism*, 24–27.
10. Historians refer to this period as the First Industrial Revolution to differentiate it from a second period of industrial growth which took place between the 1900s and early 2000s, a time of rapid advances in the steel, electric, and automobile industries.
11. Wolffe, *Expansion of Evangelicalism*, 27–28.

connection, along with the invention of the steamboat and later the railroad, created a revolutionary means for transporting goods across long distances, thus stimulating the Industrial and Market Revolutions in America. While these developments in industry, economy, and transportation had not fully come into their own by the time of the Second Great Awakening, it is clear that easier communication and faster transportation was on the rise. This trend would facilitate the expansion of evangelical Christianity and, thus, the reach of revival across much longer distances.[12] Additionally, with the invasion of people into the cities, the ability to reach the masses with the gospel became more efficient, as large numbers of people could be gathered in one place for a Christian service.

Philosophical, Religious, and Moral Conditions

Nevertheless, as the eighteenth century ended, there was a general decline in the religious and moral aptitude among the populous, especially in America. One major culprit for this spiritual setback was the heavy toll of war. The French and Indian War (1754–63), especially the American Revolution (1776–83), but also the War of 1812 all helped cause the spiritual vigor that came from the First Great Awakening to get sidetracked for the more urgent task of liberty. Even many of the ministers replaced their Bible for a weapon during this time, inevitably resulting in the vacancy of the pulpit and the neglect of ever-important spiritual matters. Alvin Reid writes, "While the revolution was being won to secure fundamental freedoms, the religious convictions of many people were being lost."[13]

As devastating as the wars were in themselves, perhaps an even greater disaster to the spiritual vitality of this new nation was the intrusion of the philosophical and religious refuse of the Enlightenment that came with an alliance with the French. While France was militarily indispensable to colonists during the American Revolution, the French also introduced the writings of Voltairé, Rousseau, and David Hume, and with them trending anti-Christian philosophies like skepticism, deism, and atheism. Many of these ideas were promoted by American writers such as Thomas Paine and Ethan Allen. J. Edwin Orr expounds on the impact, noting, "The bitter writings of Thomas Paine and the gentler utterances of Thomas Jefferson had lent great aid to the rapid spread of a kind of deism and unbelief in the newly

12. Wolffe, *Expansion of Evangelicalism*, 28–29.
13. McDow and Reid, *Firefall*, 228.

independent United States." With patriotic zeal, Orr concludes, the new nation showed hospitality to religious skeptics and political radicals, "the French revolutionists capturing the place of the evangelical moderates."[14] The egregious results were inevitable. Promiscuity, profanity, gambling, and drunkenness abounded. In a nation of less than four million people, three hundred thousand were confirmed alcoholics, with more than fifteen thousand of them dying each year.[15] Conditions deteriorated so much in America during this time that the atheist Voltaire predicted that Christianity would be forgotten in the new nation within three decades.[16] Surveying the societal landscape of post-Revolution America, Orr concludes,

> The unsettled state of society following a long-fought war and a revolution, the self-assertive feelings which accompanied independence, the changing social conditions, the lure of the western frontier, the rugged individualism of the frontiersman, the break-up of the family and church relationships due to migration—all these were factors in the decline, but they were matched by the influence of the militant French infidelity which had swept the country.[17]

Tenacious Remnants of the First Great Awakening

The First Great Awakening had weakened considerably by 1750. What had been a mighty move of God's Spirit among the masses in the first half of the 1700s had doubtlessly diminished in the second half of the same century. This is not to mean, however, that the effects of the First Great Awakening were completely gone. On the contrary, several undercurrents that caused the waves of revival then were still churning at the approach of 1800. John Wolffe explains:

> The very term "Second Great Awakening," when applied to the specific decade of the 1790s, is apt to mislead, insofar as it implies discontinuity with the first wave of the Evangelical Revival. Obviously there was generational change, both in the passing of early leaders and in the growing up of younger people who had never encountered their ministry. There was also in specific localities, especially perhaps in England and New England, an apparent

---

14. Orr, *Campus Aflame*, 31.
15. Towns and Whaley, *Worship through the Ages*, 135.
16. Towns and Porter, *Ten Greatest Revivals*, 73.
17. Orr, *Campus Aflame*, 31.

loss of initial fervor. . . . On the other hand, taking the English-speaking world as a whole, revival was never absent.[18]

He goes on to cite spectacular expansion of Methodists and Baptists in the southern United States during the 1770s and 1780s, rumblings of renewal among Presbyterian colleges, and even extensive revivalistic activity in the West Indies and the Maritimes. Wolffe concludes, "What happened in the 1790s and early 1800s is best seen as an acceleration and geographical expansion of a continuing undercurrent of revival."[19]

One of the most significant remaining undercurrents of revival that links the First and Second Awakenings is the use of small groups for spiritual growth and renewal. As discovered in the previous chapter, small groups had existed well before the spiritual explosion of the First Awakening through the efforts of Puritanism, Pietism, and the Moravians. These predecessors to the awakening set the stage for small groups to be a catalyst for the great revival. Moreover, through the mammoth works of Wesley, small groups in the form of Methodist bands and class-meetings continued to play a part in sustaining the sparks of revival in the subsequent decades. It is no wonder that Henry Ward Beecher, a prominent figure of the Second Great Awakening, continued to appreciate the small group system Wesley had created. "The greatest thing John Wesley ever gave to the world," Beecher proclaimed, "is the Methodist class meeting." Even more, Dwight L. Moody, a champion of Christianity's third great revival, continued to praise the Methodist small group system, stating, "The class-meetings are the best institutions for training converts the world ever saw."[20] Incidentally, while the Methodist class-meetings thrived, a new small group system was on the rise which caught the eye of even John Wesley himself. In 1780, Robert Raikes began the first Sunday school in Gloucester, England. The innovation caught on so quickly that when Wesley visited Leeds, England, just four years later, he found twenty-six Sunday schools with more than 2,000 students and forty-five teachers. The Sunday school movement will be discussed later in this chapter. For now it is enough to note that, while the Methodist class-meetings remained a prominent system for discipleship in the latter part of the 1700s and throughout the 1800s, it would also be accompanied by Sunday school and other small group strategies for the propagation of the Christian faith. Together, these small group methods

18. Wolffe, *Expansion of Evangelicalism*, 47–48.
19. Wolffe, *Expansion of Evangelicalism*, 47–48.
20. Quoted in Henderson, *John Wesley's Class Meeting*, 93.

not only continued to be a key element of the First Great Awakening, they would again serve as catalysts for the Second as well.

Small Groups and Revival on College Campuses in America

The heinous marks of Enlightenment philosophies left by the French in post-Revolution America are most vividly seen on college campuses. In the second half of the eighteenth century, the spiritual state among college students was abysmal. Orr laments that, so far as religion was concerned, colleges had become "seedbeds of infidelity."[21] As evidence, Orr notes that the University of Pennsylvania, Transylvania College, Columbia College in South Carolina, and other campuses hired influential freethinkers on their faculties. At Yale and Princeton, student bodies were overwhelmingly populated with skeptics, such that the number of believers at Yale could be counted on one hand and, in 1782, no more than two students at Princeton claimed to be Christian. Also, William and Mary, established in the seventeenth century to provide a pious education to Anglicans, now debated whether the Christian faith had been helpful or harmful to humanity.[22]

In such an anti-Christian environment, debauchery could not help but thrive. Orr records that when the Dean at Princeton opened the chapel Bible to read, a pack of playing cards fell out because someone had cut a rectangle out of each page to fit the pack. Christians were so unpopular that they were forced to meet in secret, keeping their minutes in code. Deist students led a mob in burning the Bible of a Presbyterian church in the Raritan Valley. In other cases, students disrupted worship services with profanity and spit, burned down buildings and forced the resignation of college presidents.[23] In an excerpt from his autobiography, Lyman Beecher gives a telling portrayal of the spiritual state of the typical campus:

> College was in a most ungodly state. The college church was almost extinct. Most of the students were skeptical and rowdies were plenty. Wine and liquors were kept in many rooms. Intemperance, profanity, gambling and licentiousness were common. . . . Most of the class before me were infidels and called each other

---

21. Orr, *Campus Aflame*, 33.
22. Dorchester, *Christianity in the United States*, 316.
23. Orr, *Campus Aflame*, 33.

Voltaire, Rousseau, etc. . . . . That was the day of the infidelity of the Tom Paine school.[24]

Hampden-Sydney College

It was in this spiritual bleakness that the flame of revival would erupt, starting in 1787 at Hampden-Sydney College in Virginia. Four students—William Hill, Cary Allen, James Blythe, and Clement Read—began to meet for prayer. Although their spiritual state has been debated,[25] what is clear is their concern about the rampant immorality of the college, prompting them to gather privately for prayer, study, and worship. At first, the small group met in a forest away from the campus, but then moved to a locked dorm room, fearing the degenerate student body. One of the four complained, "We tried to pray, but such prayer I never heard the like of." He continued, "We tried to sing, but it was in the most suppressed manner, for we feared the other students."[26]

At last, the group was discovered, and the four "fanatics" were ridiculed and threatened. The disturbance was so great that two faculty members had to intervene, and the university president came to investigate. The president, John Brown Smith, was a convert of the First Great Awakening, thus sympathetic to the four praying students. Brown sharply rebuked the persecuting students and invited the four to meet in his study to continue to pray. The four students prayed, studied, and worshipped until, at last, revival broke out. Shortly thereafter, Hampden-Sydney College was in the throes of a spiritual awakening, resulting in more than half of the student body coming to faith in Christ.[27] The impact of the revival began to reverberate to the surrounding counties, stirring local churches into revival as well. During the next three decades, revival would occasionally break out on the campus again and again, eventually spreading to other campuses. Thus, what started as a small group of fervently praying students became the stimulus for spiritual awakening among America's college campuses.

24. Beecher, *Autobiography*, 43.

25. J. Edwin Orr suggests that none of the students were active Christians (Orr, *Campus Aflame*, 39). However, Malcolm McDow and Alvin Reid report that two of the students, Cary Allen and William Hill, were converted in 1787 (McDow and Reid, *Firefall*, 229).

26. Lacy, *Revivals in the Midst of the Years*, 68-69.

27. Thompson, *Times of Refreshing*, 79.

The Haystack Revival at Williams College

Like other campuses at the time, Williams College in Massachusetts had also been a hotbed of anti-Christian demonstrations. Indeed, students had once conducted a mock celebration of holy communion to show their disdain for the faith.[28] However, in 1806, revival came to the campus. Like at Hampden-Sydney, Christians would privately meet for prayer, Bible study, and worship. One such small group, five students in all, would meet twice each week for private prayer. On a warm day in August 1806, the group decided to meet in a maple grove, but a summer storm erupted, forcing them to seek shelter under a large haystack. Protected from the storm's wind and rain, the men continued in prayer, which suddenly turned its focus to reaching the unevangelized world with the gospel. As the thunderstorm subsided, one in the group, a pastor's son named Samuel J. Mills, proposed a mission to India, insisting, "We can do it, if we will."[29]

Their passion for missions made their numbers increase. Then in 1808, immediately after graduating from Andover Theological Seminary, Mills and others from the group requested the General Assembly of Massachusetts to send them to India as missionaries. As a result, on June 28, 1810, the American Board of Commissioners for Foreign Missions was formed, becoming the first official foreign missions organization in the United States. Some of the first missionaries to come out of this organization included Adoniram Judson, Samuel Mott, Luther Rice, Gordon Hall, and Samuel Newell. Since that fateful August day, historians refer to what happened under the haystack to those praying students from Williams College as the "Haystack Revival." Moreover, because of the faithful prayers of that small group, other colleges like Princeton and Amherst began to experience revival; and societies for foreign missions were formed in denomination after denomination.[30]

28. Rudolph, *American College*, 38.

29. Spring, *Memoir of Samuel J. Mills*, 38.

30. Orr, *Campus Aflame*, 53; McDow and Reid, *Firefall*, 231. Another outcome of Williams College's Haystack Revival is the founding of the American Bible Society. The society was founded in 1816 for the purpose of distributing free copies of the Bible in local languages throughout the world. Some of its original leaders included influential American Protestants like former president of the Continental Congress, Elias Boudinot, the first Chief Justice of the United States Supreme Court, John Jay, a key figure of the First Great Awakening, Frederick T. Frelinghuysen, and the writer of American's National Anthem, Francis Scott Key. For a detailed history of the American Bible Society, see Fea, *Bible Cause*.

SMALL GROUPS IN THE SECOND GREAT AWAKENING (1780–1850)

Spread of Revival to Other Colleges

As a result of the revivals that happened at Williams, and especially Hampden-Sydney, colleges across the United States began to witness revival among their student body. Students began to form Christian fellowships on their own. Harvard, Bowdoin, Brown, Dartmouth, Middlebury, and Andover began to see new Christian societies formed, all prompted by students seeking spiritual renewal. In resistance to the godless vices that were prominent, these groups committed themselves to steadfast watchfulness, passionate prayers, frequent fellowship, mutual counsel, and friendly correction. In most cases, these societies were very small. At Brown University, just three students formed a "college praying society," which met weekly under strict privacy "for fear of disturbance from the unpenitent."[31] Around the same time, on December 11, 1802, three juniors and four sophomores came together to form the Harvard Saturday Evening Religious Society. Although these small groups began in secrecy, the Spirit of God was prompted through their prayers in such a way that revival often broke out across the entire campus and into the surrounding communities.[32]

Unfortunately, the colleges and universities in Europe did not enjoy revival like their American counterparts. Probably the major reason for this is that the European colleges were under strict control of the nation's political powers. Oxford and Cambridge, for instance, were preserves of the Church of England; and colleges in Europe at large were under the control of Napoleon and the French Revolution. On the other hand, the spiritual awakenings among American college campuses during the late eighteenth and early nineteenth centuries continued for more than fifty years. Their passionate and prolonged spiritual vitality had profound effects on evangelical Christianity and American society in general. The founding of many colleges, the increase of philanthropic endeavors, and the rise of mission work can all be traced to some extent to the campus revivals. Similarly, many of the college revivals can be traced to some small group of students who were desperate for a renewal and passionate in their prayers.

---

31. Guild, "Early Religious History of Brown University," quoted in Orr, *Campus Aflame*, 39.

32. Orr, *Campus Aflame*, 39.

Prayer Unions and Revival in Britain

The stirring waters of revival were not limited to the college campuses. Both across the Atlantic and in the New World, God was at work among local pastors and churches, planting seeds that would spring into revival. While the 1790s saw a brief recession in revivals in North America, renewal was picking up in various parts of Great Britain. One such location was Edinburgh, Scotland, where John Erskine was pastoring a local congregation. Pierced by the depravity of his country and desperate for God to change it, in 1784 Erskine published a memorial to call for prayer for an outpouring of God's Spirit. Essentially, the memorial was a republication of Jonathan Edwards's *An Humble Attempt to Promote Explicit Agreement and Visible Union of God's People in Extraordinary Prayer for the Revival of Religion and the Advancement of Christ's Kingdom*. As the memorial made its way throughout Britain, it drew a remarkable response. With what became known as "prayer unions," Christians began to set aside one Monday each month to gather in groups for the purpose of prayer. While these prayer unions began in the form of small groups, soon churches and finally entire denominations found themselves taking part in a "concert of prayer" throughout the nation.[33]

The effects of these prayer efforts were astounding, as reports of revival began to spread like wildfire across Britain. Revival found its way across the British Isles, filling church buildings that once lay all but empty, and collecting thousands more in fields to hear the message of Christ. Thomas Chalmers and brothers Robert and John Haldane testified to incredible church growth in Scotland, and Ireland saw Methodists surge by the thousands. Social reform followed and morality among the people improved. Soon, for example, the English people called for the abolition of the slave trade and the improvement of Britain's prison systems.[34] Moreover, while Robert Raikes's Sunday school in Gloucester, England, had already begun, revival caused the philanthropist's personal conviction to become a formidable movement.

Revival also broke out in Yorkshire, England, partly due to the prayer meetings of small groups. In 1791, Methodist minister William Bramwell (1759–1818) was transferred to the Dewsbury circuit in Yorkshire.

---

33. McDow and Reid, *Firefall*, 231. For more details on the revivals in England during this time see Orr, *The Eager Feet*, 13–45.

34. Cauchi, "Second Worldwide Awakening."

SMALL GROUPS IN THE SECOND GREAT AWAKENING (1780-1850)

Dismayed by the spiritual state of the Methodist societies within his purview, Bramwell chronicled that "active religion scarcely appeared."[35] Believing that revival was the only cure for the spiritual depravity and disunity among his parishioners, Bramwell began a lengthy and earnest campaign of personal prayer on behalf of his circuit. Sometime later, he was joined by the "Praying Nanny," Ann Cutler (c. 1759-94), who was known for her commitment to a life of prayer. Together, Bramwell and Cutler would meet together very early in the morning for prayer. A member of Bramwell's family wryly reflected, "Sleep there could be none for those who were within earshot of these clamorous suitors, when the spirit of supplication was strong."[36] As with anyone seeking true revival, Bramwell was not initially as interested in the salvation of unbelievers as he was in the sanctification of professed believers, leading to a deeper zeal for God and personal holiness. One year later, in the fall of 1792, attendees of small prayer meetings and class-meetings began to report some professing sanctification. This led to a spiritual upsurge that eventually led to conversions of unbelievers and church membership. Convinced that revival had come to the Dewsbury circuit because of his and Cutler's prayers, he declared that God had finally "unstopp[ed] the sluices of heaven . . . sending a mighty rain upon the land."[37]

In 1793, Bramwell transferred to the nearby Birstall circuit, and revival followed him. By 1794, virtually all of Yorkshire was becoming spiritually awakened. The renewal began to spread to other parts of Northern England, to Sheffield in 1795 and Nottingham in 1798, finding its way into Lancashire and the north Midlands. The impact of the revival brought about by the prayers of Bramwell and Cutler was impressive. Wolffe reports that Methodist membership in Yorkshire jumped from 10,397 in 1792 to 16,539 in 1797; during that same span of years in Lancashire, it increased from 6,598 to 10,963. In all, Methodist membership in Britain rose as a result of the revival: from 1.04 percent in 1792-93 to 14.19 percent in 1793-94 to 8.47 percent in 1794-95.[38]

---

35. Quoted in Wolffe, *Expansion of Evangelicalism*, 49.
36. *Memoir of the Life and Ministry of William Bramwell*, 38-39.
37. Wolffe, *Expansion of Evangelicalism*, 50.
38. Wolffe, *Expansion of Evangelicalism*, 50-51.

A "Concert of Prayer" and Revival in America

Hearing the reports of revival in Great Britain, evangelical Christians seeking an awakening in the United States began to emulate the small group model of prayer meetings among their churches. In 1784 and with the same invocation of Edwards's *A Humble Attempt* that John Erskine had used the same year, Baptist pastors Isaac Backus and Stephen Gano sent out a call for ministers of "every Christian denomination" to come together in a "concert of prayer" for revival.[39] The call was answered, with ministers from every denomination joining in. Methodists held revival-focused prayer groups from 1796 to the close of the century. In Logan County, Kentucky, Presbyterian pastor James McGready enlisted believers to pray for revival every Saturday evening, Sunday morning, and the entire third Saturday of each month. Soon Congregational and Reformed groups began to mingle with the Baptists in a network of prayer meetings. Even the Moravians joined the concert of prayer, thus bringing all of New England to its knees in prayer at noon on Mondays for revival.[40]

In response, God's Spirit began to awaken New England. Initially, prior to 1795, revival was scattered: First and Second Baptist Churches of Boston in the winter of 1791–92, in Yarmouth, Maine, in 1791 and then in New Salem, Connecticut, in 1792. By 1798, however, reports of revival began to pour in from West Simsbury, Torrington, New Hartford, Northington, and many other New England towns. Revival then spread to Maryland and Delaware. McDow and Reid write, "Methodist hymns echoed from fields, workshops, and logging camps."[41] Not stopping there, God unleashed revival onto the Maritime provinces of Canada, throughout the Mid-Atlantic states and the South, and into the Trans-Allegheny West, where a miraculous spiritual resurgence was reported.[42] The revival fires were raging such that, in its inaugural issue, *The Connecticut Evangelical Magazine* declared that "the nation was witnessing an outpouring of the Holy Spirit not seen since the 1740s."[43] Indeed, in the words of J. Edwin Orr, "The Second Great

---

39. Strickland, *Great American Revival*, 45.
40. Towns and Whaley, *Worship through the Ages*, 138.
41. McDow and Reid, *Firefall*, 233.
42. Halliday and Gregory, *Church in America*, 386.
43. McDow and Reid, *Firefall*, 233.

Awakening in America had come," and its advent was largely due to small groups of believers in desperate prayer for revival.[44]

The Presence of Small Groups in the Rise of Camp Meetings

Perhaps no other event better serves as the symbol of the Second Great Awakening than the camp meeting. Outdoor revival services that emerged first in the American frontier and then expanded eastward, these camp meetings were held by most of the Protestant denominations as a means for filling the spiritual void that largely gripped the untamed West. Camp meetings are mostly recognized for their flamboyant worship services that involved multiple preachers, drew enormous crowds, and often lasted for several days. Such a description of these meetings is certainly not without merit. Testimonies abound of hosts of people screaming, weeping, fainting in response to the emotionally charged preaching. Moreover, strange concepts such as "having the jerks," "being slain in the Spirit," and approaching the "anxious bench," are common features of these charismatic events. Yet, even with all of the hyper emotions and seemingly bizarre antics, the element of small groups has made its mark, albeit subtly, on the iconic camp meetings of the Second Great Awakening.

The Cane Ridge Revival (1801)

At the dawn of the nineteenth century, the American West was growing. The call of a life on the frontier was answered by many seeking freedom, land, treasure, and adventure. Many of these adventurers were rough and rowdy, and hardly Christian. Consequently, spiritual conditions were worse in the West than in the East. While the East battled the philosophical whims brought on by the Enlightenment, the West was filled with men who often seemed as wild as the frontier itself. This was no more apparent than in Logan County, Kentucky. Methodist revivalist Peter Cartwright describes the area well, writing,

> Logan County, when my father moved into it, was called "Rogues Harbor." Here many refugees from all parts of the Union fled to escape punishment or justice; for although there was law, yet it could

---

44. Orr, *Campus Aflame*, 34.

not be executed, and it was a desperate state of society. Murderers, horse-thieves, highway robbers, and counterfeiters fled there, until they combined and actually formed a majority. Those who favored a better state of morals were called "Regulators." But they encountered fierce opposition from the "Rogues," and a battle was fought with guns, pistols, dirks, knives, and clubs, in which the "Regulators" were defeated.[45]

It is to Logan County that Presbyterian preacher James McGready migrated from North Carolina in 1796. Having experienced an outbreak of revival in North Carolina in 1791, McGready found himself dismayed by the moral depravity of his adopted community and the spiritual deadness of his flock. McGready immediately set aside the third Saturday of each month for fasting and prayer. Like Bramwell in Yorkshire a few years earlier, he called on his three small churches in Muddy, Red, and Gasper River to join him in praying "for the conversion of sinners in Logan county, and throughout the world." He continues, "We also engage to spend one half hour every Saturday evening, beginning at the setting of the sun, and one half our every Sabbath morning, from the rising of the sun, pleading with God to revive his work."[46]

In June 1880, more than five hundred people from McGready's three congregations gathered for a joint communion service at Red River. The crowd filled the area with great expectancy coming from four years of prayer for revival. Because there were too many people for McGready alone to serve, he enlisted five local pastors to help him administer the communion elements and preach. The meeting continued to grow, forcing them to move the service outdoors. Elmer Towns and Vernon Whaley describe what happened next: "For three days, matters were orderly, serious, fervent, solemn, and sincere. Then a tangible sense of God's presence swept across the congregation . . . and scores were converted."[47] The Red River revival was so successful that McGready scheduled a second series of "sacramental meetings" to last for four days during the next month, but this time at Gasper River. Expecting large crowds, McGready held the meeting in the forest and instructed the congregants to "bring your wagons and provisions" in preparation to spend the night. The reputably wild

---

45. Cartwright, *Autobiography*, 24–27.
46. Beard, *Brief Biographical Sketches*, 7–17.
47. Towns and Whaley, *Worship through the Ages*, 141–42.

and debaucherous frontiersmen came from miles around, bringing their horses and buggies and staying for days.[48]

Among those who attended the Gasper River meetings was Barton Stone, the Presbyterian pastor at Cane Ridge and Concord, near the Kentucky state capital of Lexington. So moved by what he experienced, Stone began to inspire revival in his own churches. He invited McGready to lead a meeting at Cane Ridge in August 1801. Throughout that summer, a groundswell of excitement was building. Finally, the meetings were held, from Friday, August 8 until the following Wednesday, August 12. The estimated number of attendees range between twelve thousand and twenty five thousand and the crowd spread out for over half a mile. Since it was impossible for such a large gathering to hear a single speaker, numerous other preachers—Baptists, Methodists, and Presbyterians alike—erected stands in different locations throughout the crowd. From their make-shift pulpits, these preachers would gather smaller groups of attendees and preach the gospel to them.[49] The intensity of corporate conviction was so overwhelming, it simultaneously produced a vibrant and chaotic atmosphere. Some wept while others laughed uncontrollably, others trembled, some ran around, and some even barked.[50] Towns and Whaley report that the Cane Ridge Revival meetings also possessed a "pen" (similar to a cattle pen) near the "pulpit."[51] Tree logs were laid like pews inside the pen for those under great conviction over their sin to go sit and cry out to God. While the preaching carried on, these small groups of the convicted would be ministered to by others for salvation and edification.

Although it has been known for the abnormal activities that are largely associated with camp meetings, it should not overshadow the untold number of lives that were eternally changed during this pivotal event. Despite it lasting less than a week, the Cane Ridge Revival has served to symbolize the Second Great Awakening in the West. Since that event, one historian observed, "when the words 'evangelism' and 'revival' were used, they evoked images of Cane Ridge."[52]

More important to this study is that, despite the overshadowing of these massive crowds and abnormal occurrences that accompanied the

48. Towns and Whaley, *Worship through the Ages*, 141–42.
49. Wolffe, *Expansion of Evangelicalism*, 58.
50. González, *Story of Christianity* 2: 245–46.
51. Towns and Whaley, *Worship through the Ages*, 143.
52. González, *Story of Christianity* 2:246.

Cane Ridge Revival, a small group dynamic can still be found. Moreover, as the fervor for more camp meetings exploded across the whole of the country,[53] small groups would continue to accompany these meetings. One such example of this enduring partnership can be found in the so-called Hay Bay camp meeting that occurred in Upper Canada in September 1805. The camp meeting drew twenty-five hundred people, a full 5 percent of the province's entire population. At this meeting, attendees gathered together in little groups to pray, where they experienced an intense consciousness of both relationships between one another and oneness with Christ.[54]

The Conversion and Ministry of Peter Cartwright

One of the clearest examples of how small groups were used throughout the western frontier is through the circuit-riding preacher, Peter Cartwright (1785–1872). Circuit-riding preachers, usually Methodist, often travelled long distances and across treacherous terrains to bring the gospel to the folks along the frontier. An estimated one half of these remarkable Christian soldiers would not live beyond thirty-three years old. Yet it was largely due to the hoofprints of these preachers on horseback that revival spread to the West. In fact, one Presbyterian noted that, as he traveled the Kentucky trails, he could not "find a family whose cabin had not been entered by a Methodist preacher."[55]

One of these preachers was the strong, robust, and daunting Peter Cartwright. Throughout his ministry, Cartwright traversed those dangerous western roads for a generation, totaling eleven circuits. Along the way, he preached nearly fifteen thousand sermons and saw roughly ten thousand people come to faith in Christ.[56] In 1785, Cartwright's family moved to Logan County, Kentucky, the area infamously named "Rogue's Harbor." As stated earlier, the region was rough and dangerous, a perfect match for this undisciplined young man, who himself "was a wild, wicked boy and delighted in horse racing, card playing, and dancing." His parents tried to keep him in line ("My father restrained me a little, though my

---

53. John Wolffe estimates that two hundred to three hundred camp meetings were held in 1804, increasing to four hundred to five hundred annually by 1811; Wolffe, *Expansion of Evangelicalism*, 62.

54. Rawlyk, *Canada Fire*, 148–55.

55. Weisberger, *They Gathered at the River*, 45.

56. McDow and Reid, *Firefall*, 237.

mother often talked to me, wept over me, and prayed for me")[57] but it was the convicting power of God's Spirit that got his attention. In 1801, after an evening of drinking and dancing, the young man began to grieve over his guilt of sin. Cartwright then recalled, "It seemed to me, all of a sudden, my blood rushed to my head, my heart palpitated, in a few minutes I turned blind; an awful impression rested on my mind that death has come and I was unprepared to die. I fell on my knees and began to ask God to have mercy on me."[58] Even then Cartwright remained unconverted, and for the next three months he struggled over his sin. Though many tried to console him—his concerned parents, his wicked friends, and even the local preacher and a small group leader—he found no comfort. When he heard about a sacramental-turned-revival meeting that was going on nearby at a Presbyterian church, he decided to attend. It was there that Cartwright found the grace and forgiveness of God he was struggling to find. He recalls the moment clearly:

> On the Saturday evening of said meeting, I went, with weeping multitudes, and bowed before the stand, and earnestly prayed for mercy. In the midst of the solemn struggle of soul, an impression was made on my mind, as though a voice said to me, "Thy sins are all forgiven thee." Divine light flashed all round me, unspeakable joy sprung up in my soul. I rose to my feet, opened my eyes, and it really seemed as if I was in heaven . . . though I have been since then, in many instances, unfaithful, yet I have never, for one moment, doubted that the Lord did, then and there, forgive my sins and give me religion.[59]

In the following months, Cartwright attended several other camp meetings held by both Methodists and Presbyterians, where he saw "many souls converted to God." During the intermissions of one of these camp meetings, Cartwright recollects that he and a few other young men would gather as a small group in the nearby woods to hold prayer meetings. "If we knew of any boys that were seeking religion, we would take them along and pray for them." As a result, "Many of them obtained religion in these praying circles, and raised loud shouts of praise to God, in which those of us that were religious would join."[60] Aside from the camp meetings,

---

57. Quoted in Towns and Whaley, *Worship through the Ages*, 131–32.
58. Cartwright, "Autobiography," 42.
59. Cartwright, "Autobiography," 44.
60. Cartwright, "Autobiography," 54.

Cartwright was a regular attender in Methodist class meetings and other small groups where, whenever he felt compelled by God's love, "I would mount a bench and exhort with all the power I had."[61] Eventually, in May 1802, he was licensed to preach (called an "exhorter's license" at the time) by the Ebenezer society of the Methodist Episcopal Church. The following year, his family moved to Lewiston County in rural Kentucky, where "there was no regular circuit, and no organized classes." There, the presiding elder of the region granted Cartwright a letter of membership which he called a "Benjamin's mess," for it gave the young preacher not only the authority to exhort, but also to "travel through all that destitute region, hold meetings, organize classes, and, in a word, to form a circuit."[62] While Cartwright, an uneducated and immature Christian still in his teenage years, felt wholly unqualified for such an awesome task, he accepted it nonetheless and got to work. Although he faced much opposition in some places and, doubtlessly made many mistakes, he also records experiencing "some very powerful displays of Divine grace." As he persisted in his work, he reports, "A goodly number obtained religion, and I received about seventy into society, appointed leaders, met classes, sung, prayed, and exhorted, and, under the circumstances, did the best I knew how."[63] Such was the testimony of this bold young preacher time and time again. Cartwright established a circuit in this uncivilized and spiritually barren land, and he became a key contributor to the camp meeting revivals that spurred across the frontier. In history, Cartwright is mostly remembered for his fierce opposition to slavery and, like many revivalists of the time, for the emotionally powerful and sometimes bizarre activities that often accompanied his preaching. While both are certainly key components to his legacy, one must not overlook that he was also a champion of small groups, using them effectively to bring people to Christ and begin new churches.

Charles Finney and the "New Measures" Revivals

While the initial surge of revival was briefly dampened by the distraction of the War of 1812, the Second Great Awakening flourished once again throughout much of America during the 1820s–1840s. Camp meetings continued, new churches and Methodist societies were formed, and an

---

61. Cartwright, "Autobiography," 56.
62. Cartwright, "Autobiography," 56.
63. Cartwright, "Autobiography," 57.

army of ministers and preachers were fully immersed in the great work. However, despite the long list of champions of the Awakening, history records no one more prominent than Charles Grandison Finney (1792–1875). Indeed, Mark Noll submits there is a "good case" for ranking Finney as one of "the most important public figures in nineteenth-century America," and unquestionably "the crucial figure in white American evangelicalism after Jonathan Edwards."[64]

Finney was born in an irreligious home at the dawn of the Awakening. A lawyer by trade from Adams, New York, Finney was less than moved by the spiritual vitality of the churches he attended. Gaining a reputation for his atheism and antagonism toward evangelical Christianity, Finney began attending a church that was pastored by hyper-Calvinist George W. Gale. Finney was musically gifted and, with that, Gale saw an opportunity to form a relationship with Finney that would eventually become instrumental in the young lawyer's conversion. Finney began to serve as the church's music director, affording numerous opportunities for he and Gale to discuss the Scriptures together. Meanwhile, some young people began to quietly group up in prayer for Finney's conversion, one of whom eventually became his bride.[65] At last, after a lengthy time of conviction, Finney determined to settle the issue once and for all. On October 10, 1821, Finney left his work and climbed a hill across the street from his law office where he prayed. As the day was coming to a close, this once-cocky cynic of Christianity experienced a life-changing conversion. Journaling about the event, Finney wrote, "The Holy Spirit descended upon me in a manner that seemed to go through me, body and soul. I could feel the impression, like a wave of electricity, going through and through me. Indeed it seemed to come in waves of liquid love, for I could not express it in any other way."[66] Returning to his office that evening, Finney announced that he had been converted to Christ.

Although often met with surprise and occasional suspicion, Finney left his law practice and began his formidable career of preaching the gospel across America. He was ordained by the Presbyterian Church in 1824 but later became a Congregationalist, principally due to his preaching style and theological perspective. A powerful preacher, Finney used his oratory skills to persuade many to come to faith in Christ. His ability to draw a crowd

---

64. Noll, *History of Christianity*, 176.
65. McDow and Reid, *Firefall*, 239.
66. Finney, *Autobiography*, 21.

was so great, it was said that he could double the population of any town by having services there.[67] On the other hand, Finney used his effective organizational skills to develop what became one of the trademarks of the camp meetings during the Second Great Awakening, his "New Measures."[68]

Although not altogether new, these strategies were popularized by Finney and became a staple of most preaching services in early nineteenth-century America. In short, they helped make populist-driven, spontaneous, and often disorganized revival movements more established and socially respected. Among these innovations were so-called "protracted meetings," meetings that were held several nights consecutively, as long "as the revival season lasted." Other techniques were more controversial, such as praying in the common, "vulgar" language of the people, allowing women to pray publicly, and encouraging people to publicly pray for their unsaved family and friends by name. Two particularly interesting strategies Finney employed were his house-to-house visitations and the "anxious meetings." In Finney's eyes, the dynamic of personal relationships was crucial to bringing a person to Christ. In December 1834, as part of his series called *Lectures on Revival* which codified the "new measures" for others to emulate, Finney insisted that conversion is brought about by both the agencies of God and men. He explains:

> Men act on their fellow-men, not only by language, but by their looks, their tears, their daily deportment.... Mankind are accustomed to read the countenances of their neighbors. Sinners often read the state of a Christian's mind in his eyes. If his eyes are full of levity, or worldly anxiety and contrivance, sinners read it. If they are full of the Spirit of God, sinners read it; and they are often led to conviction by barely seeing the countenance of Christians.[69]

Keenly aware of the power of relationships, Finney often went into private homes, both before and after preaching services, to address families as a group regarding their personal salvation. He also developed "anxious meetings" to deal with those under heavy conviction. Akin to the "pens" erected during the Cane Ridge Revival and "mourner's benches" already used in

---

67. Towns and Whaley, *Worship through the Ages*, 165.

68. In truth, many of Finney's "New Measures" were not new at all, such as the "anxious meetings." However, Finney consolidated many of the innovations of others and employed them in his own highly successful preaching ministry, thereby codifying these innovations as key characteristics of the revival meetings of the Second Great Awakening.

69. Finney, "What a Revival Is," 95.

other camp meetings, Finney also employed "anxious seats" for those concerned about their salvation. However, he went further by assembling those who were "anxious" about their eternal state into a small group where they could be counseled as to how one might be saved.[70]

Although the New Measures became a target of relentless criticism, even opponents could not deny their effectiveness. One of Finney's most remarkable revivals occurred in 1830 at the Third Presbyterian Church in Rochester, New York, lasting for a staggering five-month span. Reflecting on the astounding event, one of Finney's most formidable critics, Lyman Beecher, admitted, "That was the greatest work of God and the greatest revival of religion that the world has ever seen in so short a time."[71] In the end, Finney gained the respect of Beecher, who estimated that more than one hundred thousand people had been converted and added to the churches in a single year through the revivals sparked by Finney's leadership. Part of his leadership that led to so powerful an awakening was Finney's wisdom to engage personal relationships through innovative methods of small groups.

The Sunday School Movement

In the final quarter of the eighteenth century, while churches in Europe and America clamored for ways to educate their children and constituents, the population at large remained without instruction in religion or much anything else, for that matter. For example, the conventional grammar schools of the Anglican church had declined considerably, to the point that Lord Chief Justice Kenyon described them as "empty walls without scholars, and everything neglected but the receipt of salaries and endowments."[72] Around the same time, a philanthropist and social reformer named Robert Raikes surveyed the impoverished and unruly children of Gloucester, England, and asked himself, "Can anything be done?" A voice answered him, "Try."[73] Raikes did, and the Sunday school movement began. Founded as a means of providing rudimentary education using the Bible as its main text, the

---

70. McDow and Reid, *Firefall*, 241.
71. Quoted in Towns and Whaley, *Worship through the Ages*, 167.
72. Boyd, *History of Western Education*, 281.
73. Gregory, *Robert Raikes*, 145. See also Harris, *Robert Raikes*, xix.

small group strategy of Sunday schools became a major vehicle of revival and a major contributor to the Second Great Awakening.[74]

Robert Raikes and the Rise of the Sunday School Movement in Britain

Robert Raikes (1725–1811) was a businessman and publisher of a weekly newspaper, the *Gloucester Journal*. Hearing of a complaint from a resident about the unruly behavior of some children in the slum area of the city, Raikes went to investigate. What he found turned his journalistic inquisition into a genuine concern regarding the welfare of the children. In the wake of the English Industrial Revolution, there were no labor laws to protect the children from having to work from sunup to sundown six days a week in the factories. Even worse, there was no provision for educating these masses of children, leaving them on their only day off, Sunday, to roam the streets in packs. From what he saw, Raikes came to believe that their parents were "totally abandoned themselves, having no idea of instilling into the minds of their children principles to which they themselves were entire strangers."[75] They were filthy, ignorant, irreligious, and largely unwanted except for their economic value as laborers. Raikes was convinced that if these children could be taught to read, they might read the Bible for themselves and come to Christ as a result. "The world marches forth on the feet of little children," Raikes once said, believing that the whole of society could be changed by reaching children with the gospel.[76]

In 1780, with the help of Anglican associates, he rented a meeting place, employed teachers, and began a school on Sundays for young people to receive secular instruction and knowledge of God and the Bible. While only the teachers had a copy of the Bible, its primary textbook, the curriculum of Raikes's Sunday school featured Christian instruction while also directing efforts to teach the children mathematics, reading, and writing. To maintain as small a group as possible so that each child could be given the personal attention he or she needed, Raikes employed a monitoring system, where assistants aided in the education and care of the students. "Raikes' teachers taught twenty children in four classes under four monitors, and the

---

74. For additional information on the role of the Sunday School Movement in evangelical revival, see Rice, *Sunday School Movement*.

75. Quoted in Maxey, "Raikes' Ragged Regiment."

76. Maxey, "Raikes' Ragged Regiment."

delegated responsibility lightened the load."[77] The children were fed, clothed, and educated each Sunday from 10 a.m. to 2 p.m.[78] Before entering, each child had to stand for inspection at the door, the price for admittance being a washed face and combed hair. At the end of each session, as students began to file out the door, they all received a coin for attending.

As with many successes of the Second Great Awakening, Raikes's Sunday school program came under attack. His friends labeled the group "Bobby Wild Goose and his ragged regiment." The churches in the area generally dismissed his efforts as hopeless. Many considered such a use of the Lord's Day to be sacrilege, and some came to feel that the Sunday school was an intentional competition to the local churches. In fact, some pastors began to preach against the "work of the devil."[79] Still, Raikes and his "ragged regiment" continued on and the movement took root. Over time, a significant transformation took place in Raikes's Sunday school students. The young people largely stopped their profanity, and the crime rate in Gloucester dropped dramatically. Consequently, in 1786, "the magistrates of the area passed a unanimous vote of thanks for the impact Robert Raikes and his Sunday school had upon the morals of the youth in that area."[80]

Amid its unprecedented growth, however, a problem emerged that had to be remedied before the small group strategy could be released to the public. The money to support the Sunday school was consumed by the modest wages for the teachers, leaving no money for students's Bibles or other learning materials. After three years of success, Raikes finally published an account of its work in November 1783. His article was reprinted across Great Britain and even beyond. In response, a group of affluent ladies volunteered as Sunday school teachers. Even Queen Charlotte of England summoned Raikes to hear his story of the Gloucester Sunday school.[81] In 1811, just over thirty years after launching his ambitious endeavor to evangelize and educate the street kids of Gloucester, Robert Raikes died of a heart attack. The local children of the Sunday schools—the kids and grandkids of Raikes' "ragged regiment"—attended his funeral. During the funeral, Al Maxey records, "each child, by prior

---

77. Orr, *Campus Aflame*, 46–47. See also Harris, *Robert Raikes*, 324.
78. Towns, "Bicentennial History," X–X.
79. Maxey, "Raikes' Ragged Regiment," X–X.
80. Towns, "Bicentennial History," X–X.
81. Maxey, "Raikes' Ragged Regiment," X–X.

order, was given a shilling and a large piece of Raikes' famous plum cake. Even in death he was thinking of the children!"[82]

By Raikes publicizing the work of his Sunday school, he helped lay the groundwork for an explosion historically known as the Sunday School Movement in England. One of the earliest and most powerful organizations to come out of the movement was the London Society, set up on September 7, 1785, "for the Support and Encouragement of Sunday schools."[83] The society began on the initiative of Baptist businessman William Fox and the wealthy "saint," Henry Thornton became one of its charter trustees, serving as treasurer. Almost immediately, Wolffe explains, "The new society gave respectability to Sunday schools and also supported them by providing textbooks and cash grants."[84] Even John Wesley joined the effort, writing just eight years after Raikes began his efforts, "I verily think these Sunday Schools are one of the noblest specimens of charity which have been set on foot in England since William the Conqueror."[85] For his part, Wesley began to call for volunteer teachers to replace the paid ones. Consequently, more literature and the free services of teachers poured in, contributing significantly to the preservation and extension of the Sunday School Movement in England. In 1805, the rising Wesleyan star Jabez Bunting articulated a rousing defense for Sunday schools. Basing his rationale on Nehemiah 6:3, Bunting saw teaching children to read the Bible as "a great work," for it instructed them on basic Christian doctrines and trained them in "habits of piety and virtue." Lamenting the failure of the parents to teach their own children in the things of God, he saw guiding the children toward holiness through Sunday school as a means to the conversion of their parents. This, he pronounced, would benefit the whole nation, as entire families would become moral and law-abiding members of society.[86]

In a very short time, what began as the project of a warmhearted proprietor to help neglected children find Jesus and a better life became an unstoppable force of spiritual revival and social transformation in Great Britain. In 1797, there were already 1,000 Sunday schools in England with nearly 70,000 students.[87] By the time of Raikes's death in 1811, there were

---

82. Maxey, "Raikes' Ragged Regiment," X–X.
83. Wolffe, *Expansion of Evangelicalism*, 163.
84. Wolffe, *Expansion of Evangelicalism*, 163.
85. Wolffe, *Expansion of Evangelicalism*, 163.
86. Bunting, *Great Work*, 6–21.
87. Noll, *Rise of Evangelicalism*, 245.

Sunday schools peppered across England with a combined attendance of 400,000 pupils. In 1820, half a million people in England and Wales—4 percent of the entire population—were in Sunday school. Ten years later, enrollment had climbed to 1.5 million, 10 percent of the population; and by 1850, almost 2.5 million people were in Sunday school, approximately 15 percent of the British population.[88] The English Sunday School Movement had become so seismic in its force, some have concluded that it was "the root from which sprang our system of day schools."[89] At the very least, it had a considerable impact on secular education in Britain and Europe, as well as creating a worldwide system of religious instruction, including the United States.

The Spread of Sunday Schools in America

Although its development of Sunday schools lagged a bit behind that in Britain, God began to use this small group innovation in America as well. In 1785, William Elliot began a Sunday school in Accomac County, Virginia. On Sunday afternoons, he arranged to have several white children meet in his plantation home for Bible study, while teaching the Negro slaves at a different hour. Elliot's groups are considered by many to be the oldest Sunday school in America. One year later, another Sunday school, primarily concerned with teaching Negro slaves, was established in Hanover County, Virginia by the Methodist circuit rider, Francis Asbury.[90] In 1791, the first American Sunday school union was launched in Philadelphia, followed by the New York Sunday School Union in 1816.[91]

In 1824, the American Sunday School Union (ASSU) was formed to unite churches and denominations behind the growing swell of Sunday schools in the states. Its purpose statement reads: "To concentrate the efforts of Sabbath School societies in different portions of our country; to disseminate useful information; to circulate moral and religious publications in every part of the land; and to endeavor to plant Sunday Schools wherever

---

88. Orr, *Campus Aflame*, 45.

89. Smith, *Life and Work*, 6. For an excellent description of evangelical efforts to promote education through Sunday schools and day schools, see Wolffe, *Expansion of Evangelicalism*, 175–78.

90. Maxey, "Raikes' Ragged Regiment."

91. McDow and Reid, *Firefall*, 247.

there is a population."⁹² At the time of is organization, the ASSU had 48,681 children in its groups, increasing to 301,358 by 1832.⁹³ Yet, for American Sunday schools, the best was yet to come. In 1830, Francis Scott Key (the author of the American national anthem) was the president of ASSU. At its annual meeting, Key challenged its constituents with the report that four million people lived between Pittsburgh and Denver who were lost and in need of Christ. He then laid down the robust vision of establishing at least one Sunday school in every town between the two cities—an area estimated to be 1.3 million square miles. Key's "Mississippi Valley Enterprise" called for eighty missionaries for the daunting task.⁹⁴ Perhaps the most famous of those to answer Key's call was Stephen Paxson. Born with a speech impediment and having little formal education, Paxson began attending Sunday school at the beckoning of his daughter. Shortly thereafter, he was enlisted to teach a small group of boys, where he would simply read Scripture and ask questions. Ashamed that the boys knew more of the Bible than he did, Paxson began to read the Bible for himself and was subsequently converted. Feeling the call of God to do more, Paxson began organizing other Sunday school groups in his spare time.⁹⁵ When Key's call to evangelize the West went out, Paxson could not help but heed it. He traveled on horseback from one small community to another throughout the frontier. It has been said that his horse, which he had named "Robert Raikes," never passed a child with whom Paxson would not stop to share Jesus.⁹⁶ During his many years of service as a missionary, he organized 1,314 Sunday schools, totaling 83,405 teachers and students. Many of these small groups grew into churches within the same community in which they had been established. These churches, in turn, typically retained the Sunday school strategy as a part of their organization and missional outreach.⁹⁷ In all, Key's "Mississippi Valley Enterprise" lasted fifty years. During that time, 61,297 Sunday schools were formed with 407,244 teachers and 2,650,784 students. A million books or more occupied Sunday school libraries, between eighty to one

---

92. Maxey, "Raikes' Ragged Regiment."
93. Wolffe, *Expansion of Evangelicalism*, 165.
94. Towns and Whaley, *Worship through the Ages*, 163.
95. "Paxson, Stephen," *DCA*.
96. Towns and Whaley, *Worship through the Ages*, 164.
97. Maxey, "Raikes' Ragged Regiment."

hundred missionaries were engaged in the work each year, and a total of $2,133,364 was invested in the evangelistic effort.[98]

As in Britain, the phenomenal growth of Sunday schools brought about by the likes of Elliot, Asbury, Key, Paxson and others is nothing short of remarkable. With enrollments increasing from less than 100,000 children in 1824 to greater than 600,000 in 1831 and 3.25 million by 1875, the small group strategy of Sunday schools had enveloped the country. Equally remarkable is the movement's enduring legacy. Indeed, Towns and Porter claim that the Sunday School Movement that swept the American frontier in the early 1800s is to be largely credited for the conservative bent of America's Midwest today.[99] To many students of Christianity in America, "Sunday schools did as much to 'tame the west' in the early days of our history as just about anything else. It also had a tremendous impact on the spread of Christianity westward. Although not everyone appreciated the concept of the Sunday School, few would deny its impact upon society."[100]

Principles Gleaned from Small Groups in the Second Great Awakening

John Wolffe wisely reminds that spiritual awakenings never emerge or remain on their own; there are always facilitating factors at work. In the case of the Second Great Awakening, such factors include an influx of intense prayer by individuals and groups, a growing crescendo of devotional and evangelistic activity, and an awareness that revivals were already underway in other places. He goes on to note that these conditions were almost continually present in some places and points in time, thereby helping to sustain the awakening with the anticipation of future spiritual outbreaks.[101] In light of the evidences explored in this chapter, it becomes apparent that one of the most significant facilitators of the global renewal was the dynamic but ever-present role of a small group strategy. At times during the awakening, it subtly lay in the shadows, graciously granting the limelight to the more illustrious features of the movement, like the vibrant preaching and colorful activities of the camp meetings. At other times, it was front and center for all to see and take part, such as the calls for prayer

98. "Key, Francis Scott," *DCA*.
99. Towns and Porter, *Ten Greatest Revivals Ever*, 116.
100. Maxey, "Raikes' Ragged Regiment."
101. Wolffe, *Expansion of Evangelicalism*, 89.

and the effervescent Sunday School Movement. Regardless, whether in the shadows or the spotlight, small groups continued to prove indispensable for true revival. Table 2, located at the end of this chapter, provides a snapshot summary of the key observations made regarding the role of small groups during the Second Great Awakening. Beyond these observations, several conclusions can be surmised regarding the role and special features of small groups of the time.

1. Prayer was an essential, and sometimes the only purpose of the small groups. From college campuses to industrialized cities and the American frontier, spiritual and social conditions were horrible and growing worse prior to the awakening. It was out of intense anguish—indeed desperation—that many believers gathered for nothing other than prayer. Sometimes these gathered groups would sing, study the Bible, and provide encouragement to one another, but they usually enveloped the whole of these activities with multiple moments of prayer. At other times, there was nothing but prayer—for that is what they felt was needed the most.

2. Openness to the gospel often came through personal relationships brought about by small group encounters. Wisdom suggests that the greatest evangelistic energies should be spent on those who are most receptive to the gospel. Moreover, the gospel travels with greater welcome through friendship or kinship relations. Charles Finney recognized this principle, and he brilliantly applied it in various parts of his New Measures, especially his home visits and the creation of "anxious meetings." Similarly, Peter Cartwright saw its value while praying with a group of his friends over a few souls struggling with their salvation. Both Finney and Cartwright recognized that a powerful way to address the spiritual needs of others was through the personal touch that comes through a small group.

3. People learn and are developed with greater efficiency through a small group atmosphere. The conventional methods of established churches were not working to educate and evangelize boys and girls in late eighteenth-century Britain. It took the innovation of an entrepreneur to recognize how small groups in the form of Sunday schools could not only teach children how to read and write, but also help them discover salvation in Christ, personal dignity, and hope for a brighter future.

4. Music and learning were brilliantly blended through the agent of small groups. An impressive number of songs were produced during the Second Great Awakening through the advent of Sunday schools, many of which are still sung today. Simple, catchy, and easy to sing, these songs were especially loved by children and effective for combining Bible teaching with the fun of singing. Immensely popular, these songs were often used not only in Sunday school meetings, but also in private times of devotion and at gatherings of family or friends. With lyrics set in common, everyday English, the songs of Sunday school typically emphasized three aspects of Christian thought: (1) the joys of heaven, (2) the love of Christ, and (3) satisfaction gained in living the Christian life. Perhaps the most remembered of the voluminous Sunday school tunes is "Jesus Loves Me," written by composer, musician, and publisher, William Bradbury.[102]

5. Small groups can adapt to the needs of its participants and the opportunity of the moment. Some college students gathered in private rooms, while others in wooded areas and even under a haystack. Some of the groups studied the Bible, sang hymns, and fellowshipped with each other, while other groups simply prayed. In the cities, prayer groups were often organized and scheduled for specific times, but there were also occasions when groups spontaneously formed with no such planning or preparation. Regardless, whether in a building or a barn and whether scheduled or spontaneous, small groups serve best when they are adapted for the needs of its participants at the moment.

6. Small groups, when effectively done, provide a sustainable strategy for continued spiritual growth long after revival has gone. One need only look to Sunday schools for evidence. Hints of Sunday schools in their embryonic stage can be seen in the latter part of the First Great Awakening. Since that time, Christian history has seen three other great revivals come and go; yet Sunday schools remain as a staple feature in churches across the globe even today. While, admittedly, Sunday schools have lost their effectiveness in many churches, in most cases it is due to these congregations forgetting their purpose and neglecting their requirements for success. Nevertheless, no other system has been as widely accepted as a strategy for spiritual growth than these small group Bible studies.

---

102. Towns and Whaley, *Worship through the Ages*, 167–68.

Conclusion

Perhaps most importantly, small groups can facilitate continued, steady growth when the spirit of revival has slowed. Wolffe explains, "Much evangelical church growth occurred through the slow but steady recruitment of individuals rather than through the mass conversions associated with revivals."[103] Thus, as much as small groups precede and even help to facilitate revival, perhaps more importantly, they continue to serve as an effective means for spiritual growth after revival has ended—and in preparation for the next time the Spirit chooses to awaken the church.

---

103. Wolffe, *Expansion of Evangelicalism*, 91.

Table 2: Key Observations of the Catalytic Small Groups during the Second Great Awakening (1780–1850)

Precursors to the Small Groups	• Methodist Class Meetings
Emergence of the Small Groups	• Hampden-Sydney (1787) and Williams Colleges Prayer Groups (1806) • Cane Ridge Revival (1801) • Peter Cartwright's camp meeting and circuit formation (1803) • Charles Finney's "New Measures" (1824–32) • Robert Raikes's Sunday School in Gloucester, England (1780)
Major Proponents of the Small Groups	• John Erskine (Edinburgh, Scotland) • William Bramwell, Ann Cutter (Yorkshire, England) • Robert Raikes (Gloucester, England) • Charles Finney (Oneida County, New York) • Stephen Paxson (Midwest Circuit Rider) • Francis Scott Key (Mission Valley Enterprise)
Prominent Revival Leaders, Ministries, and Movements that Emerged from the Small Groups	• American Board of Commissions for Foreign Missions (1810) • American Bible Society (1816)
Key Features of the Small Groups	• Christian instruction • Concerted prayer efforts • Sunday school initially provided basic education to children, but included Christian instruction and later expanded to adults • Used as a means for counseling those under conviction of sin and in need of conversion • Used music as a form of instruction and worship

5

Small Groups in the Layman's, Welsh, and Korean Revivals (1857–1910)

IN ONE OF HIS seminal works, John Piper thematically states, "God is most glorified in us when we are most satisfied in Him."[1] While Piper's book, within which this statement is found, focuses mainly on the individual Christian, its principal teaching aptly applies to Christians in any generation. God is most glorified when his followers exalt him above all else, and history has demonstrated that it is in these times, when God is glorified above all, that he manifests himself in amazing ways. In other words, as a rule, God brings revival only when the church is desperate for him. This desperation is most fully expressed in sincere prayer. Matthew Henry is credited with saying, "When God desires to do a fresh work, he sets his people to praying."[2] Revival is always conceived in the heart of God, but it is birthed by burdened believers overwhelmed with the urgency to plead for it. Thus, when even a few believers give themselves fully to serious, united prayer, they are stoking the embers that often rage into revival. Such prayer is nowhere better encountered than in a small group of earnest Christians, and such an awakening is nowhere more clearly seen than in the series of revivals that erupted in the second half of the nineteenth century. The most notable among these renewals are the Layman's Prayer Revival (1857–59), the Welsh Revival and Global Awakening (1904–5), and the Korean Revival, also known as the Pyongyang Revival (1907–10). While they are not historically consolidated into one general awakening, these revivals and their evangelistic aftershocks worked together to provide the third of the most significant spiritual awakenings in Christian history.

1. Piper, *Desiring God*, 50.
2. Quoted in McDow and Reid, *Firefall*, 251.

The Layman's Prayer Revival (1857–59)

As with all of the awakenings, several factors played a key role for the emergence of the renewals of the late 1800s, but no factor was more important than the clusters of prayer groups that littered the cities and countryside. The Layman's Prayer Revival of 1857–59 is a splendid example of these small groups of believers desperately seeking and finding the face of God. Of all renewals studied in history, the Layman's Prayer Revival is arguably the least appreciated. City shops shut down at midday and factories erected tents on their grounds to accommodate the concerts of prayer that became a catalyst for this revival. As a result, in its brief span, an estimated one million people came to Christ and were added to the churches.

Conditions Leading Up to the Revival

While ripples of revival from the Second Great Awakening could still be felt on occasion, by the 1840s and 1850s it was evident that renewal was waning across the globe. The excited crowds of the camp meetings gave way to the hustle and bustle of a growing society, and the powerful means of educating through Sunday schools were being threatened by innovative efforts of secular education and the rise of college fraternities. Consequently, Frank Beardsley records, "For several years, from 1843 to 1857, the accessions to the churches scarcely equaled the losses sustained by death, removal or discipline, while a widespread indifference to religion became prevalent."[3] Considering the onslaught of distractions that occurred during this period, such attrition from spiritual matters is understandable. Ironically, it would be these very factors that would incite a call for concerted prayer that ultimately brought revival.

There are many factors that contributed to spiritual decline, not the least of which was the industrial and economic advancement of the United States during this period. By the mid-1800s, the United States was on the rise as a global power. During the 1840s, the nation acquired much of the territories that would make up its southwestern states from Texas to California. At the same time, innovation continued to thrive, yielding pivotal technologies like the Conestoga wagon, the railroad, and the telegraph. These advances helped expand America westward, a land rich with coal, oil, and gold. Combined, these innovations and natural resources

---

3. Beardsley, *Religious Progress*, 40.

propelled the adolescent nation to the forefront of the Industrial Revolution. Reflecting on the American industrial machine, Alvin Reid reports that between 1820 and 1860, the number of Americans working in manufacturing grew fourfold.[4] However, these industrial and economic blessings inevitably turned the hearts of the people away from the one who granted them. Warren Candler assesses the spiritual decline of the time, quipping, "Men forgot God in pursuit of gold."[5]

Another powerful element that preceded revival was the plague of war. Revolution and turmoil had gripped large swaths of Europe by the middle of the century. The Chartist demonstrations had erupted in Great Britain, along with republican agitation in Ireland. In addition, uprisings broke out in Germany, France, and Austria, invoking a tightening hold on the present tyrannies.[6] In the United States, there was the question of slavery, a formidable contention that engulfed a great deal of the passions and energies of the American people. Although during the previous awakening, many of the prominent figures like Charles Finney and Lyman Beecher had preached fiery sermons against it, the issue raged even more during this time, yielding events such as the publication of *Uncle Tom's Cabin* by Harriet Beecher Stowe (1852), the *Dred Scott* decision by the Supreme Court (1857), and John Brown's raid on Harper's Ferry (1859). Indeed, the polarizing problem of slavery would not be resolved until the Civil War (1861–65), two years after the Layman's Prayer Revival had subsided.

A third condition that dogged spiritual vitality during the time was the moral decline among college campuses. J. Edwin Orr claims that college fraternities emerged as a reaction to the wave of evangelical revivals that had swept the campuses during the Second Great Awakening. "It was too much to expect the oncoming, unregenerate classes of students to appreciate the religious enthusiasms of their predecessors, who had experienced spiritual realities in the times of the awakening." Therefore, these fraternal organizations served as escapes from the mundane and regimented life of the campus brought about by conventional academic and religious pursuits. As brothers protected each other through the loyalty of concealment, "the fraternity provided new ways of enjoying a cigar, a drink, a song, or the company of a coquette."[7] The results were as predictable as they were

4. McDow and Reid, *Firefall*, 252.
5. Candler, *Great Revivals and the Great Republic*, 210.
6. Orr, *Campus Aflame*, 62.
7. Orr, *Campus Aflame*, 61.

disheartening, with only a handful of Christian conversions being reported among this new generation of students.[8]

Religious extremism was another major contributor to the spiritual decline, such as the failed apocalyptic claims of William Miller. In response to the claims by Miller and others that Christ would return on April 23, 1843 and then on March 22, 1844, much excitement stirred. Some even abandoned their material possessions and assembled together in anticipation for Christ's triumphant return. However, when his predictions failed, so did public confidence, not only in him but in Christianity as a whole. Many of the disillusioned left the faith, some becoming cynics while others turned to materialism. Churches became the objects of ridicule, and for several years, attrition outpaced the gain of newcomers.[9]

Serving as a final, climactic factor for the mid-century spiritual decline was the crash of the American financial market on October 14, 1857. As a result of "excessive railroad building, over-speculation, and a wildcat currency system,"[10] financial panic swept through, causing banks to fail and pivotal corporations such as the railroad to go bankrupt. In step, factories shut down, businesses closed, and multitudes suddenly became unemployed, with thirty thousand men without a job in New York City alone.[11] The gold which had replaced God as the center of people's faith was gone; now they had nothing but hunger and despair to look to. At last, desperation had come to the point that men began to pray.[12]

---

8. Orr, *Campus Aflame*, 63–64.
9. Orr, *Campus Aflame*, 63.
10. Beardsley, *History of American Revivals*, 216.
11. Beardsley, *History of American Revivals*, 217.
12. Orr notes that many historians have dismissed the Layman's Prayer Revival as artificial, having been prompted by financial ruin caused by the market crash of 1857. However, Orr goes on to argue against this notion, first by noting that "bank-panics do not automatically produce spiritual awakenings" (for example, 1929 crash), and by pointing out that many efforts of prayer and evangelism had already begun prior to the financial panic. Orr, *Campus Aflame*, 67. See also Orr, *Fervent Prayer: The Worldwide Impact of the Great Awakening of 1858*, 5; McLoughlin, *Modern Revivalism*, 163; and McDow and Reid, *Firefall*, 252–53.

Prayer Groups, Sunday School, and the Groundwork for Revival

In truth, many believers had begun praying for spiritual renewal well before the financial crisis of 1857. For instance, Samuel Prime, editor of the *New York Observer*, recorded that the market crash only elevated attendance at the already established prayer meetings. Since they found themselves suddenly unemployed, droves of businessmen, "in their want of something else to do, assembled in the meetings for prayer."[13] Accompanying the growing groundswell of prayer were the continuing evangelistic efforts of Sunday school. In this regard, Alvin Reid offers the example of a massive Sunday school outreach campaign launched in New York City in September, 1856. In this interdenominational effort, people went block by block enlisting the unchurched for Sunday school. The strategy was so successful that it was duplicated in other cities, including Hartford, Buffalo, Boston, and Detroit. All these efforts—the prayer meetings and the Sunday school outreaches—helped lay the footing for the revival that was to come.[14]

Jeremiah Lanphier and the Union Prayer Meetings

While others were already taking place, perhaps the prayer meeting primarily credited for the launch of Layman's Prayer Revival began at the Fulton Street Church (Dutch Reformed) in New York City through the leadership of Jeremiah Lanphier. Lanphier was a forty-two-year-old businessman who was converted to Christ in 1842. Filled with zeal and a deep desire for others to experience the love of Christ, this layman was hired by Fulton Street Church as a missionary to engage the city's unreached citizens with the gospel. On July 1, 1857—just four months before the market crash—Lanphier got to work in the city. After his initial efforts only yielded modest results, he was overcome with the daunting task of reaching a city full of businessmen "hurrying along their way, often with care worn faces, and anxious, restless gaze."[15] Lanphier soon changed tactics, organizing a noon prayer meeting for businessmen. With great enthusiasm, he printed and distributed invitations and flyers for the meeting. Lanphier describes his vision of the meetings, which officially began on September 23, 1857:

13. Prime and Bingham, *Power of Prayer*, 14.
14. McDow and Reid, *Firefall*, 256.
15. Prime, *Prayer and Its Answer*, 24.

SMALL GROUPS IN THE LAYMAN'S, WELSH, AND KOREAN REVIVALS

> Going my rounds in the performance of my duty one day, as I was walking along the streets, the idea was suggested to my mind that an hour of prayer, from twelve to one o'clock, would be beneficial to businessmen, who usually in great numbers take that hour for rest and refreshment. The idea was to have singing, prayer, exhortation, relation of religious experience, as the case might be; that none should be required to stay the whole hour; that all should come and go as their engagements should allow or require, or their inclinations dictate. Arrangements were made, and at twelve o'clock noon, on the 23rd day of September, 1857, the door of the third story lecture-room was thrown open.[16]

Initially, no one showed up at the designated time, so Lanphier prayed alone. Then, about twenty minutes later, one person arrived, followed by another. By the end of the hour, six people had joined him in prayer. The following week, the small group of praying businessmen had expanded to twenty; and at the third meeting, more than thirty had joined them. On October 14—at the fourth meeting of Lanphier's prayer group and on the day of the market crash—over one hundred businessmen came to pray. Before long, three large rooms were filled, and then the church's auditorium. In short order, Lanphier's prayer group had prompted other similar meetings across the city, and within six months fifty thousand were meeting daily for prayer in New York alone.[17] Elmer Towns and Vernon Whaley tell the story when, in February 1858, George Bennett of the *New York Herald* was standing near a second-floor window at the time that the church steeple chimed its noonday song. Suddenly seeing men running through the streets, he sent a reporter to investigate "why the men are running." Upon returning, the reported told Bennett, "The men are running to follow the exhortation of Jesus who said, 'Could you not pray with me one hour?'"[18]

Part of the success of Lanphier's prayer meetings was their uniqueness in style. While former meetings were often formal and routine, these meetings were free and spontaneous. It typically had no leaders or preachers, and the prayers were informal. Indeed, anyone was welcome to pray, lead in singing, or give a brief word of testimony. As a general rule, Lanphier established seven guiding policies for the prayer groups: (1) begin with a brief hymn; (2) open in prayer; (3) read a scripture passage; (4) allow time for requests, exhortations, and prayers; (5) have prayer follow each request

---

16. Quoted in Prime and Bingham, *Power of Prayer*, 22.
17. McDow and Reid, *Firefall*, 258.
18. Towns and Whaley, *Worship through the Ages*, 181; see Matt 26:40.

or at most two requests, limiting individuals to five minutes of prayer or comments; (6) avoid controversial subjects; (7) at five minutes before 1:00, sing a closing hymn, assuring the meeting ends promptly at the hour.[19] In contrast to the previous two major awakenings that emphasized evangelistic preaching, this movement focused on prayer. The prayer gatherings knew neither denominational nor socioeconomic boundaries. Even the original six businessmen who comprised the first meeting represented four denominations. Orr explains, "It was a layman's movement, in which the laymen of all denominations gladly undertook both normal and extraordinary responsibilities in the service of God and humanity."[20] Thus, these prayer gatherings were called "union" prayer meetings, emphasizing the unity amid the diverse backgrounds of their participants.[21] Though characteristically spontaneous and loosely organized, the prayer meetings and the resulting revival were uniquely devoid of the emotionalism that accompanied the camp meetings of the early 1800s. Instead, amid an atmosphere of prayerfulness, the spirit of revival largely featured calmness and sobriety. Roy Fish records one witness to the revival:

> The most crowded meetings were solemn by their deep and strange illness; the most thorough conviction and terrible anxiety showed themselves in concentrated meditation and half-suppressed and deep drawn sighs; while the joy and hope and forgiveness told of its presence by tears which made the eyes they moistened more radiant than ever.[22]

Yet in this spirit of solemnity, men often arose and cried out for salvation as others gathered around them for intercession. In general, the spirit of these prayer groups was one of deep love for Christ which spilled over to one another with such intensity that unchurched onlookers observed in amazement at the mutual compassion and answered prayers that came out of the meetings. The fame of these meetings stretched into the Midwest, drawing some from as far as St. Louis to be part of the movement.

---

19. Chambers, *Noon Prayer Meeting*, 46–48.
20. Orr, *Campus Aflame*, 68.
21. McDow and Reid, *Firefall*, 259.
22. Fish, "Awakening of 1858," 60.

Spread of Revival in America

Not surprisingly, the Layman's Prayer Revival spread via these prayer meetings—first along the eastern seaboard, then throughout the nation, and ultimately abroad. Wherever the revival reached, its effects were much the same. In America, the impact of the prayer meetings and the revival that followed was profound. In areas where churches were scarce, factory owners erected tents where workers could pray. This "zone of heavenly influence" reached the United States ports as well.[23] For example, McDow and Reid record an instance when the battleship *North Carolina* was moored in New York City's harbor with over one thousand crewmen. During the period that the ship was docked, a small group of four sailors began to meet for prayer on the ship. At some point, they were so filled with God's Spirit that they began to sing. Hearing the singing, some ungodly sailors began to ridicule the four men. Almost immediately, these mockers were gripped with conviction, and they began to cry out for mercy. Every evening, prayer meetings were held on the ship, with each night yielding more hardened shipmen coming to faith in Christ. Revival was so powerful, a team of ministers were solicited to help care for the newly converted. Even more astounding is that the *North Carolina* during this time was serving as a receiving ship for the navy. Sailors from different posts transitioned to other assignments through this ship. Thus, revival spread across the seas as a result of God using the faithful prayers of a small group of sailors.[24]

Small prayer groups began popping up on college campuses as well, so that nearly all of the denominational colleges were impacted by revival. Orr reports that New England, home of many of the country's top colleges, was incredibly moved in the awakening both on its campuses and in its cities. Yale had not experienced such a powerful revival in nearly forty years.[25] Revival fires had also spread into Pennsylvania. In fact, an excellent example of how the awakening affected American colleges can be found on campuses in Philadelphia. On February 3, 1858, a group of young men affiliated with the YMCA moved their prayer meeting which had begun three months earlier into a small waiting room adjacent to a large venue known as Jayne's Hall. At first, the small room was plenty to

---

23. Hoffman, *Revival Times in America*, 114.
24. McDow and Reid, *Firefall*, 262.
25. For a more detailed account of the effects of the Layman's Prayer Revival on American colleges, see Orr, *Campus Aflame*, 68–83.

accommodate the group of only a few. However, the group began to grow—from twenty, to thirty, on to sixty in attendance. With the small room no longer adequate, the sponsors decided to move the meeting into the main hall, a venue of twenty-five hundred seats. At its first meeting on March 10, the hall was overflowing with those eager to pray. At the peak of the revival, six thousand people gathered daily to pray.[26] Similarly, in the South at Davidson College, students who had been suspended for drunkenness and immorality just a few years earlier found themselves in weekly prayer meetings (besides attending chapel). Indeed, according to Orr, "a score of colleges which experienced campus revivals between March and May of 1858 reported more than five hundred conversions, and it was supposed that at least five thousand students declared their faith in the general revival throughout the country."[27] Perhaps the clearest glimpse into the impact of the revival on college campuses—and the role of small groups in it—can be seen through the lens of a student at the time. On May 27, 1858, college student G. L. P. Wren briefly journaled the following:

> Monday April 19, 1858: Yesterday I went to hear preaching, but little did I think of hearing such as sermon as I did. . . . Tuesday April 20: Being some rain in the fore part of the day, we could not meet in the woods for prayer and we met in the Phi Gamma Hall, and in a very few minutes there were six or eight converted and we repaired to the church where there were several more converted before we left.[28]

Across America, groups of believers earnestly seeking revival met for prayer; and revival came on a seismic scale. At a time when the population of the United States was about thirty million, the Layman's Prayer Revival resulted in more than one million people—3 percent of the entire nation—coming to faith in Christ and joining a local church in a single year![29]

Spread of Revival Abroad

While addressing the Convention of the Diocese of Ohio on the Revival of Religion, Bishop Charles P. McIlvaine noticed at least six significant

---

26. Orr, *Campus Aflame*, 73–74.
27. Orr, *Campus Aflame*, 78.
28. Cited in Godbold, *Church College*, 137.
29. Orr, *Campus Aflame*, 68.

SMALL GROUPS IN THE LAYMAN'S, WELSH, AND KOREAN REVIVALS

characteristics of the Layman's Prayer Revival. As discussed earlier, he observed that the revival was simple in means, quiet and calm, harmonious, and restrained. Additionally, McIlvaine stated that the revival was far-reaching to the widest extent and that it commanded the respect of the world in unprecedented ways.[30] Because the revival was so reputable and extensive, God's Spirit used it to bring spiritual awakening to other countries around the world. Reports of revival came from Northern Ireland, England, Scotland, Wales, South Africa, Scandinavia, Switzerland, and Germany. With these spiritual stirrings also came the small group dynamic as a catalyst for renewal. For instance, A. B. Earle was a Baptist evangelist whom God used to reach the people of Canada during the revival's zenith. On one occasion, Earle wrote concerning a typical village he would visit, "I went out at midnight near my boarding house and could distinctly hear the voice of prayer in the houses, in the barns, in the fields, in the streets."[31] As a result, revival was so powerful that Earle was one of five ministers who were simultaneously baptizing new converts due to the staggering numbers of them. Ireland also experienced revival partly through the agency of a small group. In 1856, a woman came to the island to evangelize from house to house. One man whom she had spoken to was James McQuilken. In response, McQuilken and a small group of other believers began to meet for prayer in September 1857. The group eventually became what is known as the Believer's Fellowship Meeting. Over the next two years, McQuilken's small group grew to about fifty and fanned the flame of revival that engulfed the country—an awakening later known as the Ulster Revival of 1859.[32]

Similarly in Wales, a powerful awakening erupted in 1859. Writing about the revival, Thomas Phillips quipped, "The work of a century is crowded into a year."[33] It began with Humphrey Jones, a church leader in Wales who had been in the United States when the revival erupted. When he returned, Jones began to pray for God to do a similar work in his homeland. Influenced by Humphrey, another Welsh pastor named David Morgan began to assemble people to pray for revival on the island. As a result, revival gripped the heart of Wales with such fervor that Morgan testified that his people "appear as if they had been shot by the truth."[34] Thomas Phillips

30. McIlvaine, *Bishop McIlvaine's Address*.
31. Earle, *Bringing in Sheaves*, 59.
32. McDow and Reid, *Firefall*, 268–69.
33. Phillips, *Welsh Revival*, 1.
34. Quoted in Towns and Whaley, *Worship through the Ages*, 163–64.

writes that drunkenness had all but disappeared in many towns, and that the revival had even reached the coal mines. One mine in particular had been so gripped by revival that all but one miner had been converted, "and that calloused, remaining sinner was being deluged with a torrent of earnest prayers for his conversion."[35] Thus, what started in a small room of a church in New York City exploded into a global movement of spiritual renewal that would find its way into the coal mines of Wales.

Impact of the Layman's Prayer Revival

To only have lasted two or three years, the Layman's Prayer Revival had an immeasurable impact throughout the world. Indeed, revered scholar of revivals J. Edwin Orr claims that it was the greatest revival he ever studied, and Perry Miller of Harvard called the revival "The Event of the Century."[36] Such accolades are well-deserved when one considers the fruit of the awakening. As is true with generally all spiritual awakenings, the effects of the Layman's Prayer Revival developed in four systematic phases: reviving, evangelizing, missionary, and social.[37] This chapter has already reported the vast wave of prayer groups that prompted renewal among believers. Evangelistically, virtually every denomination boasted of significant increases in the late 1850s, and the overall percentage of churchgoers in America jumped by 50 percent.

Another significant outcome of the awakening is the tsunami of missions involvement which it stirred.[38] One of the most formidable examples of missional efforts coming out of this revival is the Student Volunteer Movement. British athlete C. T. Studd had given his life to Christ and missions during a D. L. Moody crusade, another outcome of the revival. In 1885, Studd was joined by six other believers to form a small group called the "Cambridge Seven." This small group steadily grew to become the Student Volunteer Movement, a mighty missional force that would yield

---

35. Phillips, *Welsh Revival*, 72, 106.

36. Miller, *Life of the Mind in America*, 88.

37. Orr, *Campus Aflame*, 104.

38. This is not to imply that modern missions began with the Layman's Prayer Revival but that it picked up even more steam. Indeed, when considering the numerous reform societies, evangelistic outreach efforts, and philanthropic endeavors that sprang up during the early to mid-1800s, a case can and should be made that the modern missions movement was born from the Second Great Awakening.

approximately 20,500 students being involved in international missions over the next half century.

Perhaps no greater evidence regarding the social effects of the revival can be found than how it spiritually prepared the American nation for the storms of war that were churning. Some historians have concluded that the revival was of divine providence, preparing America for these sinister years of conflict. Henry and Richard Blackaby believe, "Even as churches across America were celebrating the influx of new converts into their ranks, God knew that the most horrific war in America's history was just a few years away. More than 600,000 young men would die in the carnage of the Civil War, thousands of whom had only recently given their lives to Christ during the awakening of 1857–1858."[39] Orr agrees, stating that the revival "served and fortified the churches for the great trauma. While the younger generation sallied forth for battle, home churches, as the war progressed, showed no diminishing of zeal."[40] Similarly, Fred Hoffman noted, "As a result of the revival the nation entered the dark days of the Civil War with a deeper faith in God and a firmer belief in the efficacy of prayer."[41]

With the advent of the Civil War came an ebbing of the spiritual renewal that had brought light and vitality to so many just a few years earlier. As a result, most historians claim that the Layman's Prayer Revival ended around the year 1859. Nevertheless, though the revival itself may have concluded at that time, much of the prayer efforts and evangelistic impacts that characterized the revival continued, its banner being carried forth by Christian revivalists such as D. L. Moody.

The Continuation of Revival through the Ministry of Dwight L. Moody

Moody's Early Years and Conversion

Perhaps the Layman's Prayer Revival's most profound and long-lasting impact can be found in the life of one individual, Dwight Lyman Moody (1837–99). Born on February 5 on a small farm in Northfield, Massachusetts, Moody was the sixth of nine children. Moody's father, a bricklayer steeped in alcoholism, died when he was just four years old. One month

---

39. Blackaby et al., *Fresh Encounter*, 159.
40. Orr, *Event of the Century*, 50.
41. Hoffman, *Revival Times in America*, 114.

later, his mother, now widowed, gave birth to twins. Growing up in abject poverty, Moody only had four years of formal schooling. When he turned seventeen, Moody ventured to Boston and began working for his uncle as a shoe salesman. While in Boston, he joined what he called "the Christian saciation [sic]," the YMCA of Boston. Founded only three years earlier, it was the second YMCA established in North America (the first was in Montreal one week prior) and the first in the United States. For one dollar per year, Moody had a place where he could get away on his own "and I can have all the books I want to read free of expense . . . they have a large room and the smart men of Boston lecter to them for nothing and they get up a question."[42] As part of his agreement with his uncle, Moody attended the Mount Vernon Church and Sunday school each week. To the young man, church was the same regardless of the denomination, and he reported in a customary demeanor of dutiful disinterest to the local church's Sunday school superintendent. After spending a few moments with Moody, the superintendent allotted Moody to the class of Edward Kimball, a strikingly tall man in his early thirties who worked as a salesman in a dry-goods store. As the group meeting continued, Kimball noticed that Moody was struggling to find his place in the Gospel of John, so the keen mentor quietly handed Moody his own Bible open at the right place. At this gesture, Moody said to himself that he would "stick by the fellow who had stood by him and had done him like that."[43] With that, a life-changing—indeed world-altering—relationship had begun. For the next eleven months, Moody absorbed the teaching of Kimball and the preaching of Mount Vernon Church's pastor, Dr. Edward Norris Kirk. Over the course of this time, he struggled intensely with the lostness of his soul. Forty years later, Moody recalled, "When I came to Jesus Christ, I had a terrible battle to surrender my will, and take God's will." Finally on Saturday morning, April 21, 1855, while the church was holding revival services, Kimball "decided to speak with Moody about Christ and about his soul." He found Moody in the back of his uncle's store stacking shoe boxes. As Kimball looked down into the young man's eyes, he asked Moody plainly "to come to Christ, who loved him and who wanted his love and should have it." Kimball recalled what happened next: "It seemed that the young man was just ready for the light

---

42. Pollock, *Moody*, 9.
43. Pollock, *Moody*, 11.

that broke upon him, for there, at once, in the back of that shoe store in Boston, [Moody] gave himself and his life to Christ."⁴⁴

Small Groups in Moody's Sunday School Mission

In 1856, eighteen months after his conversion, Moody moved westward to Chicago to work for another uncle at a different shoe store. Now in Chicago, he joined the Plymouth Congregational Church, and soon became enamored with the spiritual renewal that was sweeping the city a year later. Biographer John Pollock wrote, "The revival of early 1857 tossed Moody out of his complacent view of religion as primarily an aid to fortune."⁴⁵ Writing to his mother about the revival, Moody admitted, "There is a great revival of Religion in this city. I go to meeting every night. How I do enjoy it. [It] seems as if God was here himself."⁴⁶ Soon thereafter, Moody gave himself over to the newfound passion of sharing the gospel with children. Moody was so effective, worship services at the church commonly found four pews full of young men that the young evangelist had brought. Eventually, Moody would serve as a full-time employee of the YMCA. Remembering how the organization had been so instrumental in his life during his first days in Boston, Moody embraced the ministry with passion, eventually becoming its national president.⁴⁷

However, it would be Sunday school that would become the primary platform during the early years of Moody's goliath evangelistic ministry. Searching for a Christian activity that could command his full spare-time energy, Moody began a Sunday school mission in the slums of northern Chicago. Appropriating an abandoned freight car on North State Street, Moody invited some young hoodlums he had befriended to "assist him in starting a mission Sunday school." On the following Sunday afternoon, extraordinary sounds began to erupt. "Shouts, whoops, cheers, a moment of silence, a sacred song in a baritone voice swept up into a shouted chorus." Pollock reports that "after a few Sundays, with boys bringing pals to the new adventure . . . the sides of the old car bulged."⁴⁸ Hearing about Moody's mission, Lawyer King offered the Mansion House—a one-story empty

---

44. Pollock, *Moody*, 13.
45. Pollock, *Moody*, 19.
46. Pollock, *Moody*, 19.
47. Bebbington, *Dominance of Evangelicalism*, 46.
48. Pollock, *Moody*, 25–26.

saloon—for the Sunday school to use. The group grew even more and Sunday afternoons became noisier. As a way to give the children more attention, Moody would gather smaller groups together during the weeknights. King describes the attraction of Moody in eyes of the youngsters: "All loved him, because he took such an interest in their welfare. No one forgets the pleasant smile and the cordial handshake, both of which were characteristic."[49] Similarly, a Chicago pastor, G. S. F. Savage, recalls Moody's magical appeal to these rowdy kids, stating he "went out on the streets with candy and knickknacks and got the good will of the children." Later, Savage was invited to attend one of the weekday small groups for a Thanksgiving Day "service." He testifies of what he saw:

> There were no gas fixtures in the house and he was trying to light it with a half-dozen candles, but the darkness had rather the best of it. I found him with a candle in one hand and a Bible in the other, and a child on his knee who he was trying to teach. There were twenty-five or thirty children in all, and they were as sorry a lot of little ragamuffins as could have been found in Chicago.[50]

Moody's Sunday school mission continued to thrive, capturing more than six hundred children each week for Bible study. By 1859 Moody's motley crew had become the largest Sunday school in Chicago, and Moody was subsequently elected president of the Illinois Sunday School Association. Towns and Whaley state, "Sunday school had become so popular that there was a local Sunday school organization in every county from Illinois to the Atlantic Ocean. Massive Sunday school conventions attracted thousands and motivated teachers to reach children for Jesus Christ and teach them the Word of God."[51] Near the beginning of one such convention in Illinois, Moody stood before the assembly and declared, "This [meeting] so far is dead, we will not start until God sends us revival." At this point, he dismissed the meeting and scattered the assembly into small groups to pray to the Lord for revival. Among those at the convention was H. J. Heinz, who said, "I'd rather be known as a Sunday school man, not a ketchup man."[52]

49. Pollock, *Moody*, 26.
50. Pollock, *Moody*, 26.
51. Towns and Whaley, *Worship through the Ages*, 183.
52. Towns and Whaley, *Worship through the Ages*, 183.

Small Groups in Moody's Evangelistic Ministry

Moody's Sunday school work with children eventually led to the founding of the nondenominational Illinois Street Church in 1864, with Moody as its pastor. The church gradually blossomed through the ministry and preaching of Moody, along with his newly acquired friend and worship leader, Ira Sankey. However, Moody was in a constant struggle with God over his call to itinerant evangelism. In the midst of this struggle, Moody experienced another life-altering event, the great Chicago Fire of 1871. Moody's beloved city and church lay in ashes. Yet in the midst of such terrible devastation, God claimed Moody's heart for a gospel ministry that would shake the world. Pollock describes the moment when Moody, collapsing in a spare room of a friend's house, fully surrendered to God:

> The room seemed ablaze with God. Moody dropped to the floor and lay bathing his soul in the Divine. Of this Communion, this mount of transfiguration, "I can only say that God revealed Himself to me, and I had such an experience of His love that I had to ask Him to stay His hand." Turmoil of mind glided into peace, conflict of character snapped into integration. That masterful strength which has hammered at the gates of hell and charged full tilt at the world, the flesh and the devil was melted and remolded, to leave him gentle as a babe, utterly dependent on a power beyond his own. Not for him to see and choose his path, nor pride to rule his will. God must lead, and God supply. Moody need never thirst again. The dead dry days were gone. . . . Crazy Moody became Moody the man of God.[53]

Fully surrendered to whatever God had in store, Moody was now set for what would be a quarter century of one of Christian history's most illustrious ministries in itinerant evangelism. While his evangelistic crusades are most widely known by the synergistic efforts of Moody's preaching and Sankey's leading of worship, the famed preacher never abandoned the use of small groups for reaching the lost. Indeed, there is evidence that small groups were employed in at least two strategic ways which helped his evangelistic campaigns become so powerful. One such strategy was the blanketing of surrounding communities with personal engagement of the gospel. In a lecture before a crowd of church leaders eager for revival,

---

53. Pollock, *Moody*, 90–91.

Moody explained that when people do not come to Christians, Christians are to go to them:

> If people will not come to the churches, why not send others out after them, and why not have meetings outside? That will soon give them an interest so that they will come to the house of God. Another way is to have prayer-meetings in the homes. A good many mothers cannot come out to church; but we can go down to their homes, and have four or five families come together, and pray with them and get them interested. Many a mother cannot go to the house of God for years, they have no servants to take care of their families, and the only way to reach them is to have cottage prayer-meetings.[54]

Moody concludes, "Let every man, woman and child help us a little and we pray that as they go into these attics and these households, the Holy Spirit may help them to present Christ in all His glory and loveliness."[55]

A second means by which Moody engaged a small group strategy in his evangelistic efforts is through the "enquiry room," an adaptation to Finney's "anxious bench." At the conclusion of an evangelistic meeting, Moody would typically invite anyone who wanted to become a Christian to stand and make their way to a private room. Here, respondents were broken up into small groups where they were given personal counseling regarding their decision for salvation. Church historian, David Bebbington, estimates that nearly four-fifths of everyone who came to Christ under Moody's evangelistic ministry did so through the enquiry room.[56]

Although he was never officially ordained into the ministry, Dwight L. Moody has been revered as one of the most famous and successful servants of the Lord in Christian history. His city-wide campaigns yielded amazing results. For example, McDow and Reid report that a three-month campaign in Chicago in the winter of 1876 had a cumulative attendance of nine hundred thousand (in a city of four hundred thousand), six thousand converts, and a multitude of new members added to local churches.[57] Consequently, Moody's ministry helped perpetuate the evan-

---

54. Moody, "How Can Non-Church-Goers Be Reached?" in McLoughlin, *American Evangelicals*, 173.

55. Moody, "How Can Non-Church-Goers Be Reached?" in McLoughlin, *American Evangelicals*, 175.

56. Bebbington, *Dominance of Evangelicalism*, 46. See also Dale, *Life of R. W. Dale of Birmingham*, 319.

57. McDow and Reid, *Firefall*, 266. Moreover, Moody and Sankey's strategy of

gelistic effects that the Layman's Prayer Revival had initiated. Conversely, when asked if Moody started the revival, Orr answers, "No, Moody did not start the '58 revival, the '58 revival started Moody."[58] Indeed, the interdependence between Moody and the awakening is unmistakable, as is Moody's love affair with the small group strategy for evangelism. From his conversion to Christ in the back of a shoe store through the help of a loving Sunday school teacher, to his Sunday school mission in a boxcar that reached the street kids of Chicago, to his house-to-house visitation and enquiry rooms which fortified his evangelistic campaigns, D. L. Moody was a small groups man—and they served him well.

The Welsh Revival and Global Awakening (1904–5)

Building upon the spiritual stirrings that had occurred during the Layman's Prayer Revival and subsequent evangelism campaigns like those by Moody and Sankey, another wave of revival would rise in the British principality of Wales. While the small European island had already been repeatedly blessed by earlier revivals, this time it would find itself as the epicenter of another worldwide awakening.[59] Indeed, many have considered the Welsh Revival to be the greatest awakening in history,[60] and J. Edwin Orr called it "a blaze of evening glory at the end of the great century."[61] Further explaining the immense impact of the awakening, Alvin Reid writes, "The Global Awakening did not penetrate as deeply as earlier great revivals, nor did it continue as long in influence as did the First and Second Great Awakenings. Still, the awakening is significant because God visited not only America and Europe but also many regions around the world."[62] As a result, some

---

blanketing a city with an evangelistic campaign featuring worship services and gospel preaching would serve as a basic model for the phenomenal ministries of Billy Graham and George Beverly Shea.

58. Orr, "Revival and Evangelism," 6; quoted in McDow and Reid, *Firefall*, 266.

59. Wales has historically benefited so often from spiritual awakenings that it has been called the "Land of Revival" and the "Land of Song." McDow and Reid, *Firefall*, 275.

60. For a brief account of the survey, see Towns and Whaley, *Worship through the Ages*, 215–16n1.

61. Towns and Whaley, *Worship through the Ages*, 201.

62. McDow and Reid, *Firefall*, 275. According to Paul Dienstberger, J. Edwin Orr documented how all six of the inhabited continents experienced a remarkable and spontaneous spiritual revival around 1905. See Dienstberger, *American Republic*, 295.

have estimated that over five million people came to faith in Christ within the two years of this worldwide revival.[63]

Precursors to Revival

Much like the aftermath of the Second Great Awakening prior to the Layman's Prayer Revival, a spiritual decline was again taking shape at the passing of the mid-nineteenth-century awakenings. The following generation did not retain the spiritual vitality of its parents, and the ebb-and-flow cycle that often characterized God's people continued. By 1900, church membership was once again in decline and apathy toward spiritual matters was on the rise. Church services were stiff and formal, and the common Christian was cold and callous toward God's presence. As so often before, revival was desperately needed again.

Yet revival was already on its way, with one of its earliest glimpses coming through the leading of Joseph Jenkins, a pastor in New Quay, Cardiganshire. Several months before revival erupted, Jenkins had been earnestly praying for a change to come over the area churches. In the fall of 1903, Jenkins formed a small prayer group called the Young People's Meeting in an effort to specifically combat the rising worldliness among the younger generation. In early February 1904, during one of these prayer meetings for young people, he asked the individuals in the group to share about how they viewed God. One attendee said, "Jesus is the light of world," to which Jenkins replied, "Yes, but what does He mean to you?" It was at that moment that a twenty-year-old Welsh girl named Florrie Evans stood and declared, "I love the Lord Jesus Christ with all of my heart."[64] At that moment, God's Spirit captured the room and gripped the hearts of the youth. Virtually everyone in the group began to weep and declare their love for Christ. Slowly but surely, this spiritual brokenness began to spread to other places nearby, including Blaenannerch, where God would capture another champion of revival, Evan Roberts.

---

63. Towns and Porter, *Ten Greatest Revivals Ever*, 23–44.
64. "1904 Welsh Revival."

Evan Roberts and the Welsh Revival

Serving as a popular evangelist at the time of this emerging spiritual renewal, Seth Joshua traveled to Newcastle Emlyn for a series for special services. During the last service, a student from a nearby Methodist Bible school named Evan Roberts (1878–1951) was in attendance. Roberts was a former coal miner from an humble Christian family. Even early in his life, Roberts had been known to carry his Bible everywhere he went.[65] Captivated by Joshua's message, Roberts followed the itinerant preacher to Blaenannerch. At the end of one of the meetings, Joshua said something to the effect of, "Bend the church and save the world." Struck by the prayer, Evan knelt and prayed fervently for himself, saying, "Oh Lord, bend *me*." Roberts later reflected on that moment and its impact on his life: "I felt ablaze with a desire to go through the length and breadth of Wales to tell of my Savior; and had that been possible, I was willing to pay God for doing so."[66]

Immediately Roberts began experiencing a divine call to bring revival to his native land. Publicly, he traveled to various towns and spoke of his changed life and vision from God, while privately, Roberts spent long hours in Bible study, prayer, and worship. During this time, God impressed upon him a sense that a revival was coming to Wales such that large numbers of people would come to Christ—and he was to be intricately a part of it. So overwhelmed by this vision, Roberts once commented to his friend, Sydney Evans in late 1904, "Oh Syd, we are going to see the mightiest revival that Wales has ever known—the Holy Spirit is coming just now." With anticipation, he continued, "We must get ready. We must get a little band and go all over the country preaching." He then stopped and, looking at his friend, Roberts asked, "Do you believe that God can give us 100,000 souls now?"[67]

In October 1904, Roberts felt God's leading to speak to his home congregation. With the permission of his college's administrator, he left his studies and traveled home to the village of Loughor, near Swansea. He asked his pastor for permission to deliver a message he claimed God had given

---

65. McDow and Reid report that while Roberts was a young coal miner, a page of his Bible was scorched which consisted of 2 Chr 6 where Solomon prayed for revival. After he became famous, the Bible was displayed in the photographs around the world; McDow and Reid, *Firefall*, 277.

66. Orr, *Flaming Tongue*, 5. For a detailed recount of Roberts's reflections, see Lewis, "Christ among the Miners," 37–42.

67. Stewart, *Invasion of Wales*, 28–29.

him for the church. The pastor agreed to allow the young man to speak, but only after the regular Monday evening prayer service. Just a small group of seventeen young people stayed behind to listen to Roberts; yet for nearly three hours, the twenty-six-year-old evangelist led the group in a prayer beckoning God to send revival. Towns and Whaley record that by the end of the meeting, "almost all of the young people were visited by the convicting power of the Holy Spirit, confessed their sins, and called on God for mercy."[68] The revival continued the next evening in the nearby town, Moriah. There, Roberts gave four requirements for revival that later became known as the "Four Points": (1) confess any known sin to God and put right any wrong done to others; (2) put away any doubtful habit; (3) obey the Holy Spirit promptly; and (4) confess faith in Christ openly.[69]

The results were instant and profound. The services continued each evening, and by the end of the week people from the surrounding churches were gathering for worship. The following week, these gatherings continued without any formal publicity. The crowds grew so large that people stood in the vestibule and near open doors to hear the word of God preached. Many went straight to the church from work just to make sure they could get a seat.[70] Henry and Richard Blackaby write, "There had been no organized campaign. There was no advertising, public relations, radio broadcast, or program for outreach. God did a sovereign work that captured the attention of the world."[71]

In his survey of the revival, Orr rightly declares, "The influence of the revival upon life in Wales is beyond calculation."[72] Within two months, seventy thousand people had come to Christ; within five months, the number had risen to eighty-five thousand; and, just as Roberts had envisioned, God had converted more than one hundred thousand souls. In less than a year, the whole of society within these Welsh communities had changed. Taverns shut down for lack of business. Sporting events and dancing socials stopped because people were flocking to churches instead. Crime dramatically dropped, leaving the police with little to do. McDow and Reid write, "Judges were presented with white gloves signifying no cases to be tried. Alcoholism was halved. At times hundreds would stand

---

68. Towns and Whaley, *Worship through the Ages*, 203.
69. Davis and Jones, *When the Fire Fell*, 79.
70. Towns and Whaley, *Worship through the Ages*, 203.
71. Blackaby, Blackaby, and King, *Fresh Encounter*, 164.
72. Orr, *Campus Aflame*, 111.

to declare their surrender of Christ as Lord. Restitution was made; gamblers and others normally untouched by the ministry of the church came to Christ."[73] Remembering a conversation he had had with the manager of a local mine during that time, G. Campbell Morgan stated that the coal production—which had typically been driven by profanity-commanded horses—was slowing dramatically because of the awakening. "The haulers are some of the very lowest. They have driven their horses by obscenity and kicks. Now they can hardly persuade their horses to start working, because there is no obscenity and kicks."[74] Evan Roberts never returned to Bible school, for revival had come at last. Moreover, the Welsh Revival's dating of 1904–05 only reflects the time in which the awakening was at a fever pitch; the revival, however, continued to impact the nation for years to come. In fact, Orr believes that the total number of conversions that came out of the revival was one-tenth of the entire Welsh population.[75] Yet the awakening was far from limited to Wales. The Spirit of God who had captured Wales in the opening years of the twentieth century would expand his reach globally, including the United States.

Impact of the Awakening in America and the World

In the late 1800s, America found itself in the ironic position of experiencing pain and prosperity. During the final years of the century, the nation was still licking its wounds brought about by the Civil War. At the same time, it was continuing to thrive industrially. By the turn of the century, both the automobile and the motion picture were born, while other inventions like the telephone, typewriter, lightbulb, phonograph, and electric motor further generated many more commercial enterprises. As an output of these advances, urbanization was growing swiftly as well. These new enterprises offered jobs both for Americans and an unprecedented number of immigrants—an estimated nine million in the first decade of the twentieth century. America also continued its territorial advance, annexing Hawaii and receiving the territories of Guam, the Philippines, and Puerto Rico from Spain after the Spanish-American War. By 1900, the United States had become a world power.

---

73. McDow and Reid, *Firefall*, 278.
74. McDow and Reid, *Firefall*, 279. See also Orr, *Flaming Tongue*, 15.
75. Orr, *Flaming Tongue*, 15.

Inevitably, these societal changes had an impact on the spiritual condition of the nation. Overall, religious life began to wane as it had in Europe during this time. Although the evangelistic campaigns of Moody had been effective for decades, even their impact began to diminish by the end of the century. "The religious excitement that followed Moody and Sankey in the mid-1870s was not equaled in the remainder of the nineteenth century."[76] Added to the demands of a bustling society, numerous religious and philosophical daggers began to fly at the heart of American churches. The rise of theological liberalism and scientific discoveries, especially Darwin's *Origin of Species*, began to take its toll on the American perspective on God, Jesus, and the Bible. The Social Gospel Movement, honorable in its attempts to combat societal ills, served as a distraction to the evangelistic imperative. If that were not enough, several religious sects had also emerged, including the Church of Christian Science founded in 1879 by Mary Baker Eddy, and the organization of Jehovah's Witnesses in 1884 under the headship of Charles Taze Russell. Despite the spiritual decline, there were some glimmers of renewal. Such vast urbanization, for instance, helped set the stage for the movement of the Spirit to impact masses of people who are concentrated in the cities. Also, the South found its former slaves thronging to the churches. Indeed, McDow and Reid report that the chief post-Reconstruction institution for blacks was the local church, and "virtually every African-American was a church member."[77]

Added to these spiritual factors was a growing groundswell of prayer in places scattered across the United States. Following the lead of Moody, another revered Christian revivalist that emerged during this time was Reuben Archer Torrey (1856–1928), the first evangelist to take the gospel message literally around the world. During the years from 1899 to 1901, Torrey led some three or four hundred people to gather in prayer each Saturday night in Chicago with the special focus of beseeching God for revival. Even after the gatherings ended in the evening, Torrey and a small group of others would often continue to commune in prayer at his home, sometimes until three in the morning. It was during one such occasion that Torrey specifically prayed that God would allow him to travel around the world and preach the gospel. Consequently, from 1902 to 1906, Torrey did just that, including holding services in Japan, China, and Australia.[78]

76. Robertson, *Chicago Revival*, 2.
77. McDow and Reid, *Firefall*, 282–83.
78. McDow and Reid, *Firefall*, 286.

The story of R. A. Torrey is just a microcosm of the spiritual wave that crashed through the United States in 1905 out of the overflow of the Welsh Revival. No part of the American lands was untouched. Philadelphian Methodists attested that 6,101 people had come to Christ that year, and pastors in Atlantic City, New Jersey, said that only fifty adults were left in the city who were unconverted. In the South, Southern Baptists reported a 25 percent increase in baptisms in one year, and First Baptist Church of Paducah, Kentucky, saw a thousand members added to its flock. Midwest Methodists reported "the greatest revivals in their history." A day of prayer was declared in Denver, resulting in churches filling to capacity by ten o'clock that morning. The Colorado State Legislature, every school, and virtually every business in the entire city was shut down, and by eleven thirty in the morning, twelve thousand people gathered in downtown theaters and halls for prayer. In the West, multi-denominational gatherings brought in 180,000 people for prayer and worship. The Los Angeles Grand Opera House found itself besieged by prostitutes and alcoholics seeking conversion to Christ, and the entire city of Portland stopped business between 11:00 a.m. and 2:30 p.m. so noonday prayer meetings could be attended.[79]

Spiritual Awakening on College Campuses

In a short amount of time, these prayer meetings-turned-revivals among the American churches found its way to college campuses. Several Christian schools were founded during this time in North America such as Toronto Bible College, Winnipeg Bible Institute, Toccoa Falls College, Nyack Missionary College, and Columbia Bible College.[80] However, this time the Spirit's movement was not limited to Christian colleges but also spread into secular and state institutions as well. A key to this movement, the World's Student Christian Federation declared February 12, 1905 as a Universal Day of Prayer, in hopes that "revival may spread until all the colleges in the country are reached." On campus after campus, the Universal Day of Prayer was implemented by both small prayer groups meeting in rooms and prayer services in congregating in larger venues. As an effect, the Universal Day of Prayer became a fulcrum of spiritual renewal that caused simultaneous outbreaks of revival to occur on campuses great distances from each other. Serving as a sampling of the revival's impact, the small prayer and Bible

79. Towns and Whaley, *Worship through the Ages*, 214.
80. Towns and Whaley, *Worship through the Ages*, 215.

study groups at Cornell University in 1907–8 doubled their numbers to 350 students, nearly 12 percent of the student body.[81] Moreover, the effects of the American Awakening continued well beyond 1905, particularly in the form of small group Bible studies on college campuses. In fact, the increasing interest in these Bible studies became so prominent that the Collegiate YMCA announced that in one particular state with eleven thousand students, 2,790 were members of Christian organizations, 1,660 were engaged in Bible study groups, and 312 in missionary studies.[82]

The Pentecostal Revival

Another key outcome of the awakening in America was the birth of Pentecostalism through what has been known as the Azusa Street Revival (1906–08). Although many of its elements can be found in earlier movements, Pentecostalism can be traced to Charles Parham (1873–1929) and William Joseph Seymour (1923). Parham was a nondenominational evangelist from 1894 to 1899, who, in 1900, founded a Bible school in Topeka, Kansas called Bethel College. During a specially called prayer group meeting on December 31, 1900, Parham and others laid hands on a woman named Agnes Ozman for her to receive the Holy Spirit to go into the mission field. According to Parham, God's Spirit fell on her like "a halo [that] seemed to surround her head and face," and Ozman began to speak in the Chinese language.[83]

After experiencing similar occurrences like that of Ozman, Parham founded another school like his Topeka campus in Houston, Texas. One of its students was William J. Seymour, the son of recently freed slaves, who instantly embraced Parham's controversial teachings. Seymour was later called to serve as pastor of a church in Los Angeles where, in his first sermon, he explained the Pentecostal experience he had encountered in Houston under Parham's tutelage. Offended by Seymour's doctrine, the church rejected their new pastor and led him out of the building at the beginning of the service that evening. Seymour was then invited to lead prayer meetings in a church member's home, and then to conduct services

---

81. Orr, *Campus Aflame*, 115–16.

82. Orr, *Campus Aflame*, 125. Orr goes on to cite several specific examples of the impact of Bible study groups on college campuses: 125–29.

83. Parham, *Life of Charles Parham*, 52–53.

at 214 North Bonnie Brae Avenue, the home of Richard and Ruby Asberry.[84] Several members from Seymour's former church came to hear him preach, a mixture of both whites and blacks. On April 9, 1906, Seymour and a small group of eight others prayed on their way to the worship meeting. That evening, "the power fell" on those who had gathered, and they began to speak in other tongues. Three days later, Seymour began worshiping God in an unknown language.[85] News spread throughout the city, and the house suddenly became too small to accommodate the crowds. Eight days later, on April 14, 1906, Seymour and his congregation moved to 312 Azusa Street, and the revival that had erupted continued for the next three consecutive years. More significantly, it was from Azusa Street that Pentecostalism would spread around the world.[86]

The Global Awakening

The reshaping of Wales and the spiritual revitalization of America were not the only works of the 1904–5 Welsh Revival. It traveled to lands across the globe, effectively shaking the world with spiritual fervor.[87] Reports of revival began pouring in from nations across Europe: Great Britain, Norway, Sweden, Denmark, Germany, and France. Historian Paul Dienstberger writes, "Scandinavia was especially moved after the 1904 earthquake took place in Norway,"[88] and Norwegian Bishop Eivind Berggrav claimed the awakening to be "the greatest revival of his experience."[89] Similarly in France, the awakening effectively unified its one million evangelicals under one banner and mission, and multitudes were saved in Germany through evangelistic tent meetings. Even parts of politically turbulent Russia saw revival with thousands coming to Christ.[90]

If that were not enough, testimonies from distant lands like Asia, Australia, New Zealand, and South America were being heard. In Asia, Bible

---

84. Alexander, *Black Fire*, 118.
85. Alexander, *Black Fire*, 118–19.
86. McDow and Reid, *Firefall*, 292.
87. It is due to the global spread of revival during this period that McDow and Reid label the revivals of the first decade in the twentieth century "The Global Awakening;" McDow and Reid, *Firefall*, 294.
88. Dienstberger, *American Republic*, chap. 8 (n.p.).
89. Towns and Porter, *Ten Greatest Revivals Ever*, 15–17.
90. Towns and Whaley, *Worship through the Ages*, 212–13.

studies turned into times of confession of sin and conversion of souls, yielding baptisms by the droves as Hindus and Buddhists came to Christ. Indians were being saved at a rate sixteen times greater than converts to Hinduism, and Burmese missionaries reported that people were converting to Christ at a rate "surpassing anything known in the history of the mission." Similarly, Latin America saw a 180 percent increase in Christian conversions over the course of seven years during that time. After an earthquake in August 1906, Valparaiso, Chile became a center for spiritual renewal; and revival spread throughout Brazil through the distribution of Bibles.[91]

The Korean Revival (1907–10)

One of the most phenomenal episodes of spiritual awakening that came as aftershocks of the Welsh Revival occurred on the Korean peninsula, especially in the city of Pyongyang. J. Edwin Orr states, "The moral transformations occurring in Korea were without precedent in the peninsular country."[92] Indeed, the powerful impact of God's Spirit and the spread of the gospel in the city led to it being called among missionaries the "Jerusalem of the East."[93]

Conditions Prior to Revival

Surprisingly, during the final two decades of the nineteenth century, the Korean land bustled with Christian missionary activity. The king of Korea officially welcomed Christians to evangelize the country in 1884, and by the turn of the century, North American Presbyterians and Methodists had started missions throughout the peninsula. Presbyterians opened a mission in Pyongyang in 1895, which soon became the headquarters for missionaries from all nationalities and denominations. Accordingly, Pyongyang and its surrounding region became the most heavily Christian area of Korea, and the hub for Presbyterian mission activity throughout Asia.[94]

---

91. Towns and Whaley, *Worship through the Ages*, 213. Towns and Whaley report that among the Karen people group in Burma there were two thousand baptisms in 1905, ten times the usual number. One church alone among the Shan people group baptized 1,340 people in one month during that same time.

92. Orr, *Campus Aflame*, 135.

93. Kim, "Forgotten American Missionaries."

94. Kim, "Forgotten American Missionaries."

By 1907, however, Pyongyang had the dishonor of being known for its debauchery, a city full of wine, women, and music. Mathew Backholer describes it as "a dark city in the early twentieth century with sin abounding. It even had its own Gisaeng (Korean geisha) training school."[95] Added to this flesh-filled way of life was the long-standing and insatiable hatred for the Japanese. During this period, the Japanese occupied Korea, claiming sovereignty over the land, and exercising severe brutality against its people. Anyone who refused to bow to the Japanese Emperor was subjected to imprisonment, torture, and even execution. Journaling his impressions, missionary William Blair summarizes the condition of these broken people:

> The simple truth is that the Koreans are a broken-hearted people. Corrupt and unworthy as their old government was, nevertheless they loved it, and all the more, no doubt, in proportion as it seems to be taken away from them. It is pitiable to see them grieve, to see strong men weep over national loss. . . . But it means much that their eyes are open.[96]

In light of the humiliation of the Koreans, Blair concludes, "By brokenness of spirit Korea has been prepared for the Gospel."[97] In response to their broken spirit, God's Spirit would soon revive the Koreans in a profound way.

The Outbreak of Revival in Pyongyang

The first revival recorded in Korea happened in 1903, known as the Wonsan Revival Movement, when Presbyterians and Methodists united their efforts to reap large spiritual harvests. During that revival, thirty thousand were converted to Christ in Pyongyang, ten thousand in 1904 alone. By the middle of 1906, however, the revival had subsided.[98] After months of persistent prayer, the spiritual stagnation was short lived, and Korea was set ablaze by a second revival in January 1907, yielding fifty thousand people converted in that same year.

In the fall of 1906, reports of the Khasi Hills Revival (1905–6) and the great Welsh Revival (1904–05) found their way onto the Korean peninsula. American missionary Howard Agnew Johnston visited Pyongyang

95. Backholer, "Pyongyang Great Revival."
96. Blair and Hunt, *Korean Pentecost*, 25.
97. Blair and Hunt, *Korean Pentecost*, 25.
98. Backholer, "Pyongyang Great Revival."

for a few services at the Central Church, where he reported to the Korean Christians about the Khasi Hills Revival in India. Over the Christmas period the Pyongyang Christians gathered in groups each evening for prayer, rather than conducting their usual festive celebrations. William Blair writes, "That winter we had no heart for social gatherings." Prayer meetings were held each evening, until the Presbyterian General Class began on January 2. It was customary among Korean Presbyterian churches to send delegates to the two-week Bible study in Pyongyang at the beginning of each year. This study was open to pastors and leaders from throughout the nation. However, "so strong was our desire to pray that we decided to hold noon prayer meetings daily during the class for those who could attend." These prayer meetings connected with the class began on January 6 in the Central Church, with over fifteen hundred men in attendance representing leaders from hundreds of churches. The congregation broke off into smaller groups with missionaries and Korean pastors leading the groups. Blair goes on to report that the gathering was not looking for some spectacular occurrence; rather, everyone was merely "seeking to show the need of the Spirit's presence and the necessity of love and righteousness." He continues, "Nothing unusual happened. We were not looking for anything unusual. Only a hushed solemn sea of unturned faces and eagerness to lead in prayer showed how the Spirit was working."[99] Believers from other assemblies throughout Korea also heard of God's stirring in the Indian and Welsh Revivals, leading many of these churches to unite in prayer for revival.

On January 12, a Saturday evening, Blair preached on 1 Corinthians 12:27, about how "if one member suffers, all the members suffer with it." Blair was seeking to demonstrate how hatred in a brother's heart injures not only the whole church but also brings pain to the church's head, Jesus Christ. After the sermon, Blair recalls that "many testified to a new realization of what sin was," and "a number with sorrow confessed lack of love for others, especially for the Japanese."[100] It seemed that the hateful hearts of the people were beginning to crack as the prayers they had offered for so long were being answered. However, the next night Blair noticed what looked to be a significant setback. "There was no life in the meeting. The church was crowded as usual, but something seemed to block everything . . . the devil had been present, apparently victorious."[101]

---

99. Blair and Hunt, *Korean Pentecost*, 68–69.
100. Blair and Hunt, *Korean Pentecost*, 69.
101. Blair and Hunt, *Korean Pentecost*, 70.

SMALL GROUPS IN THE LAYMAN'S, WELSH, AND KOREAN REVIVALS

At noon on the following day, Monday, January 14, the missionaries gathered to pray for God's blessing on the upcoming evening's service, refusing to allow Satan to dampen the gathering. In response, "each felt as he entered the church that the room was full of God's presence... impossible of description." After a brief message was shared, another missionary, Graham Lee, invited people to offer prayers. So many began praying that Lee said, "If you want to pray like that, all pray," to which the entire audience began praying out loud at the same time. Blair recalls, "The effect was indescribable—not confusion, but a vast harmony of sound and spirit, a mingling together of souls moved by an irresistible impulse of prayer. The prayer sounded to me like the falling of many waters, an ocean of prayer beating against God's throne."[102] Suddenly, a Korean man named Gil Seon-ju came forward and confessed to stealing $100. He claimed his sin was like that of the sin of Achan, and it was blocking God's blessing. Immediately following, "Man after man would rise, confess his sins, break down and weep, and then throw himself to the floor and beat the floor with his fists in perfect agony of conviction." Lee writes, "Sometimes after a confession, the whole audience would break out in audible prayer, and the effect of that audience of hundreds of men praying together in audible prayer was something indescribable.... And so the meeting went on until two o'clock a.m., with confessions and weeping and praying."[103]

During the Tuesday evening meeting, God began to deal with a well-known conflict between two believers, a Mr. Kang, Blair's assistant, and a Mr. Kim, who was an elder at the Central Church. The night prior, Kang had confessed his hatred for Kim, but Kim remained silent and refused to reconcile. Tuesday night, however, Kim got up from his seat, approached the pulpit, and made this confession: "I have been guilty of fighting against God. An elder in the church, I have been guilty of hating not only Kang You-moon, but Pang Mok-sa [the Korean name for William Blair]." Then, turning to Blair, Kim beckoned, "Can you forgive me, can you pray for me?" Blair stood up to pray, but he could only get out two words: "Apa-ge, Apa-ge ("Father, Father")." Blair describes what happened next:

> It seemed as if the roof was lifted from the building and the Spirit of God came down from heaven in a mighty avalanche of power upon us. I fell at Kim's side and wept and prayed as I had never prayed before. My last glimpse of the audience is photographed

---

102. Blair and Hunt, *Korean Pentecost*, 71.
103. Quoted in Swearingen and Swearingen, "1907–1910 Pyongyang Korea Revival."

indelibly on my brain. Some threw themselves full length upon the floor, hundreds stood with arms outstretched toward heaven. Every man forgot every other. Each was face to face with God. I can hear yet that fearful sound of hundreds of men pleading with God for life, for mercy.[104]

After a while, Graham Lee began singing a hymn, which briefly restored order to the meeting. However, Blair reports:

> Then began a meeting the like of which I had never seen before, nor wish to see again unless in God's sight it is necessary. Every sin a human being can commit was publicly confessed that night. Pale and trembling with emotion, in agony of mind and body, guilty souls, standing in the white light of that judgment, saw themselves as God saw them. Their sins rose up in all their vileness, till shame and grief and self-loathing took complete possession; pride was driven out, the face of men forgotten. Looking up to heaven, to Jesus whom they had betrayed, they smote themselves and cried out with bitter wailing, "Lord, Lord, cast us not away for ever!"[105]

The Presbyterian General Class ended that Tuesday evening, and its attendees returned to their churches, carrying with them the "Pentecostal fire."

The Impact of the Korean Revival

The revival that broke out in Pyongyang spread to their respective churches and soon the nation was engulfed with revival. Personal conviction, confession and repentance from sin, and restitution among Christians became the hallmark of this revival. As a result, tens of thousands of people came to Christ and were added to the Korean churches. Despite the increase of Japanese persecution, the Korean Christian population continued to grow exponentially: two thousand people by March 1907 and thirty thousand by July of the same year. By 1911, there were two hundred thousand Korean Christians; by 1912, the number had increased to three hundred thousand.[106] Orr reports that 90 percent of the students at Union Christian College in Pyongyang professed conversion.[107] Writing of his experiences during his visit to the peninsula in June 1907, Chinese missionary

---

104. Blair and Hunt, *Korean Pentecost*, 72–73.
105. Blair and Hunt, *Korean Pentecost*, 74.
106. Swearingen and Swearingen, "1907–1910 Pyongyang Korea Revival."
107. Orr, *Campus Aflame*, 135.

Jonathan Goforth (1859–1936) said, "Those missionaries seemed to carry us right up to the throne of God. The Korean movement was of incalculable significance in my life, because it showed me at first hand the boundless possibilities of the revival method. Korea made me feel, as it did many others, that this was God's plan for setting the world aflame."[108] Largely due to the Korean Revival of 1907–10, today the largest churches in the world are found in Seoul, Korea, and Koreans have launched more than ten thousand missionaries into other countries to spread the gospel.

Principles Gleaned from Small Groups in the Layman's, Welsh, and Korean Revivals

Although not historically considered one great awakening, the late 1800s and first decade of the 1900s experienced a cluster of significant spiritual revivals. While they were certainly not the only recorded movements of God's Spirit, the most notable awakenings during this time are the Layman's Prayer Revival of 1857–59, the Welsh Revival and Global Awakening of 1904–05, and the 1907–10 Korean Revival that began in Pyongyang. After surveying the revivals in greater detail, a key element that can be found in each is the presence of some kind of small group that helped facilitate the movement of the Spirit toward renewal. Table 3, located at the end of this chapter, offers a summary of the key observations of these revivals. Admittedly, the small group factor played a notably different and perhaps less significant role in some of these revivals than the two previous awakenings. Nevertheless, their presence is found, and from these instances a number of important lessons can be learned about how small groups may be influential in prompting and sustaining a revival movement.

1. A central and common feature of small groups in these revivals was the focus of prayer. Like those of the Second Great Awakening, these revival occurrences feature small groups with the primary—and sometimes only—purpose to pray for God's moving hand. Such motivation has become the namesake of the Layman's Prayer Revival, and it was in the midst of these prayer meetings that revival broke out. Similarly, with the obvious exception of Evan Roberts's historic post-service

---

108. Quoted in Backholer, "Pyongyang Great Revival." Goforth went on to have a powerful ministry and experienced revival in 1907–09 and again in 1915 in various cities throughout China and Manchuria.

Bible study, the Welsh Revival and subsequent Global Awakening were impacted by small groups with no other noted purpose than that of prayer. Not to be left out, the Korean revival erupted partly as a result of a small group of missionaries fervently seeking God to break the callous hearts of the people. Even though the actual occurrence of revival came through daily worship services, the hardened ground of the Welsh and Korean cultures was doubtlessly tilled through the concerted prayer of its resident Christians.

2. The spontaneous and adaptable nature of small groups is an equally important feature among these revival movements. For instance, most historians mark the beginning of the Welsh revival with Evan Roberts's preaching to a group of seventeen young people after a Monday evening prayer service. Similarly, D. L. Moody's Sunday school tactics—such as meeting in an empty boxcar and then an abandoned saloon—demonstrate how, unlike most other dynamics of Christian ministry, small groups can happen anytime, anywhere, and with anyone. Arguably, it is for this reason that Moody continued to utilize small group strategies throughout his illustrious ministry that saw thousands come to Christ. Such adaptability and spontaneity are emblematic of small groups and increasingly important in their role of sustaining revival.

3. Small groups need not be formal, highly emotional, or even with a leader to be effective. Several of the small groups observed in these revival movements were informal and without an official leader. Such as in the case of Lanphier's Union prayer meetings, at any point an individual if so moved could rise to lead in a song, confess sin, or share a message of encouragement. Other times, as in the case of Joseph Jenkins's Young People's Meeting, small groups may consist of a simple conversation among the group regarding the things of God. What is consistent among these groups, and in stark contrast to many of the emotion-charged gatherings of the Second Great Awakening, is that the prayer groups during this awakening were less animated and more somber. These prayer groups were unequivocally serious about their intense focus on the task at hand—earnest prayer for a movement from God.

4. While revivals are inherently focused on the spiritual renewal of believers in Christ, including those prompted by a small group endeavor,

they inevitably result in significant evangelistic and missional outputs. The Layman's Prayer Revival was prompted by prayer groups peppered throughout the United States seeking a fresh movement of God, yet American churches increased by 50 percent during that time, including thousands coming by way of conversion. Additionally, an incredible influx of evangelistic and missional activities erupted from these groups as well, including the Student Volunteer Movement started by the "Cambridge Seven," and Moody's evangelistic crusades. The Welsh Revival saw incredible numbers of those converted as well, including the Roberts-prophesied one hundred thousand new believers during the first year. Similarly, the Korean Revival was clearly a movement of God to rejuvenate his church, yet it yielded hundreds of thousands of new Christians and thousands being called into the gospel ministry.

5. A key to sustaining the revival fires is the continued use of small groups in some way. This becomes even more apparent when considering the Layman's, Welsh, and Korean Revivals. Although some of these renewals remained more faithful to a small group strategy than others (such as the Layman's Prayer Revival), as the revival fires raged small groups were largely replaced with very large gatherings for prayer and worship. As stated earlier, the small group factor generally played a different and more minor role in these revivals and, perhaps, the fact that they were often overtaken by larger assemblies is a key reason why. Obviously, such assemblies have an important and powerful part in spiritual renewals. In contrast to the earlier multi-decade awakenings that championed small groups throughout their respective tenure, however, none of the revivals discussed in this chapter are recorded to have lasted more than five years. This offers all the more evidence that the longevity of an awakening is directly correlated to the sustained use of a small group strategy.

Conclusion

If the fuel that fed the flames of the Layman's, Welsh, and Korean Revivals had to be summarized in one word, it would indisputably be *prayer*. Although prayer has been a prevailing theme in all of the revivals, it seems that Christians collectively and sincerely seeking God's face was even more of a phenomenon in these awakenings. While these intense prayer efforts often manifested themselves in very large gatherings, they inevitably began with a handful of people joining together as a small group to beseech God. Thus, as with the prior revivals, the small group factor continues to demonstrate its significance in the rise of awakenings. Although renewals only come from the hand of God, it seems clear that a tool of preference is the intimate fellowship of a small group of believers.

Table 3: Key Observations of the Catalytic Small Groups during the Layman's, Welsh, and Korean Revivals (1857–1910)

Precursors to the Small Groups	• Methodist Class Meetings • Sunday School • "Anxious" seats and meetings
Emergence of the Small Groups	• Jeremiah Lanphier's Union Prayer Meetings (1857) • Revival prayer groups in factories, ports, churches, and college campuses (1857–59) • D. L. Moody's freight car Sunday School and "Gospel Wagon" (1856), and evangelistic house visits and "enquiry rooms" (1871) • Joseph Jenkins's Young People's Meeting (1903–04) • Evan Roberts's initial service in Loughor, Wales (1904)
Major Proponents of the Small Groups	• Jeremiah Lanphier (New York) • James McQuilken (Ireland) • D. L. Moody (Chicago) • William Blair (Pyongyang, Korea)
Prominent Revival Leaders, Ministries, and Movements that Emerged from the Small Groups	• Student Volunteer Movement (1885) • Dwight L. Moody (1855–57) • Reuben A. Torrey (1902)
Key Features of the Small Groups	• Sunday School designed for the evangelism and Christian instruction for children • Many of the small group events were spontaneous prayer and Bible study events • Emphasis on repentance from sin, personal holiness, prayer, and worship through singing • Often informal and without a leader, but directed and focused • Primarily, and sometimes only, focused on prayer for revival

6

Small Groups in the Mid-Century Revival (1949–1979)

THE FINAL OF THE four great awakenings is generally named the Mid-Century Revival, roughly from 1949 to 1979. Like the Layman's, Welsh, and Korean Revivals discussed in chapter 5, the Mid-Century Revival is better understood as a cluster of regional or specialized awakenings that coincided with one another, rather than one unified movement. Unlike any of the other revivals in this study, however, the Mid-Century Revival has not enjoyed indisputable consensus as a major spiritual movement. To be sure, widespread agreement is found that the middle third of the twentieth century was a time of spiritual movement and effective evangelism, but its labeling as a spiritual awakening has been debated. Revivalists and historians J. Edwin Orr, Clifford Olmstead, Alvin Reid, and Fred Hoffman all confirm that spiritual renewal and fervor was a key feature of the period,[1] albeit Orr and Reid are more tempered in their view of the era, referring to it as the "Mid-Century Resurgence." Orr goes further to qualify that it "by no means reached the effectiveness of either of its predecessors in the eighteenth century or the nineteenth."[2]

On the other hand, Edward Elson claimed that "the days since World War II have been days of expanding religious activity" in America,[3] and Arthur Johnston called it the "Fourth Great Awakening."[4] Gerald I. Gingrich compared the 1950s with a dozen other revival movements,

---

1. McDow and Reid, *Firefall*, 299. See also Orr, *Good News in Bad Times*, 250–62; Olmstead, *History of Religion*, 589–91; Hoffman, *Revival Times in America*, 155–80.

2. Orr, *Good News in Bad Times*, 254.

3. Elson, "Evaluating Our Religious Revival," 55.

4. Johnston, *Battle for World Evangelism*, 126.

including the Wesleyan Revival; the Great Awakening; the Revival of 1800; Finney's Revivals; the 1857 Revival; the evangelistic campaigns of Moody, Chapman, Torrey, Gypsy Smith, and Billy Sunday; the Welsh Revival, and the Korean Revival. From his comparative survey, Gingrich noted several common characteristics between these preceding revivals and that of the 1950s: key leaders, deep prayer, a high regard for Scripture, open confession of sin, and massive numbers of conversions. Thus, Gingrich concluded that he was "in the midst of a revival of Christianity" in his day.[5] Despite the ongoing debate regarding the magnitude of the renewal, the Mid-Century Revival provided arguably the last significant installment of the movement of God's Spirit the world has seen,[6] and it serves as the fourth example of how small groups were present as a key player in its emergence. More specifically, there are three primary aspects of the awakening in which the small group factor can be found: highly effective evangelistic campaigns that arose, campus revivals, and the youth-oriented counterculture known as the Jesus People Movement.[7] How and to what degree small groups influenced the emergence of each these key features of the revival will be considered in turn.

Conditions Prior to the Awakening

The years immediately after World War II proved in many ways to be a time of incredible increase, especially among churches. The close of the devastating war gave way to a time of booming growth. Due to the return of soldiers home to their greatly-missed loved ones, there was a vast surge in the North American population during the years that followed. Known as the post-war Baby Boom, countless new families emerged for whom attachment to Sunday morning church services became as normal as moving to the suburbs. This surge led to a dramatic increase both in church membership and the construction of church buildings. From 1945 to 1949, Southern Baptists increased its rolls by nearly three hundred thousand

---

5. Gingrich, *Protestant Revival*, 9.

6. Alvin Reid states that although there have been regional and specialized awakenings during the twentieth century, there has been a glaring "absence of a great revival in our lifetime." McDow and Reid, *Firefall*, 299.

7. Certainly, there were many other dynamics that characterized the Mid-Century Revival, such as the Charismatic Revival featuring such ministries as Oral Roberts and the Vineyard. However, none of these other dynamics manifest to a significant degree the use of a small group strategy.

members; Catholics baptized approximately one million infants each year; and Methodists reported a more rapid growth during this time than any other since the mid-1920s. By 1950, Protestant seminaries were enrolling double their prewar numbers, and Catholic institutions grew at a similarly substantial rate. In 1953, religious literature outsold all other categories. One year later in 1954, Congress included the words "under God" to the American Pledge of Allegiance and installed a prayer chamber in the Capitol Building. By 1955, approximately 49 percent of all Americans went to church on an average Sunday, the all-time high in church attendance in history.[8] In Canada, the boom appeared even greater, with innumerable new Sunday schools and Bible study groups popping up and drawing tens of thousands to them. During the two decades after the war, the United Church of Canada alone built fifteen hundred churches, a figure generally matched by other denominations in the country.[9]

Ironically, McDow and Reid remind that "religious activity and revival are not synonymous."[10] Such was the case of the mid-1900s when religious prosperity did not necessarily translate into a proportionately moral society. As with other major awakenings—or any revival, for that matter—the American society after World War II was largely in spiritual decline. One fourth of marriages ended in divorce, an alarmingly high rate for the time, and an estimated six million citizens were alcoholics. Added to these statistics was unprecedented prosperity that accompanied the growing pursuit for the "American dream" which eclipsed spiritual matters. If that were not enough, theological and philosophical liberalism had become entrenched in colleges and universities, and even many seminaries.[11] Following these doctrinal deviations came political and cultural shifts away from the things of God. On June 25, 1962, in the landmark case *Engel v Vitale*, the US Supreme Court declared school-sponsored prayers unconstitutional. Ten years later, the court ruled that a woman had the right to abort her unborn child (*Roe v Wade*, 1973). Beyond these rulings, unwed cohabitation and homosexuality became much more socially acceptable than they had in prior years. The 1960s saw political conflict turn into anti-government social unrest, which often became violent. By the end of the decade, one could

---

8. McDow and Reid, *Firefall*, 301. See also Orr, *Good News in Bad Times*, 72; and Hoffman, *Revival Times in America*, 163–64.

9. Noll, *History of Christianity*, 437–38.

10. McDow and Reid, *Firefall*, 301.

11. McDow and Reid, *Firefall*, 300.

identify at least three types of anti-government demonstrations: civil rights protests, anti-Vietnam War demonstrations, and a youth-led counterculture known as the Hippie Movement. Consequently, despite the incredible increases in religious activities in the 1940s to the 1950s, most of these gains were lost from church decline.[12] In short, the middle decades of the twentieth century were in great need for a stirring of God's Spirit.

Small Groups and the Rise of Evangelistic Enterprises and Revival Abroad

The Mid-Century Revival was a reaction against the moral decline brought about in large part by liberalism and the Social Gospel Movement.[13] As powerful as these two opposing forces were to Christianity, the ensuing revival had equally powerful help at its side. As it had been in prior revivals, concerted efforts of sincere prayer among followers of Christ played a vital role. As one profound example, thirty thousand people (the largest prayer assembly ever recorded in the state) gathered at the steps of the Iowa state capitol in Des Moines to pray. Technology also had a hand in bringing about revival. As instrumental as the telegraph was to the propagation of the Layman's Prayer Revival, so the innovations of radio and television broadcasting became even more beneficial to this new awakening.[14] These two media innovations played an especially important part in bringing about revival, as they became the conduit for simultaneously spreading the gospel to multitudes, such as in the mighty evangelistic ministry of Billy Graham.

---

12. Towns and Whaley, *Worship through the Ages*, 295.

13. An important caveat should be provided here that not all aspects of the Social Gospel Movement should be considered as contributors to moral decline. Indeed, while the church was trying to reach the masses with the gospel message, many of the physical needs (for example, hunger, homelessness, sickness) of the ones it was trying to reach had been largely overlooked. That the Social Gospel Movement shed light on this blind spot is important. However, much of the Social Gospel Movement also ignored the spiritual and intellectual needs of people. It is this extreme version of the movement, one that neglected biblical doctrines and the message of salvation, that took a toll on the moral aptitude of society at the time.

14. McDow and Reid, *Firefall*, 300–301.

BIG THINGS START SMALL

The Influence of Small Groups in the Life and Ministry of Billy Graham

The legendary ministry of Billy Graham alone as an outcome of the Mid-Century Revival demonstrates the mighty work of God during this time. Gerald Gingrich considers Graham to be the premier leader of the revival,[15] and Graham himself spoke of the spiritual stirrings, saying:

> A religious revival unparalleled in modern history is sweeping like a prairie fire across the English-speaking world. It is a spiritual awakening in which millions are turning to God. . . . I have talked with hundreds of thousands of men, women, and children in America, England, continental Europe, and Asia. Everywhere I have seen living evidence of this groping for spiritual foundations.[16]

Certainly, a distinction should be made between a crusade of evangelistic campaigns and the outpouring of God's Spirit. As was stated in the first chapter of this work, a spiritual revival may ultimately result in the conversion of a multitude of unbelievers, but a revival necessitates that its primary target is the church of God, as believers in Christ recapture their passion for Christ and obedience to his Word. Nevertheless, as was in the case of Moody, spiritual renewals and evangelistic harvests can overlap. This same phenomenon was true of Graham's ministry, especially in his initial years. While numerous books and documentaries have traced the incredible ministry of Billy Graham, such is not the point in this work. Instead, attention here will be focused on key moments in Graham's early years when, through a small group of peers, Graham encountered Christ in a profound way that inevitably charted the course for his future.

William Franklin Graham Jr. (1918–2018) converted to Christ in 1934 during a crusade event in his hometown of Charlotte, North Carolina, led by evangelist Mordecai Ham. Prior to his conversion, Graham's father along with a small group of godly businessmen had been gathering to pray specifically that "out of Charlotte the Lord would raise up someone to preach the gospel to the ends of the earth."[17] It was this small group that had invited Ham to come to the city in hopes that the beginnings of their prayer would

---

15. McDow and Reid, *Firefall*, 300.

16. Graham, "Our Greatest Secret Weapon," 19, cited in Gingrich, *Protestant Revival*, 80, and in McDow and Reid, *Firefall*, 300.

17. Lockard, *Unheard Billy Graham*, 13.

be answered. In 1949, while president of Northwestern College in Minneapolis, Minnesota, Graham was invited to speak at an evangelism crusade at Los Angeles. At some point during this time, Graham invited a group of his close associates to his office in Minneapolis for a midnight prayer meeting. Those attending the prayer group included William Dunlap, J. Edwin Orr, and Jack Franck. According to F. W. Hoffman, it was this midnight prayer meeting that originally started the stirring of revival.[18]

Prior to the crusade, Graham attended an annual conference for Christian colleges at Forest Home, a Christian retreat center in the San Bernardino Mountains in Southern California. Forest Home was founded by Henrietta Mears, a dynamic and powerful Christian leader who served as the director of Sunday school in the First Presbyterian Church of Hollywood. Commenting on the impact of Mears on his life and ministry, Graham said, "She has had a remarkable influence, both directly and indirectly, on my life. In fact, I doubt if any other woman outside of my wife and mother has had such a marked influence. . . . She is certainly one of the greatest Christians I have ever known!"[19] While at this conference, organized for a small group of executives of a dozen organizations, Graham had what his biographers quote him as saying, "a transformative experience."[20] J. Edwin Orr, who also attended the conference, recalls a contemplative Graham coming to talk to him about total commitment:

> When Graham sought a more perfect commitment of life during that startling awakening at Forest Home, he began his inquiry by mentioning that he had offered his life to God during the 1943 awakening at Wheaton College. I recalled discussing evangelism and revival with him when we first met at Trinity College near Tampa in Florida and again at Lincoln College in Oxford, where the conversation concerned a possibility of "revival in our time." Graham's transforming experience took place out in the woods, a mile high, alone with God.[21]

Graham would see the results of his commitment at Forest Home a month later during the Los Angeles crusade.

At the beginning of the crusade, Mears asked Graham to lead a series of Bible studies for a small group of Hollywood celebrities in her home on

---

18. Hoffman, *Revival Times in America*, 163-64; see also Orr, *Campus Aflame*, 171.
19. Powers, *Henrietta Mears Story*, 7.
20 Orr, *Campus Aflame*, 174.
21. Orr, *Campus Aflame*, 174.

Hollywood Boulevard. Orr and some movie stars who had recently come to Christ had gathered with Mears to form the Hollywood Christian Group. Some of the celebrities involved in the group included Roy Rogers, Dale Evans, Tim Spencer, Ronald Reagan, and Stuart Hamblin.[22] Graham's Bible study messages captivated Hamblin, an influential West Coast radio personality. Convinced he could fill the venue if he endorsed Graham, Hamblin interviewed Graham on his radio program, ending with, "Go down to Billy's tent and hear the preaching. I'll be there." That evening, Hamblin's prediction came true; people thronged into the tent nightly. Hearing of the large crowds and the conversion of Hamblin,[23] powerful newspaper mogul William Randolph Hearst, prompted his employees to strongly promote Graham and the meetings.[24] As a result, the crusade went on for eight weeks—five weeks longer than planned, and Graham's "Canvas Cathedral With the Steeple of Light" drew in 350,000 people, with about 3,000 committing their lives to Christ.[25] Stories of the Los Angeles crusade ran in newspapers from Detroit to Miami and from Chicago to New York, as well as in *Time* magazine. Thus, by virtue of the efforts of his father's prayer group in Charlotte years earlier, because of his transformative experience at Forest Home, and through the Spirit's work on Stuart Hamblin during a Bible study for celebrities, Billy Graham's long and successful evangelistic ministry was launched. In a reflection of Graham's life, *USA Today* reports, "More than 214 million people in 195 cities and territories heard God's call in Graham's stentorian voice and witnessed him deliver the Gospel—pure and uncritical—in person or by satellite links. Beyond his 417 crusades were rallies and services adding up to 226 events in the USA and 195 in foreign cities."[26] Arguably no one in the history of Christianity has shared

---

22. McDow and Reid, *Firefall*, 303.

23. Towns and Whaley, *Worship through the Ages*, 270. Ironically, Hamblin strangely stormed out early each night of the meetings. Finally, after having succumbed to his struggle over sin, Hamblin gave his heart to Christ one night in Graham's hotel room at 4:30 a.m.

24. Hearst ordered his editors to "puff Graham"; that is, to publish glowing descriptions of the young evangelist whose conservative attitudes matched those of the powerful publisher. Later, when some criticized that the Los Angeles crusade was just another tent revival made successful by Hearst, Graham responded, "If God were not doing something supernatural, and if souls were not being transformed, there would be nothing to 'puff.'" See Rasmussen, "Billy Graham's Star," and Towns and Whaley, *Worship through the Ages*, 270–71.

25. Towns and Whaley, *Worship through the Ages*, 270–71.

26. Grossman, "Billy Graham Reached Millions."

the gospel with so many—yet Graham's story traces back to those pivotal moments when a small group of believers had gathered.

The Influence of Small Groups in the Birth of Campus Crusade for Christ

The Mid-Century Revival also revived Christian non-profit organizations (commonly known as parachurch ministries)[27], and gave birth to arguably the largest and most influential evangelistic parachurch ministry among college students—Campus Crusade for Christ. Like Graham, William R. Bright (1921–2003), the founder of Campus Crusade for Christ, owes much of his early Christian experience to the ministry of Henrietta Mears and the Forest Home Christian Conference Center. In 1947, while at Forest Home, Bright experienced a rush of revival during a small group conversation between himself, Mears, Louis Evans Jr., and Richard Halverson. "As we continued to talk," Bright reminisced, "suddenly the Holy Spirit enveloped us."[28] Later, Bright remarked how the other two men subsequently had incredible ministries: Halverson became the chaplain of the United States Senate and Evans became an influential Presbyterian pastor, including time as overseer of the National Presbyterian Church.[29]

The beginnings of Crusade came in 1951. While he was up late at night preparing for a Greek exam, Bright recalls the moment when "a sovereign act of God . . . gave me the vision for Campus Crusade for Christ."[30] Orr states,

> Bright had an uncanny but real sense of the presence of God and felt sure that he had received direction for the rest of his life. So strong was the impression that he was to devote his life to helping win and disciple the students of the world to Jesus Christ that he dropped out of seminary, even though he had only a few units of study to complete for graduation.[31]

---

27. For a detailed survey regarding the history of Christian parachurch ministries, see Scheitle, "From Religious Societies." Although Christian nonprofits and the parachurch movement have gained much attention over the past two decades, Scheitle argues that when the window of observation expands beyond the past few decades, non-profit ministries have been active in American Christianity since at least the mid-1800s.

28. Bright, *Coming Revival*, 83.

29. McDow and Reid, *Firefall*, 303.

30. Bright, *Coming Revival*, 83.

31. Orr, *Campus Aflame*, 188.

Bright and his family moved to Westwood in hopes to reach students at the University of California at Los Angeles (UCLA). After organizing a twenty-four-hour prayer chain for the campus, Bright began to recruit, train, and organize students into groups to visit the various fraternities, sororities, and dormitories. In a few short months, Bright reports that more than 250 students, including the student body president, the campus newspaper editor, and several athletes "had committed their lives to Christ."[32] Much of the appeal of these early Crusade efforts was found in the intimacy of its small group gatherings. Orr writes of his experience during those formative years of Crusade:

> I participated in those early meetings on the U.C.L.A. campus and nearby. As chaplain of the Hollywood Christian Group, in which famous movie stars met in one another's homes, I found the Campus Crusade for Christ gatherings in comfortable drawing rooms very similar. The students sat on sofas, chairs, floor rugs, hassocks, stairs, and the like—just as the movie stars. Fellowship was the penetrating influence.[33]

Bright had always envisioned Crusade being the very definition of a parachurch ministry—one that walks alongside of the church as a partner in Christian ministry. He and his team understood their special role was to introduce students not only to Christ but to local churches and area ministries for discipleship. However, as the ministry flourished wildly, hundreds of students were coming to Christ, effectively overwhelming the churches and localized ministries in the area. To assimilate this influx of new believers into further Christian growth, Crusade developed an array of special discipleship strategies, including small group Bible studies, ministry groups, and correspondence courses.[34] Thus, just as small groups played a part in its origin, so Campus Crusade for Christ continues to take advantage of the strategy for evangelizing and discipling generation after generation of college students.

---

32. Bright, *Come Help Change*, 30.

33. Orr, *Campus Aflame*, 189.

34. Orr, *Campus Aflame*, 189. Today Cru (formerly Campus Crusade for Christ) has a ministry presence in 190 countries, representing 99.6 percent of the world's population. See "History of Cru" at www.cru.org.

SMALL GROUPS IN THE MID-CENTURY REVIVAL (1949–1979)

The Influence of Small Groups in the Hebrides Revival

In 1949—the same year of Billy Graham's historic Los Angeles Crusade—the Mid-Century Revival was beginning to manifest itself across the Atlantic among Presbyterian churches in the Scottish Hebrides Islands. In the traumatic wake of World War II, spiritual life was at a dismal low in the Hebrides. Peggy Smith, an eighty-four-year-old blind woman and her eighty-two-year-old equally impaired sister Christine had been praying constantly for revival in their home near Barvis on the Isle of Lewis, the northwest and largest of the Scottish islands. In the midst of their praying, God began to show Peggy visions of a coming revival. Months later, as the sisters were praying one winter's morning, God imposed on them an unyielding conviction that revival was near. Peggy sent for James Murray MacKay, beseeching their pastor to call the church leaders to concerted prayer. For three months, on Tuesdays and Fridays of each week, the small group of leaders met together in a farmer's barn to pray. One late evening in their prayer gathering, a young deacon from the Free Church read Psalm 24 and challenged the group to be clean before God. "It seems to me so much humbug to be waiting and praying, when we ourselves are not rightly related to God," the deacon confessed. Then, with uplifted hands, he prayed, "O God, are my hands clean? Is my heart pure?"[35] Suddenly, as if that was what God was waiting for, the Holy Spirit swept over them, sparking what many believe to be the beginning of the Hebrides Awakening.

In the following weeks, Mackay invited evangelist Duncan Campbell to come and lead ten days of meetings at the Presbyterian parish in Barvis. At the close of the first meeting, the travel-weary preacher was asked to join an all-night prayer meeting. Thirty people gathered for prayer in a nearby cottage. Campbell describes the tremendous scene that night:

> God was beginning to move, the heavens were opening, we were there on our faces before God. Three o'clock in the morning came, and God swept in. About a dozen men and women lay prostrate on the floor, speechless. Something had happened; we knew that the forces of darkness were going to be driven back, and men were going to be delivered. We left the cottage at 3 a.m. to discover men and women seeking God. I walked along a country road, and found three men on their faces, crying to God for mercy. There was a light in every home, no one seemed to think of sleep.[36]

35. Towns and Porter, *Ten Greatest Revivals Ever*, 145.
36. Quoted in Whittaker, *Great Revivals*, 159.

When the group arrived at the church that morning, it was already crowded with people from all over the island, some coming in buses and vans. It is not discovered how they were compelled to come or who told them. Nevertheless, large numbers who had been in deep and visible anguish over their sins were converted to Christ. After hours of experiencing the extraordinary movement of God's Spirit, Campbell attempted to conclude the Spirit-charged service. Suddenly, a young man began to pray out loud, going on for forty-five minutes. Once again, the sanctuary filled with more people seeking salvation, until the service ended at 4 a.m. the next morning. Amazingly, even then the weary evangelist was unable to retire to bed. As Campbell was leaving the parish, a messenger accosted him, saying, "Mr. Campbell, people are gathered at the police station, from the other end of the parish; they are in great spiritual distress. Can anyone here come along and pray with them?" Sleepless for nearly thirty-six hours, Campbell went with the messenger and encountered droves of men and women—along the road, by the side of a cottage, and even behind a pile of compost—all crying out to God for mercy.[37]

The revival raged on for five weeks with services lasting for over twelve hours each day. Soon the awakening spread to the neighboring districts, with Campbell traveling to other churches. Thus, the waves of revival that occurred in Barvis washed over again and again.[38] However, the movement of God's Spirit was not limited to church houses. Towns and Porter speak of one occasion during the weeks of revival when a successful factory worker invited Campbell to visit his factory. Even then, God's Spirit moved mightily; for as the evangelist walked through the rows of mills, convicted workers began falling to the floor begging for salvation. Towns and Porter report, "Some factory owners shut down their machines and gathered their employees in a common area so Campbell could preach. As a result, thousands were saved in factories, businesses, and plants."[39] Geoff Waugh logs that, in God's answer to the continued prayer of his people, the Hebrides Revival continued in the area into the fifties, peaking again on the previously resistant island of North Uist in 1957. Again, night after night, meetings were crammed with people crying

---

37. Waugh, "20th Century Revival." For a videotaped account of Campbell's personal testimony of the Hebrides Awakening, see "Hebrides Revival 1949."

38. Whittaker, *Great Revivals*, 160.

39. Towns and Porter, *Ten Greatest Revivals Ever*, 147.

out to God for salvation.[40] The vision of the awakening seen by two blind sisters became a vivid reality, as the Spirit of God honored the persistent prayers of a small group of saints earnestly seeking revival.

Small Groups and the Reemergence of Revival on College Campuses

Another significant feature of the Mid-Century Revival was its powerful influence on evangelical schools around the year 1950. As theological compromise had crept into many institutions by means of liberalism, so spiritual renewal arose among the fertile ground of students and faculty as well. In several of these instances, the influence of a small group can be found.

In 1949, for instance, J. Edwin Orr was asked to present a series of lectures at Bethel College in Minneapolis. The series was gloriously interrupted by a sudden stirring of God's Spirit. The university's president, Henry C. Wingblade, later discussed the event, which he stated was "certainly one of the greatest experiences we have ever had." He explains, "I think none of us will forget that week, especially the climactic day, which was Thursday. The student body as a whole were on their faces before God in prayer, asking for His heart-searching, confessing before Him every known sin, and being willing to make any restitution that might be necessary."[41]

Scores of other colleges began to experience revival to varying degrees, some of which were as a direct result of the awakening that took place at Bethel. Asbury College in Wilmore Kentucky, having already caught a glimpse of revival in 1905, was the scene of two other renewals, both in 1950 and 1970. In early 1950, students were gathering engaged in small groups with the specific purpose of earnestly interceding for another awakening. Finally on Thursday, February 23, a normally-scheduled chapel was interrupted by the Spirit of revival that led to its participants experiencing wave after wave of brokenness and confession. Professor of philosophy at Asbury, W. W. Holland, recounted, "So mighty was the presence of the Holy Spirit in that chapel service that the students could not refrain from testimony." He continues, "Testimonies were followed by confessions, confessions by crowded altars, crowded altars gave place to glorious spiritual

---

40. Waugh, "20th Century Revival."

41. Orr, *Good News in Bad Times*, 72. See also Hoffman, *Revival Times in America*, 163–64.

victories."[42] Reverend Dee Cobb, the scheduled speaker for the chapel, cut his message short to give way to the Spirit's movement. "It was as though an electric shock moved over the whole place," he recalled, "and there was such a sense of the presence of God . . . like a gentle breeze sweeping across a broad field of wheat."[43] The chapel began at 9 a.m. that Thursday, and continued uninterrupted for 118 hours, with few leaving the chapel. Finally, after midnight on Sunday, the dean requested the female students to return to their dormitories, where small groups of students continued to meet; the male students remained in the chapel. It was not until Tuesday, March 1, that the chapel service concluded.[44] Everyday for the rest of the week, the school auditorium was filled to capacity with hundreds seeking a movement of God's Spirit in their lives. Asbury students who had experienced the extraordinary event began to share testimonies to other campuses across many parts of the nation, thus effectively spreading revival throughout much of collegiate America.

Wheaton College near Chicago also experienced revival during this time. Beginning on Sunday, February 5, 1950, Reverend Edwin S. Johnson, pastor of Mission Covenant Church in Seattle, addressed the student body in a series of meetings. After a couple of uneventful services, a day of prayer was announced for Tuesday, in which students were broken up into small groups to entreat God's Spirit.[45] During the afternoon service that day, voice after voice of both faculty members and students began to confess sins and affirm repentance. Such testimonies continued without a break, except for occasional prayer, for thirty-eight hours. The entire campus was besieged with revival. Mary Dorsett gave the following report of the revival:

> As with other revivals, the testimonies and confessions followed a Spirit-ordained order. Most were very brief, lasting only a few minutes, and although specific in the naming of sins such as cheating, pledge-breaking, pride, bitterness, resentment, etc., they avoided the sensational. . . . In addition to the main meeting, faculty and staff also counseled and prayed with students in a smaller room in Pierce Chapel.[46]

---

42. Quoted in Orr, *Campus Aflame*, 177.
43. Orr, *Campus Aflame*, 177.
44. Orr, *Good News in Bad Times*, 80.
45. Orr, *Good News in Bad Times*, 75.
46. Dorsett, "Wheaton's Past Revivals," 62.

Small Groups in the Mid-Century Revival (1949–1979)

The campus awakenings caught the attention of news reporters across the nation in early 1950, with weekly news magazines and daily newspapers carrying reports and featuring articles about the awakening. *Life* magazine offered two pages full of pictures of the spiritually awakened; *Time* magazine filled two pages on the revival; and *Newsweek* also provided ample reporting of the event.[47] Some publications unfortunately described the events at Bethel, Asbury, Wheaton, and others as a "prayer marathon." Orr protests such a description, understanding a "marathon" to be "any long contest with endurance as the primary factor," such as a dancing contest or a long-distance run. "This was simply not the case at Wheaton or Asbury or any other such college," Orr defends,

> At Bethel College, the necessity of confession was met by dividing the whole assembly in classes and by subdividing according to sex; the school was able to return to its normal schedule within the day. Such a procedure adopted at Asbury or Wheaton would have achieved the same results. But, although, the humanly unguided movements at Asbury and Wheaton were prolonged, there was utterly no thought of an endurance contest.[48]

In Orr's protest, he offers an important glimpse into how college revivals used a small group strategy. The awakening events that peppered the American campuses were not merely confined to worship services; rather, many included small pockets of participants in classrooms and dorm rooms, all of which became venues for personal repentance and spiritual renewal.

Small Groups in the Jesus People Movement (1967–1971)

The latter part of the Mid-Century Revival, particularly in the late 1960s and early 1970s, was the time of a third major wave of renewal which had small groups as a key factor. Those born in the middle of the twentieth century likely recall some elements of the Christian counterculture that emerged at the time, such as the "one way" symbol (an index finger pointing upward), youth musicals and choir tours, and Christian t-shirts and bumper stickers. "These are only a sampling," writes Alvin Reid, "of the

---

47. "College Revival Becomes Marathon," 40–41; see Orr, *Campus Aflame*, 180.

48. Orr, *Campus Aflame*, 180. Orr further quotes one of the college presidents's comments in the *Time* article as saying, "These kids are tired out. The testimonies have mostly to do with private matters. After all, the principal confessions are to Almighty God—not to a public audience."

youth awakening known as the Jesus Revolution, the Jesus Generation, or the Jesus Movement."[49] Labeling it primarily as a youth movement, Reid lists several features common in past revivals that reappeared once again: brokenness over sin, a passion for the lost, a spirit of prayer, and sacrificial obedience. The Jesus People Movement was a cultural alternative to many of the protests and anti-government demonstrations that were also going on at the time. "The war in Vietnam, the Civil Rights movement, environmental concerns, campus dissent, and other phenomena formed the milieu out of which this youth movement arose."[50]

Perhaps the most enigmatic and powerful anti-authoritarian sentiment of the time was what came to be known as the Hippie Movement. A key characteristic of the culture was the refutation of traditional values. Many caught in the fervor gave themselves over to promiscuity, illicit drug use, and "free living." Many more committed themselves to anti-materialism, anti-conformity, anti-education, anti-Christianity, and the like. In pursuit for answers for society's ills and peace from their inner turmoil, several people found themselves dabbling in skewed versions of eastern mysticism, pseudo-Christian sects, and even the occult. Historian Paul Baker describes the culture accordingly: "When it came to spiritual values, the young people were more disillusioned than ever. The motto 'In God We Trust' seemed to them not a creed but a mockery. The youth were convinced that there must be a better way to do things."[51] Emblematic of the era was the infamous 1969 Woodstock Music Festival held in White Lake, New York, with thirty-two concerts over the course of four days. Commenting on the music festival, Paul Dienstberger said the event was "almost unanimous in the use of marijuana and hallucinogenic drugs like LSD."[52] Yet, despite all of the societal conflicts and moral debauchery that characterized the late sixties, they proved to be fertile fields for the work of the Holy Spirit that transpired in the Jesus People Movement. One of the essential tools for the harvest, once again, would be a small group strategy—especially in the innovative form of coffeehouses.

---

49. McDow and Reid, *Firefall*, 307. Reid affectionately recalls the Jesus People Movement a "watershed" period for him personally, for it was in 1970—in the midst of the renewal—that Reid came to "the same Jesus so many young people were proclaiming with such passion."

50. McDow and Reid, *Firefall*, 307–08.

51. Baker, *Contemporary Christian Music*, 4.

52. Dienstberger, *American Republic*, 437.

SMALL GROUPS IN THE MID-CENTURY REVIVAL (1949–1979)

The Small Group Innovation of Coffeehouses for Evangelism and Worship

In 1965–66, tens of thousands of hippies had descended upon San Francisco's Haight-Ashbury district to openly celebrate personal expression, drug experimentation, and easy sexuality. By the spring and early summer of 1967, somewhere between seventy-five thousand and one hundred thousand young people came to Haight-Ashbury, attracted by national publicity it was drawing. Sadly, many of them became homeless, hungry, and sick. Also converted to Christ out of the drug-infested Hippie Movement in 1966, Ted Wise knew something had to be done. With the aid of several pastors in the Bay Area, Wise and his friends began sharing the gospel of Christ in Haight-Ashbury. In 1967, Wise and his wife started a coffeehouse called The Living Room, one block north of the Haight and Ashbury intersection. He made every effort to reach the disillusioned hippies, homeless, and drug addicts who walked by every day. For two years this ministry flourished, drawing between thirty and fifty thousand young people into the coffeehouse. While many came to sip soup, eat donated doughnuts, and drink coffee, many others came seeking to hear the message of these so-called "Street Christians."

Before long, coffeehouses with names like "The Belly of the Whale" and "The Upper Room" began springing up in cities and small towns across the nation.[53] They served well as small-group gathering places for young people seeking to have "church services" that were aligned with their own culture. One of the most visible of these efforts was the work of Southern Baptist preacher Arthur Blessitt, who sought to reach the runaways and drug addicts on the Sunset Strip. In 1968, he opened a storefront mission called His Place, a unique blend of a traditional skid-row mission and psychedelic coffeehouse. Through the simple offerings of Kool-Aid and peanut butter sandwiches, Blessitt's His Place ministered to a steady stream of young people with the hip message to drop "Matthew, Mark, Luke, and John" instead of LSD and to get "high on Jesus."[54] Another such example comes through the vision of Linda Miessner. In 1968, Meissner moved to Seattle from New York to begin an outreach ministry called the Teen Center. Accompanying this center, she also opened a coffeehouse called The Eleventh Hour. As the coffeehouse grew in popularity,

---

53. *The Conversation*, "'Jesus People.'"
54. Blessitt, *Life's Greatest Trip*, 26.

Meissner moved it into a larger building, renaming it the Catacombs. By 1971, the Catacombs was one of the largest coffeehouses in the nation. Out of these coffeehouses came innovations in Christian music and worship, commonly known as "Jesus Music." For instance, in Hollywood the same year that the Living Room began, the First Presbyterian Church sponsored the Salt Company coffeehouse, which has been described as "a cross between Disneyland's Main Street and Knott's Berry Farm."[55] Larry Norman, a leader in the rising "Jesus Music," was a regular performer at the coffeehouse. Alvin Reid summarizes the powerful role of small-group engagements found in these coffeehouses:

> Coffeehouses were a common phenomena, becoming evangelistic centers where refreshments were served, music was played, and youth off the street could take refuge. Most evenings featured a Bible study, group discussion, and spiritual help. The coffeehouses became fertile ground for the rise of Christian rock music. Hundreds spread across the country: The Vine coffeehouse near Los Angeles; The Fisherman's Net in Detroit; Agape in Columbus, Ohio; Powerhouse in Las Vegas; and the Apple in Fort Wayne, Indiana, where the Christian group Petra began.[56]

The Small Group Innovation of Communes for Evangelism, Ministry, and Discipleship

As misery, drug addiction, and homelessness festered, small groups in the form of communal homes (rescue missions or halfway houses) were becoming a vital part of the hippie culture. Seeing another opportunity to reach these dejected youth, Ted Wise established a Christian communal home to undergird his already thriving coffeehouse, the Living Room. This home, called the House of Acts and located in northern San Francisco, provided care and discipleship for recently converted hippies. In 1969, a former Penn State statistics professor named Jack Sparks founded the Christian World Liberation Front as a proportionate evangelical response to the radical left wing of the American culture. Launched adjacent to the radical campus of the University of California at Berkeley, Sparks began the organization with a commune in his home. Two years later, in 1971, his ministry had

---

55. Williams, *Call to the Streets*, cited in McDow and Reid, *Firefall*, 309.
56. McDow and Reid, *Firefall*, 310.

ballooned into thirty-two communes, housing six hundred so-called "Jesus People," and spread throughout the Bay Area.

Both one of the Jesus People Movement's greatest beneficiaries and contributors is the ministry of Calvary Chapel in Costa Mesa, California. The church's pastor, Chuck Smith (1927–2013), had come to the modest but growing church in 1965. Seeing tremendous opportunity to reach many for Christ, Smith led his congregation to minister to runaways and drug addicts through a live-in small group and mentoring strategy championed by evangelist David Wilkerson. In the spring of 1968, Smith was introduced to nineteen-year-old Lonnie Frisbee (1949–93), an instrumental hippie convert who had been part of the team to start the Living Room and the House of Acts. Smith was impressed with Frisbee's passion and evangelistic gifts, and he invited him to join Calvary Chapel's ministry to lead a new endeavor to house hippie converts. In May 1968, the church opened its first commune in Costa Mesa, called the House of Miracles. The home was soon overflowing, and other communes were opened in Costa Mesa, Santa Ana, Newport Beach, Riverside, and other cities. More and more, the church was able to reach hippies, druggies, and other societal outcasts. As Towns and Whaley note, these "Jesus People" embraced Jesus as Lord "but did not abandon aspects of their subculture, including informal dress, rock music, casual speech, and simple living."[57] Therefore, with Smith as the wise, fatherly pastor and Frisbee as the vivacious "hippie preacher," along with ministry and discipleship-based small groups and an increasing latitude toward upbeat pop and rock music, the church's personal atmosphere began to attract masses of young people. Before long, Calvary Chapel moved to multiple services, outgrew its sanctuary, and relocated to a large circus tent in the middle of an old farm field between Santa Ana and Costa Mesa. At the time Frisbee joined Calvary Chapel, the congregation only averaged about eighty people in attendance. A year and a half after Frisbee's arrival, attendance soared to over fifteen hundred people every Sunday, and attracted hundreds more to near-nightly small group Bible studies.[58]

Chet and Phyllis Swearingen highlight many of the outcomes of Calvary Chapel's ministry at the height of the awakening: (1) an average of two hundred people were converted to Christ weekly; (2) about five hundred baptisms occurred every month for a period of two years; (3) crowds of three thousand would often gather at these baptism services, and the occasion was

---

57. Towns and Whaley, *Worship through the Ages*, 299.
58. Eskridge, "Jesus People Movement."

used to preach the gospel, with many more coming to Christ;[59] (4) Calvary Chapel trained hundreds of church planters who launched other churches—first in California, then along the Pacific Coast, and then throughout the United States—birthing well over seventeen hundred churches in all.[60] As an important part of Calvary Chapel's church-planting strategy, the fledgling churches typically began as small group Bible studies in a family's home. From there, many of the start-ups became solid congregations that influenced their communities with the message of Christ, and some even grew into megachurches with international outreach.[61]

One of Calvary Chapel's greatest successes during the revival, and one who perpetuated the use of small groups to plant multiple churches and reach thousands with the gospel, was a free-spirited young man named Mike MacIntosh, born in 1944. Quite literally a "beach bum" in the 1960s, MacIntosh was divorced, emotionally dejected, and spiritually desperate. On his twenty-sixth birthday, while attending a music service at Calvary Chapel, he received Jesus as Lord. Under Chuck Smith's guidance, MacIntosh entered one of Calvary Chapel's communes to escape the treachery of his old life of sin and be discipled in his new life in Christ. As was characteristic of Calvary Chapel communes, the boarding house in which MacIntosh found himself, dubbed "Mansion Messiah," had a culture of uncompromising Christian values that required small group fellowship, Bible study, personal discipline, and hard work. Towns and Whaley explain, "In this spiritual boot camp, MacIntosh and his colleagues spent time in the Bible morning, noon, and night. They learned how to follow Jesus, how to get along with others, how to witness, and how to earn a living."[62] It proved to be an effective means of discipleship, for MacIntosh's marriage was eventually restored, and he was ordained in the ministry, joining the Calvary Chapel staff.

In 1974, MacIntosh was invited by friends to lead a weekly small group Bible study. At first, the group consisted of twelve people and met in a home in Point Loma, California. The group soon grew to forty-five young Christians and, in August, moved to the Ocean Beach Women's

---

59. In his book *Reproducers*, Chuck Smith stated that in the span of just two years, there were more than twenty thousand who accepted Christ and over eight thousand baptized at Pirate's Cove, which is part of the Corona del Mar State Beach. See Smith and Steven, *Reproducers*.

60. Swearingen and Swearingen, "1967–1972."

61. Towns and Whaley, *Worship through the Ages*, 301.

62. Towns and Whaley, *Worship through the Ages*, 301.

Club. There it hosted evangelistic concerts along with Bible studies. As a result, attendance grew so fast that the group had to move again—just three months later—to the House of Hospitality in Balboa Park near San Diego. In February 1975, the fledgling fellowship relocated to Linda Vista, where it offered childcare and Sunday school along with Sunday morning and evening services, as well as Monday night concerts. Their rapid growth continued, prompting a search for new facilities that resulted in the purchase and renovation of San Diego's old North Park Theater in the summer of 1976. By 1980, Horizon Christian Fellowship had planted nine churches in the surrounding communities, including Encinitas, El Cajon, Escondido, Chula Vista, Poway, Pacific Beach, Point Loma, and Alpine. To date, more than one hundred churches and parachurch ministries have grown out of the congregation worldwide.[63]

The Impact of the Jesus People Movement

In a matter of just a few years, the Jesus People Movement had captured the Pacific Coast, with its ripples of revival spreading across North America. During the years 1971–75, the Southern Baptist Convention recorded more than four hundred thousand baptisms each year, the most baptisms on record in the denomination's history.[64] By early 1971, the fires of revival had found its way into Canada. Reports out of Vancouver, British Columbia, for instance, claimed that by that year more than a dozen communes and three coffeehouses had been established, along with numerous small prayer groups that were meeting in high schools and universities.[65] Moreover, Paul Dienstberger explains that the movement was far from superficial, finding the effects of revival to be as deep as they were wide. He writes:

> When they were converted, their long hair, bell-bottoms, and barefoot appearance was overlooked because of their smiling faces, emotional joy, and bold, unabashed words of praise for Jesus. They were referred to as Jesus People, Jesus Freaks, Jesus Kids, and

---

63. Towns and Whaley, *Worship through the Ages*, 302. Information also gathered from Horizon Christian Fellowship's webpage; "HCF History."

64. McDow and Reid, *Firefall*, 313. McDow and Reid go on to note that during those same years, the percentage of youth baptisms outpaced the growth of total baptisms. "In other words," they write, "the primary numerical growth in the early 1970s was due to youth baptisms."

65. McDow and Reid, *Firefall*, 312.

> Street Christians.... While the movement originated in Southern California, spontaneous ministries sprang up in many places and in many forms. These new Christians made a fanatical effort to know the Scriptures and to quote chapter and verse... spread the gospel in the streets, coffeehouses, rescue missions, communes, [and] rock festivals.... Bible studies were the central emphasis in every segment of the new Jesus culture.[66]

When a Christian movement has the power to rescue so many from the clutches of a sin-steeped culture in so short of time, an enormous and long-lasting impact can be expected. Alvin Reid offers at least three pieces of evidence that the effect of the Jesus People Movement is still present today.[67] The first is found in the revolution in Christian music and church worship styles. What is now known as contemporary Christian music was birthed in churches that had embraced the movement. As a result, believers today are blessed with an array of radio and satellite stations that play a variety of Christian music genres, all of which are full of praise and encouragement. A second outcome of the movement that can still be seen today is the presence of megachurches throughout America and the world. While the Jesus People Movement did not give rise to modern megachurches, many of these very large congregations were born out of the womb of the revival, such as Calvary Chapel and Horizon Christian Fellowship. A third residual effect of the movement that can still be seen is the growing interest in spiritual awakening over the decades since. Looking back on the revival, Walker Knight comments on the current anticipation for revival, stating, "One thing is certain, more Southern Baptists are talking about spiritual awakening today than at any time in the past 50 years. More than 2,000 Southern Baptist churches have groups praying for spiritual awakening."[68] Reid agrees, remarking that those numbers have only increased in recent years and that a similar sentiment can be found among other denominations. What is especially interesting is the subtle but pervasive influence small groups have had or do have on each of these residual effects. It was out of the small group fellowships of the coffeehouses where contemporary Christian music was born. It is through small group strategies, whether Sunday school groups or home

---

66. Dienstberger, *American Republic*, n.p. Quoted in Towns and Whaley, *Worship through the Ages*, 298.
67. McDow and Reid, *Firefall*, 314–17.
68. Knight, "Prelude to Spiritual Awakening," 19.

cell groups, that facilitate fellowship which keep megachurches intimate and "small" no matter how large they may grow. Finally, as so often in the past, the current beckoning for revival continues to occur in small groups of people coming together to pray for another awakening. Thus, as much as the Jesus People Movement continues to impact today's society, even more so does the small group dynamic of Christian ministry which played a significant part in the movement coming about.

Principles Gleaned from Small Groups in the Mid-Century Revival

The Mid-Century Revival was not only the most recent of Christianity's four most historical awakenings but arguably the most eclectic. Through evangelistic campaigns, college students, coffeehouses, and communes, the Spirit of God moved across America and into other nations largely as a counterculture of hope to an ailing society. Consequently, the gospel of Christ offered a remedy to the world's woes in a multiplicity of ways. The results were unmistakable. Membership in Christian churches were at an all-time high, with 60 percent of Americans associating themselves with a local congregation. This growth prompted a substantial increase in the building and buying of new properties for Christian use. Financial giving was also setting records, including record sums being distributed by Americans for missionary work around the world. Such was the contagious spread of this latest awakening.[69] In a review of the effects of the Mid-Century Revival by the year 1956, the editor of InterVarsity's magazine noted, "The year ending seemed to mark, in North America at least, the zenith of Christianity's popularity during the twentieth century."[70]

Equally unmistakable is the significant influence small groups have played in the prompting and sustaining of the various aspects of the Mid-Century Revival. Table 4, located at the end of this chapter, offers a general overview of how the various small group strategies became instrumental in the success of the awakening. Like the previous three revivals, this renewal consisted of an emphasis on prayer, Bible study, and spiritual introspection. However, it also offered innovative features such as long-term discipleship and unique evangelistic efforts. An analysis of the catalytic

---

69. Marty, *New Shape of American Religion*, 14–15.
70. Editorial, *HIS Magazine*, 1–4. Quoted in Orr, *Campus Aflame*, 194.

role of small groups in the Mid-Century Revival yields several important principles for today's church.

1. Small groups can be diverse in their format, location, and leadership structure. During the few decades of the revival's breakout, small groups took on a number of different sizes, structures, and foci. Billy Graham and Bill Bright experienced personal revival through a small group of believers reflecting on their own spiritual state. The mighty Hebrides Revival began with two praying sisters, followed by a group of others beseeching God throughout the night. A similar scope could be found among the college campuses that were invaded by God's Spirit. Yet the small groups that emerged during the Jesus People Movement were predominantly a means to reach hippies and vagrants with the love of God and the gospel of Christ. Indeed, variation and versatility are some of the most powerful characteristics of a small group strategy. Unlike most other Christian ministries, small groups can be adapted to its current environment for maximum effect in reaching the lost and reviving the saved. It is a versatile tool to be used as the occasion demands and, thus, a powerful weapon in the arsenal of the evangelical.

2. Small groups are most effective when they have a personal touch. Despite their versatility, the small groups of the Mid-Century Revival were clearly and consistently a platform for genuine and wholesome relationships. This can be seen simply by observing the common venues where the groups met: in homes, in dorm rooms, and in coffeehouses. The close proximity of these settings provided an incredible atmosphere of intimacy whereby friendships were fostered. It is no wonder why these commonly become the epicenter of a spiritual awakening. However, perhaps the most vivid example of the power of a personal touch to foster discipleship and invite revival are the communes that emerged during the Jesus People Movement. A remarkable reflection of the third- and fourth-century monasteries, these commune homes offered a haven from the devilish distractions of the outside world, while providing an intimate atmosphere to grow young believers in Christ. Such long-term small group situations were necessary for these new believers, most of whom had been hardened by the corrupt culture from which they came. Although spiritually saved in an instant, many experienced a life-conversion after extended periods

of discipleship that came from these homes. In these communes, these new Christians lived together, prayed together, and learned about Christ together. Likewise, their close quarters and constant presence gave the commune's occupants the necessary venue to encourage one another and lovingly hold one another accountable. Thus, this unique and powerful small group strategy yielded an entire generation of Christian converts who know what a lost life looks like and continue to effectively engage their world for Christ.

3. Earnest prayer, serious Bible study, personal introspection, and accountability to others are consistent components of small groups that have helped prompt revival. These components are present in virtually every kind of small group found in the Mid-Century Revival. Continual prayer gatherings, full of confession of sin and genuine repentance, was the staple trait of the Hebrides Revival and the awakenings on college campuses. The coffeehouses and communes of the Jesus People Movement centered around ministry, worship, and Bible study. Even many Hollywood celebrities gathered in the home of Henrietta Mears to hear the teaching of God's Word. Having also been found in the small groups during the other awakenings, the perpetual presence of these characteristics in this renewal only gives more evidence that they are essential ingredients required for revival.

4. Small groups offer a powerful platform for singing and worship. While small groups in each awakening have contained an element of music, singing, and worship, these features were clearly more prominent during the Mid-Century Revival. Indeed, Towns and Whaley assert that music may have been the principal driver of the awakening. "Music was a tool for evangelism, and it provided an outlet for Jesus People to express deep emotions."[71] Coffeehouses were the typical setting for local musicians to lead in grassroots worship, but the dynamic quickly spread into other avenues of Christian gatherings, including corporate worship services in local churches. As a result, several new genres were born out of the awakening that have continued to thrive half a century later, such as Black Gospel Music, Traditional Gospel Music, Southern Gospel Music, and Contemporary Christian Music. Each genre has been recognized by its own unique culture, style, regional following, and even record companies. Out

---

71. Towns and Whaley, *Worship through the Ages*, 323.

of this phenomenon came notable Christian artists, such as Keith Green, Petra, Edwin Hawkins, and Bill and Gloria Gaither.[72] Thus, while today's churches and music outlets celebrate the diversity that Christian music and worship have become, these prominent features of the modern Christian culture can be traced back to many small group settings found during the Mid-Century Revival.

5. Small groups are often the incubator for the rise of powerful men and ministries of God. Perhaps one of the most overlooked yet prolific features of small groups is that these intimate times of discipleship are common places for the birth of a major Christian figure, ministry, or movement. Take Billy Graham, for instance. It was through the prayers and personal investment of a small group of Christian men (including Graham's father) whereby a revival was launched that yielded the salvation of the evangelist. It was also in an intimate group of friends that Graham reflected on God's call to evangelism; and it was through a small group of celebrities that he met Stuart Hamblin, the radio personality who promoted Graham's now-famous Los Angeles crusade which effectively launched the preacher's worldwide ministry. A similar story could be said of others, such as Bill Bright and Mike MacIntosh. Likewise, Calvary Chapel found the most effective means by which to expand its evangelistic reach was by planting new congregations through small group Bible studies. Likewise, what began as a small group Bible study has exploded into Horizon Christian Fellowship, a church with more than one hundred affiliated ministries worldwide. Small groups, then, have not only become a proven way to grow disciples but also to produce powerful men and ministries through which God's Spirit will exponentially expand the kingdom of Christ.

Conclusion

Revival is a sovereign work of Almighty God. As such, it has no parameters, programs, or policies that inhibit its emergence. God can and does use whoever and whatever he wishes to get his determinations done. This reality is no more vividly shown than through his work in the eclectic array of colleges and coffeehouses, mega-churches and recuperation homes

---

72. Towns and Whaley, *Worship through the Ages*, 328–35.

found throughout the Mid-Century Revival. Although the Almighty is free to use whatever methods he wants, it is noteworthy that one method that seems to always appear during awakenings is the small group.

Table 4: Key Observations of the Catalytic Small Groups during the Mid-Century Revival (1949–79)

Precursors to the Small Groups	• Methodist Class Meetings • Sunday School • Small Group Prayer Meetings
Emergence of the Small Groups	• Bible studies for celebrities in Los Angeles (1949) • Christian coffeehouses (late 1960s) • Calvary Chapel home Bible studies (1970) • Home Bible studies with Mike MacIntosh (1974)
Major Proponents of the Small Groups	• Henrietta Mears • Chuck Smith • Lonnie Frisbee • Arthur Blessitt • Mike MacIntosh
Prominent Revival Leaders, Ministries, and Movements that Emerged from the Small Groups	• Billy Graham (1949) • Campus Crusade for Christ (1951) • Calvary Chapel, Costa Mesa, California (1968) • Contemporary Christian Music (1970s)
Key Features of the Small Groups	• Used as an evangelistic strategy to reach the unsaved • Located for most effective purposes, including homes and the new innovation of coffeehouses • High regard for the Scriptures and intense focus on prayer • Discipleship through personal investment and accountability • Music and worship incorporated in gatherings

Epilogue
How Small Groups Can Help Ignite the Flames of Revival Again

OVER THE PAST SEVENTY-FIVE years historical research regarding the most pivotal revivals in Christianity has offered invaluable contributions to our understanding of how these world-changing spiritual awakenings began and continued." However, I have contended in this work that there has been a major deficiency within the available research on revivals regarding the role of small groups. It seems that most studies on spiritual awakenings have presented the small group dynamic as a mere sidekick of more important aspects of the revivals (for example, vibrant preaching and city-wide gospel campaigns) instead of a major player itself.

Yet the Scriptures are clear that small groups had an indispensable place in the life of the Hebrews in the Old Testament and among the first Christians in the New. Moreover, Christian history demonstrates that small groups were front and center in much of the development and spread of the faith throughout its first several centuries. Indeed, some type of small group strategy has always been present throughout the history of the Christian faith, serving as a critical tool for reaching unbelievers, discipling believers, and growing the church. Considering the significance of small groups throughout the history of the Christian faith, I have tried to make the case that a small group strategy played an equally potent part in the rise of its four greatest revivals: The First Great Awakening (1726–91); the Second Great Awakening (1780–1850); the Layman's, Welsh, and Korean Revivals (1857–1910); and the Mid-Century Revival (1949–79). In our exploration of each of these awakenings, we have discovered a well-documented history concerning the presence of small groups during these spiritual awakenings. Indeed, we have found that a small group element has consistently been a key contributor in each of these revivals, having been both present prior to or near the beginning of each awakening as well as a continuing force in the longevity of the revival. In light of the evidence, the small group strategy should no longer be overlooked as a major player in the rise of revivals.

Six Common Features of Small Groups to Emulate Today

One of the most important findings of this book is the fact that, as the role of small groups in these awakenings have been unveiled, key commonalities between the small groups have also surfaced. Admittedly, the four awakenings evaluated span across two centuries and the small groups that were found in each awakening have certain distinctions related to their place in time. Still, several key common features have been discovered among them, features that, if emulated in our time, may serve well to prepare God's church for another significant revival.

At the end of each chapter that analyzed one of the four awakenings, a list of principles gleaned from the study have been provided. These principles encapsulate many of the key features found in each awakening. When analyzed together, at least six significant features are found in common among the small groups across all four awakenings. Sadly, while small groups continue to be prominent in many modern churches, these key features among the groups during the major awakenings are all too often foreign to those today.[1] Thus, if small groups in today's churches are to contribute to a fresh spiritual awakening, the following characteristics held in common among the catalytic groups of Christianity's former awakenings should become conspicuous priorities once again.

1. *Bible study was a centerpiece of small groups across all awakenings.* While not every small group employed during these revivals had a specific agenda for studying the Scriptures, there were groups in every awakening that were intensely engaged in Bible study, and all groups seemed to have a very high regard for the Scriptures in general. During the First Great Awakening, evidence of Bible study given priority can be found in the Oxford "Holy Club," Frelinghuysen's small groups in

---

1. Citing a number of proofs for her conclusions, Joanne Jung doubts whether small groups in modern evangelical churches are actually producing the type of spiritual transformation that is needed for an awakening today. See Jung, *Godly Conversation*, 158–64.

the Raritan Valley, and Edwards's conferences in Northampton. Obviously, during the Second Great Awakening and the Layman's Prayer Revival (including D. L. Moody's ministry) Sunday schools held the predominant focus of studying Scripture. Moreover, the Welsh Revival actually began out of a Bible study with seventeen young people. Finally, during the Mid-Century Revival, small groups focused on Bible study could be found among Hollywood's celebrities as well as the coffeehouses and communes peppered across America.

In contrast, biblical illiteracy is one of the great epidemics plaguing Christians today. David Gibson states that in a society where the Bible continues to be a best seller, it remains essentially unread.[2] As it was in the eighteenth century, there is no greater weapon in the modern church's arsenal to efficiently educate God's people in God's Word. Sadly, Robert Wuthnow finds that, in a typical two-hour small group Bible study, only fifteen minutes are devoted to the study of the Scriptures.[3]

2. *On an equal or higher plane as Bible study, the small groups of the major awakenings were venues of intense, earnest, and focused prayer.* Such intense prayer is clearly seen among college students in each of the awakenings gathering together to beg God for revival. Likewise, prayer groups can be found in churches around the world during these revivals. Indeed, evidence of prayer as a priority is most clearly found during the Layman's Prayer and Korean Revivals, both of which possess small groups that stressed prayer almost exclusively as their purpose for gathering. In every instance, these gatherers recognized that such a spiritual stirring comes only by the hand of a willing God, as he rewards his children who have sought him in deep humility, true repentance, and spiritual hunger. Thus, with a demeanor of desperation, each awakening testifies of Christians—college students and businessmen, teenagers and widows, missionaries and philanthropists—coming together in a time of intimacy and intensity to beg God for revival.

These moments of prayer, unfortunately, do not typically define today's small groups. Indeed, while Wuthnow confesses that only fifteen minutes are spent in Bible study, he goes on to lament that even

---

2. Gibson, "America's Favorite Unopened Text."
3. Wuthnow, *Sharing the Journey*, 243.

less time is spent in prayer. Moreover, what prayer that does happen among these modern gatherings is generally relegated to a list of felt needs and personal problems their members want God to fix. To be sure, the Scriptures teach that God loves his children and wants them to come to him in time of need. However, Scripture is also clear that he wants his children to gaze upon him and only glance at their requests. In other words, true prayer comes not out of a felt need but out of a yearning desire to commune with a holy God. If small groups are to ignite a spiritual awakening, they must invoke spiritual transformation among believers; and if small groups are going to bring about this transformation, they must place a serious study of Scriptures and a time of intense prayer at the center of their gatherings.

3. *Small groups during the four great awakenings are also characterized by a bold but loving stress on discipleship and personal holiness.* This focus often manifested itself in a time of introspection, confession of sin, peer accountability, and personal admonishment. Indeed, this was a staple in Wesley's class meetings, having a set place in the typical gathering's itinerary. Moreover, many of the prayer groups on college campuses included a time of introspection and accountability. In fact, it was often the case that open confession of sin was the trigger that launched renewal, such as in the revivals in Edwards's Northampton church, Pyongyang, Korea, and several of the campus renewals, to name a few. Additionally, the "anxious seats" of the camp meetings, the "enquiry rooms" of Moody's campaigns, and the altar calls of Graham and Torrey incorporated a personal consultation within a small group for the purpose of making spiritual decisions. Indeed, many of the small groups found in each of these awakenings demonstrate that while one's relationship with God was intensely personal, it was never private; for it often included the peering in of others for the purpose of deeper discipleship.

While attempting to attract members, however, the typical small group today accommodates the felt needs of its members rather than their spiritual needs—a focus that has backfired. In a 2010 study, Barna Research Group reported that "few adults believe that their faith is meant to be the focal point of their life or to be integrated into every aspect of their existence."[4] The reason for this,

---

4. "Six Megathemes Emerge from Barna Group Research in 2010."

EPILOGUE: HOW SMALL GROUPS CAN HELP IGNITE REVIVAL AGAIN

Joanne Jung asserts, is because small group leaders and participants have become too polite, being hesitant to delve into each other's lives. Small group meetings have become more of a support group than one where a Spirit-led life is encouraged and challenged.[5] While most today would recoil at the practice of examination as prying and judgmental, the revivalists considered it loving and necessary—and the most effective way to refine a life toward godliness.

4. *Another of the most prolific features of the small groups found among the four major spiritual awakenings was the engagement and worship of its members through music.* Indeed, the act of worship through music was both present in and influenced by the small groups of these awakenings. According to Elmer Towns and Vernon Whaley, the First Great Awakening "gave rise to a campaign by clergy in England and America to educate congregations in the art of singing."[6] Often this education came in the context of small groups, as Christian hymns by John and Charles Wesley, Isaac Watts, and others were composed and used regularly for the purpose of both worship and instruction in Christian doctrine. Much of the same was true during the Second Great Awakening as well, as learning and singing were used synergistically in small groups, such as Sunday school. Worship and song were incorporated in many of the small groups of the Layman's Prayer Revival as well, where during its prayer union meetings a participant may spontaneously rise and lead the group in singing. And Moody's Sunday school bunch created a weekly ruckus as they cheered, shouted, and sang together. Finally, one of the most impactful aspects of the small groups during the Jesus People Movement was the rise of a new genre of music that came out of the informal worship of its coffeehouses. In short, worship, music, and singing were an integral part of the small groups that helped stimulate revival, for it afforded a safe and intimate place where believers could express their love, awe, and admiration to God.

Unfortunately, small groups today largely neglect the aspect of worship in their meetings. As a result, contemporary Christians often have a severely insufficient understanding of the nature and character of God. God has become small and impersonal. Instead of the omnipotent

---

5. Jung, *Godly Conversation*, 114.
6. Towns and Whaley, *Worship through the Ages*, 125.

Creator who is intimately yet sovereignly involved in the world, God fits into a man-made mental box, becoming a god who serves the believer rather than the God who is worthy of worship and praise.

5. *A fifth feature of small groups during these major waves of revival is that the effects of these gatherings were not confined to the gatherings themselves.* Instead, the spiritual stirrings that occurred in these groups poured out into the neighboring communities, churches, and organizations. While revival *per se* is not defined as an evangelistic occurrence, notoriously spiritual awakenings result in evangelistic and missional outputs. The reason is simple: those who experienced revival could not help but to share it with others. In other words, as D. L. Moody is credited with saying, "Get on fire for Jesus and the world will come to watch you burn." It was largely the testimony of Jonathan Edwards's *A Humble Attempt* near the beginning of revival that caused Whitefield and the Wesleys to sail to America to fan the flames of the First Awakening. It was greatly due to the college prayer groups, camp meetings, and Sunday schools that the Second Awakening yielded a wave of Christian organizations purposed for missions, evangelism, benevolence, and social reform. It was out of the small groups that the likes of D. L. Moody, R. A. Torrey, and Evan Roberts emerged during the third major awakening. It was the diaspora of Korean Christians who took their experience of renewal in Pyongyang to their respective communities, thereby infecting the peninsula with revival. Finally, it was out of small group Bible studies and Christian encouragement that Campus Crusade for Christ, the Billy Graham Crusades, and several other missional and evangelistic ministries were launched. Thus, the small groups that helped start each of these awakenings did so in part because their members applied their spiritual experience to their lives in personal and practical ways, thereby making the spirit of revival a glorious contagion in places well beyond their reach.

Unfortunately, in many small groups today where there may be serious Bible study, there is still typically a serious lack of personal and tangible application of the biblical truths discovered. This disparity becomes evident in a disconnect between studying the Scriptures and Christian living, especially in the realms of caring for others and sharing the gospel. Bible knowledge must permeate into one's personal nature which will translate into a change in his or her life. Gallup presents this challenge: "We need to work toward closing the gap between belief and practice—we need to turn professed faith into lived-out faith. What is called for is not new communities, new strategies, or position papers; we need nothing less than changed hearts."[7] The small groups of these revivals can help here as well.

6. *A final key feature among the small groups of the four major revivals is their latitude toward logistics.* These small groups took a seemingly unending variety of shapes and sizes, while remaining faithful to their core purposes. Indeed, small groups were often designed in such ways as to better fulfill their revival-driven objectives. Some groups, such as the Methodist class meetings, were organized according to age, gender, spiritual maturity, or station of life. Others were a collection of "whosever wills," all of whom shared the common cause of seeking spiritual transformation, such as the "anxious meetings" and "enquiry rooms." Some small groups, like Robert Raikes's Sunday school, were structured with a clear and organized agenda, while others maintained a culture of informality, spontaneity, and freedom, such as Jeremiah Lanphier's prayer union meetings and the coffeehouses of the Jesus People Movement. Moreover, the locations where these groups met were equally as diverse, including dorm rooms, private homes, business offices, mineshafts, barns, and even freight cars and saloons. Part of the effectiveness of these small groups lay not in their proper placement and structure, but in their freedom, agility, and adaptability, as they empowered people to meet when and where they could for as long as they could in pursuit of personal transformation and spiritual awakening.

On the other hand, sometimes small groups fail today because they are forced to fit into a preconceived mold. Congregants who cannot—or will not—be formed into that mold usually do not participate in a small group, which often leaves them to themselves to find another way to grow in Christ—or not grow at all. However, in order to reach as many as possible for spiritual transformation, small groups must be flexible enough to "become all things to all men" (1 Cor 9:22), not by compromising its purpose or core principles, but by changing its look into whatever way is needed.

To accompany the findings of this study provided above, Table 5 offers a summary of the key observations made regarding all four of the major

7. Gallup and Lindsay, *Gallup Guide*, 14.

spiritual awakenings evaluated in this study. Based on the findings of this project, small groups were not only found before the rise of each of these major awakenings; they also helped set the stage for each revival, and they were equally influential in determining how long each awakening lasted. Moreover, the small groups that were found in each of these awakenings held in common at least six key features which may have served as stimulants for their respective revival. While each of the small groups contained additional characteristics unique to their own time and culture, these six features are commonalities among the groups across all four of the awakenings. Likewise, not all of the unique traits from these small groups of old can be feasibly practiced today. However, these six features are held in common among revivals that have spanned two centuries and found in a plurality of societies. Therefore, they have proven to transcend such chronological and cultural boundaries, thereby proving their relevance and applicability for small groups today.

Conclusion

Christianity is a relational faith. Its primary attraction is a saving relationship with almighty God. Secondary to this, but still quite fundamental, are the relationships a believer has among a community of other believers, the body of Christ. It is largely for this reason that small groups can be found throughout the Old and New Testament Scriptures, as well as Christian history. It is also for this reason that in many parts of the world today congregations continue to engage some type of small group model to facilitate and nurture spiritual transformation and Christian community. It has long been proven to be effective for discipleship and, in the case of this study, for helping to invoke a culture-shifting spiritual awakening. Yet, as many contemporary believers have commonly complained, "My generation has never seen a mighty outpouring of the Spirit."[8] Many reasons may be given as to why such a spiritual drought prevails, but what is more important is to discover the factors that may prompt another much-needed stirring to return. Small groups are one of these factors, so long as their members genuinely worship the Lord, lift high the Scriptures, are earnest in prayer, and are intentional in their walk with God. As today's Christians sincerely seek, pray, and prepare for another awakening, they will discover that spiritual revival big enough to reach the masses begins with spiritual renewal in small groups.

8. McDow and Reid, *Firefall*, 299.

Table 5: A Summary of the Key Observations of the Catalytic Small Groups During Christianity's Four Major Awakenings

British Revivals and 1st Great Awakening (1726–91)	2nd Great Awakening (1780–1850)	Layman's Prayer and Welsh Revivals (1857–1910)	Mid-Century Revival (1949–79)
Precursors to the Small Groups			
Puritan Conference Pietist Conventicles Moravian Bands	Methodist Class Meetings	Methodist Class Meetings Sunday School "Anxious" seats and meetings	Methodist Class Meetings Sunday School Small Group Prayer Meetings
Emergence of the Small Groups			
Bible Studies in Raritan Valley, NJ (1726) "Holy Club" at Oxford (1729) Conferences in Northampton, MA (1734) Methodist Class Meetings (1742)	Hampden-Sydney (1787) and Williams Colleges Prayer Groups (1806) Cane Ridge Revival (1801) Peter Cartwright's camp meeting and circuit formation (1803) Charles Finney's "New Measures" (1824–32) Robert Raikes's Sunday School in Gloucester, England (1780)	Jeremiah Lanphier's Union Prayer Meetings (1857) Revival prayer groups in factories, ports, churches, and college campuses (1857–59) D. L. Moody's freight car Sunday School and "Gospel Wagon" (1856), and evangelistic house visits and "enquiry rooms" (1871) Joseph Jenkins's Young People's Meeting (1903–04) Evan Roberts's initial service in Loughor, Wales (1904)	Bible studies for celebrities in Los Angeles (1949) Christian coffeehouses (late 1960s) Calvary Chapel home Bible studies (c. 1970) Home Bible studies with Mike MacIntosh (1974)

Table 5: A Summary of the Key Observations of the Catalytic Small Groups during Christianity's Four Major Awakenings (continued)

Major Proponents of the Small Groups			
Philip Jakob Spener (Frankfort, Germany)	John Erskine (Edinburgh, Scotland)	Jeremiah Lanphier (New York)	Henrietta Mears (Forest Home)
Ludwig Von Zinzendorf (Herrnhut, Germany)	William Bramwell, Ann Cutter (Yorkshire, England)	James McQuilken (Ireland)	Chuck Smith
Theodore Frelinghuysen (New Jersey)	Robert Raikes (Gloucester, England)	D. L. Moody (Chicago)	Lonnie Frisbee
John Wesley (England)	Charles Finney (Oneida County, New York)	William Blair (Pyongyang, Korea)	Arthur Blessitt
Jonathan Edwards (Northampton, Massachusetts)	Stephen Paxson (Midwest Circuit Rider)		Mike MacIntosh
	Francis Scott Key (Mission Valley Enterprise)		
Prominent Revival Leaders and Organizations that Emerged from the Small Groups			
George Whitefield (1737)	American Board of Commissions for Foreign Missions (1810)	Student Volunteer Movement (1885)	Billy Graham (1949)
John Wesley (1738)	American Bible Society (1816)	Dwight L. Moody (1855–57)	Campus Crusade for Christ (1951)
Jonathan Edwards (1734)		Reuben A. Torrey (1902)	Calvary Chapel, Costa Mesa, California (1968)
Methodist Movement (1742)			Contemporary Christian Music (1970s)

Key Features of the Small Groups			
Open group, often mixed in terms of gender, age, social standing, and spiritual condition Relational, casual but structured Spiritual outputs of evangelism and missions Emphasis on unity, discipleship, and holiness Worship through hymns, extensive prayer, Bible study, personal inspection, and peer accountability and exhortation	Christian instruction Concerted prayer efforts Sunday school initially provided basic education to children, but included Christian instruction and later expanded to adults Used as a means for counseling those under conviction of sin and in need of conversion Used music as a form of instruction and worship	Sunday School designed for the evangelism and Christian instruction for children Many of the small group events were spontaneous prayer and/or Bible study events Emphasis on repentance from sin, personal holiness, prayer, and worship through singing Often, informal and without a leader, but directed and focused Primarily, and sometimes only, focused on prayer for revival	Used as an evangelistic strategy to reach the unsaved Located for most effective purposes, including homes and the new innovation of coffeehouses High regard for the Scriptures and intense focus on prayer Discipleship through personal investment and accountability Music and worship incorporated in gatherings

Bibliography

Alexander, Estrelda Y. *Black Fire: One Hundred Years of African American Pentecostalism*. Downers Grove: IVP Academic, 2011.
The Apostolic Fathers. Translated by John Lightfoot. Chicago: Moody Bible Institute, 2009.
Atkinson, Harley T., and Joel Comiskey. "Lessons from the Early House Church for Today's Cell Groups." *Christian Education Journal* 11.1 (2014) 75–87.
Atwood, Craig D. *The Theology of the Czech Brethren from Hus to Comenius*. University Park, PA: Penn State University Press, 2009.
Augustine. *Confessions*. Translated by Maria Boulding. Hyde Park, NY: New City, 2002.
Autrey, C. E. *Renewals before Pentecost*. Nashville: Broadman, 1968.
Bacher, Wilhelm, and Lewis N. Dembitz. "Synagogue." JewishEncyclopedia.com. http://jewishencyclopedia.com/articles/14160-synagogue.
Backholer, Mathew. "Pyongyang Great Revival (1907-1910) - Korea." https://www.byfaith.co.uk/paulbyfaithtvmathewthoughts18.htm.
Baird, Robert. *Religion in the United States of America*. Glasgow/Edinburgh: Blackie and Son, 1844.
Baker, Derek, ed. *Renaissance and Renewal in Christian History: Papers Read at the Fifteenth Summer Meeting and the Sixteenth Winter Meeting of the Ecclesiastical History Society*. Oxford: Basil Blackwell, 1977.
Baker, Paul. *Contemporary Christian Music: Where It Came From, What It Is, Where It's Going*. Westchester, IL: Crossway, 1985.
Banks, Robert, and Julia Banks. *The Church Comes Home: A New Base for Community and Mission*. Sutherland, New South Wales: Albatross, 1986.
Barclay, William. *The Lord's Supper*. Louisville, KY: Westminster John Knox, 2001.
Beard, Richard. *Brief Biographical Sketches of Some of the Early Ministers of the Cumberland Presbyterian Church*. Nashville: Southern Methodist, 1867.
Beardsley, Frank G. *A History of American Revivals*. 3rd ed. New York: American Tract Society, 1904.
———. *Religious Progress through Religious Revivals*. New York: American Tract Society, 1943.
Bebbington, David W. *The Dominance of Evangelicalism: The Age of Spurgeon and Moody*. Vol. 3. A History of Evangelicalism: People, Movements and Ideas in the English-Speaking World, Ed. David W. Bebbington and Mark Noll. Downers Grove: IVP Academic, 2005.
Beecher, Lyman. *Autobiography, Correspondence, Etc*. New York: Harper, 1865.

Blackaby, Henry T., Richard Blackaby, and Claude King. *Fresh Encounter: God's Pattern for Spiritual Awakening*. Nashville: Broadman & Holman, 2009.

Blair, William N., and Bruce F. Hunt. *The Korean Pentecost and the Sufferings Which Followed*. Edinburgh: Banner of Truth, 1977. https://archive.org/details/koreanpentecostsooblai.

Blessitt, Arthur. *Life's Greatest Trip*. Waco, TX: Word, 1970.

Boyd, William L. *The History of Western Education*. 8th ed. London: Adam & Charles Black, 1966.

Bright, Bill. *Come Help Change the World*. Old Tappan, NJ: Revell Company, 1970.

———. *The Coming Revival: America's Call to Fast, Pray, and Seek God's Face*. Orlando, FL: Here's Life, 1995.

Bunting, Jabez. *A Great Work Described and Recommended, in a Sermon, Preached on Wednesday, May 15, 1805, at the Rev. Mr. Thorp's Meeting-House, in New Court, Carey-Street, London, before the Members of the Sunday School Union*. London: Richard Edwards, 1805.

Bunton, Peter. "300 Years of Small Groups—The European Church from Luther to Wesley." *Christian Education Journal*, 3, 11, no. 1 (Spring 2014): 88–106.

Burns, J. Patout, and Robin M. Jensen. *Christianity in Roman Africa*. Grand Rapids, MI/Cambridge: Eerdmans, 2014.

Butalia, Tarunjit Singh, and Dianne P. Small. *Religion in Ohio: Profiles of Faith Communities*. Athens, OH: Ohio University Press, 2004.

Cairns, Earle E. *Christianity Through the Centuries*. Grand Rapids: Zondervan, 1954.

Candler, Warren A. *Great Revivals and the Great Republic*. Nashville: M. E. Church, 1904.

Carden, Allen. *Puritan Christianity in America: Religion and Life in Seventeenth-Century Massachusetts*. Grand Rapids, MI: Baker, 1990.

Carrick, J. C. *Wycliffe and the Lollards*. Edinburgh: T & T Clark, 1908.

Cartwright, Peter. *Autobiography of Peter Cartwright: The Backwoods Preacher*. Edited by William P. Strickland. New York: Nelson & Philips, 1856.

Cauchi, Tony. "The Second Worldwide Awakening of 1792." The Revival Library. Accessed February 5, 2020. http://www.revival-library.org/index.php/catalogues-menu/1792.

Chambers, Talbot W. *The Noon Prayer Meeting of the North Dutch Church, Fulton Street, New York: Its Origin, Character and Progress, with Some of Its Results*. New York: Board of Publication of the Reformed Protestant Dutch Church, 1858.

"College Revival Becomes Marathon." *Life*, February 22, 1950.

Comba, Emilio. *History of the Waldenses of Italy*. London: Truslove and Shirley, 1889.

Comiskey, Joel. *2000 Years of Small Groups: A History of Cell Ministry in the Church*. Moreno Valley, CA: CCS, 2015.

Couvares, Francis. *Interpretations of American History*. Vol. 1: Patterns and Perspectives. New York, NY: Simon and Schuster, 2000.

Dale, A. W. W. *The Life of R. W. Dale of Birmingham*. London: Hodder and Stoughton, 1898.

Davis, George T. B., and R. B. Jones. *When the Fire Fell*. Salem, OH: Schmul, 1983.

Dienstberger, Paul R. *The American Republic: A Nation of Christians*. Ashland, OH: Paul R. Dienstberger, 2000.

Dorchester, Daniel. *Christianity in the United States*. New York: Hunt and Eaton, 1895.

Dorsett, Mary. "Wheaton's Past Revivals." In *Accounts of a Campus Revival: Wheaton College*, edited by Timothy K. Beougher and Mary Dorsett. Wheaton, IL: Harold Shaw, 1995.

BIBLIOGRAPHY

Dowley, Tim, ed. *Eerdman's Handbook to the History of Christianity*. Grand Rapids: Eerdmans, 1977.

Duffy, Eamon. "Primitive Christianity Revived: Religious Renewal in Augustan England." In *Renaissance and Renewal in Christian History*, edited by Derek Baker, 287–300. Oxford: Blackwell, 1977.

"Dura Europos and the Early Christian 'House Church.'" The Saylor Foundation. Accessed July 13, 2018. https://www.saylor.org/site/wp-content/uploads/2011/03/ARTH401-1.1.3-Dura-Europos-FINAL.pdf.

Durnbaugh, Donald F. "Intentional Community in Historical Perspective." In *The House Church Evolving: Studies in Ministry and Parish Life*, edited by Arthur L. Foster. Chicago: Exploration, 1976.

Dyson, Hague. *The Life and Work of John Wyclif*. London: The Church Book Room, 1935.

Earle, Absalom B. *Bringing in Sheaves*. Boston: J. H. Earle, 1884.

Elson, Edward L. R. "Evaluating Our Religious Revival." *The Journal of Religious Thought* 14 (Autumn-Winter -1957 1956).

Eskridge, Larry. "Jesus People Movement." *World Religions and Spirituality* (blog), October 15, 2016. https://wrldrels.org/2016/10/24/jesus-people-movement/.

Estep, William R. *Renaissance and Reformation*. Grand Rapids: Eerdmans, 1995.

Etheridge, J. W. *The Life of Adam Clarke*. 2nd ed. London: John Mason, 1858. Google.

Fea, John. *The Bible Cause: A History of the American Bible Society*. Oxford: Oxford University Press, 2016.

Filson, Floyd V. "The Significance of the Early House Churches." *Journal of Biblical Literature* 58, no. 2 (1939): 105–6.

Finney, Charles G. *The Autobiography of Charles G. Finney*. Edited by Helen Wessel. Minneapolis: Bethany House, 1983.

Finney, Charles G., and William G. McLoughlin. "What a Revival Is (1834)." In *The American Evangelicals, 1800-1900: An Anthology*. Gloucester, MA: Harper & Row, 1968.

Fish, Roy J. "The Awakening of 1858 and Its Effect of Baptists in the United States." ThD diss., Southwestern Baptist Theological Seminary, 1963.

Gallup, George, and D. Michael Lindsay. *The Gallup Guide: Reality Check for 21st Century Churches*. Loveland, CO: Gallup Organization Group, 2002.

Gauvreau, Michael. "Protestantism Transformed: Personal Piety and the Evangelical Social Vision." In *The Canadian Experience, 1760-1990*, edited by George A. Rawlyk. Montreal: McGill-Queen's University Press, 1990.

Gehring, Roger W. *House Church and Mission: The Importance of Household Structures in Early Christianity*. Peabody, MA: Hendrickson, 2004.

Gibson, David. "America's Favorite Unopened Text." *Beliefnet*, December 2000. http://www.beliefnet.com/Faiths/Christianity/2000/12/Americas-Favorite-Unopened-Text.aspx.

Gingrich, Gerald I. *Protestant Revival Yesterday and Today*. New York: Exposition Press, 1959.

Godbold, Albea. *The Church College of the Old South*. Durham, NC: Duke University Press, 1944.

Gonzalez, Justo L. *The Story of Christianity*. Vol. I: The Early Church to the Dawn of the Reformation. New York: Harper Collins, 1984.

———. *The Story of Christianity*. Vol. II: The Reformation to the Present Day. New York: Harper Collins, 1984.

Graham, Billy. "Our Greatest Secret Weapon." *The American Magazine* 158 (November 1954).

Green, Michael. *Evangelism in the Early Church*. Grand Rapids: Eerdmans, 1970.

Gregory, Alfred. *Robert Raikes, Journalist and Philanthropist: A History of Sunday Schools*. London: Hodder and Stoughton, 1880.

Grossman, Cathy Lynn. "Billy Graham Reached Millions through His Crusades. Here's How He Did It." *USA Today*, February 22, 2018, sec. Nation. https://www.usatoday.com/story/news/nation/2018/02/21/billy-graham-crusades-how-evangelists-reached-millions/858165001/.

Guild, Reuben. "Early Religious History of Brown University," n.d.

Hall, Christopher A. *Learning Theology with the Church Fathers*. Downers Grove, IL: IVP Academic, 2002.

Hall, Louis Brewer. *The Perilous Vision of John Wyclif*. Chicago: Nelson-Hall, 1983.

Halliday, Samuel B., and Daniel S. Gregory. *The Church in America and Its Baptisms of Fire*. New York: Funk & Wagnalls, 1896.

Hambrick-Stowe, Charles E. *The Practice of Piety: Puritan Devotional Disciplines in Seventeenth-Century New England*. Chapel Hill, NC: University of North Carolina Press, 1982.

Hamilton, Kenneth G., and J. Taylor Hamilton. *History of the Moravian Church*. Bethlehem, PA: Moravian Church in America, 1967.

Harmless, William. *Augustine and the Catechumenate*. Collegeville, MN: Liturgical Press, 2014.

———. *Desert Christians: An Introduction to the Literature of Early Monasticism*. Oxford: Oxford University Press, 2004.

Harris, Josiah H. *Robert Raikes: The Man and His Work*. Bristol: J.W. Arrowsmith, 1899.

Henderson, D. Michael. *John Wesley's Class Meeting*. Nappanee, IN: Evangel, 1997.

Herrin, Judith. *The Formation of Christendom*. Princeton, NJ: Princeton University Press, 1987.

History.com Editors. "Industrial Revolution." History, October 29, 2009. https://www.history.com/topics/industrial-revolution/industrial-revolution.

History of Cru. Cru.org. Accessed March 7, 2020. https://www.cru.org/us/en/about/what-we-do/milestones.6.html.

Hoffman, Fred. *Revival Times in America*. Boston: W. A. Wilde, 1956.

Hunter, George G. *Church for the Unchurched*. Nashville: Abingdon, 1996.

Hurston, Karen. "Home Groups: Channels for Growth." *Ministries Today*, June 1987.

Jenson, Robert W. *America's Theologian: A Recommendation of Jonathan Edwards*. New York, NY: Oxford University Press, 1988.

"'Jesus People'—A Movement Born from the 'Summer of Love.'" *The Conversation*. https://theconversation.com/jesus-people-a-movement-born-from-the-summer-of-love-82421.

Johnston, Arthur. *The Battle for World Evangelism*. Wheaton, IL: Tyndale House, 1978.

Joncas, Jan M. "Clergy, North African." In *Augustine Through the Ages: An Encyclopedia*, edited by Allan D. Fitzgerald, 213–17. Grand Rapids: Eerdmans, 1999.

Jones, Jeffrey M. "U.S. Church Membership Falls Below Majority for First Time." *Gallup*, March 29, 2021. https://news.gallup.com/poll/341963/church-membership-falls-below-majority-first-time.aspx.

Jones, Maldwyn A. *The Limits of Liberty: American History, 1607-1992*. Oxford: Oxford University Press, 1995.

Jung, Joanne J. *Godly Conversation: Rediscovering the Puritan Practice of Conference.* Grand Rapids, MI: Reformation Heritage, 2011.
Kim, Robert. "The Forgotten American Missionaries of Pyongyang." *Atlas Obscura* (blog), April 25, 2017. https://www.atlasobscura.com/articles/american-pyongyang-missionaries-north-korea.
Knight, Walker. "Prelude to Spiritual Awakening." *Missions USA*, April 1982.
Krautheimer, Richard. *Early Christian and Byzantine Architecture.* 3rd ed. The Pelican History of Art. Harmondsworth, Eng./New York: Penguin, 1979.
Kreider, Alan. "Protest and Renewal: Reformers Before the Reformation." *Christian History* 9 (1984). https://christianhistoryinstitute.org/magazine/article/reformers-before-the-reformation/.
Lacy, Benjamin R. *Revivals in the Midst of the Years.* Richmond, VA: John Knox, 1943.
Latham, Jane H. "In Search of the True Church: An Examination of the Significance of Small Groups within Early Anabaptism and Pietism." M. A. thesis, Acadia University, 1992.
Latourette, Kenneth S. *A History of Christianity.* Vol. 1 and 2. New York, NY: Harper & Row, 1975.
Lewis, H. Elvit. "With Christ among the Miners." In *Glory Filled the Land: A Trilogy on the Welsh Revival (1904-05),* edited by Richard O. Roberts. Wheaton, IL: International Awakening, 1989.
Lindberg, Carter. *The European Reformations.* Cambridge: Blackwell, 1996.
Lockard, David. *The Unheard Billy Graham.* Waco, TX: Word, 1971.
Lucas, Henry. *The Renaissance and the Reformation.* 2nd. New York: Harper & Row, 1960.
Luther, Martin. "The German Mass and Order of Service." In *Luther's Works,* edited by Ulrich S. Leupold, Vol. 53. Philadelphia, PA: Fortress, 1965.
Lutton, Robert. *Lollardy and Orthodox Religion in Pre-Reformation England: Reconstructing Piety.* Suffolk, England: Boydell & Brewer, 2006.
Marsden, George M. *Jonathan Edwards: A Life.* New Haven, CT: Yale University Press, 2003.
Marty, Martin E. *The New Shape of American Religion.* Westport, CT: Greenwood, 1979.
Maxey, Al. "Raikes' Ragged Regiment: Reflecting on the Sunday School and Non-Sunday School Movements." *Reflections*, no. 184 (April 14, 2005). http://www.zianet.com/maxey/reflx184.htm.
McDow, Malcolm, and Alvin L. Reid. *Firefall: How God Has Shaped History Through Revivals.* Nashville: Broadman & Holman, 1997.
McGowan, Andrew B. *Ancient Christian Worship: Early Church Practices in Social, Historical, and Theological Perspective.* Grand Rapids: Baker Academic, 2014.
McGuire, Brian Patrick. *Friendship and Community.* London: Cornwell University Press, 2010.
McIlvaine, Charles P. *Bishop McIlvaine's Address to the Convention of the Diocese of Ohio on the Revival of Religion: Delivered in Trinity Church, Newark, June 3d, 1858, and Published by Special Request of the Convention.* Cincinatti: C. F. Bradley, 1858.
McLoughlin, William G., ed. *The American Evangelicals, 1800-1900: An Anthology.* Gloucester, MA: Harper & Row, 1968.
———. *Modern Revivalism: Charles Grandison Finney to Billy Graham.* New York: Ronald, 1959.
McLynn, Neil B. *Ambrose of Milan: Church and Court in a Christian Capital.* Berkeley: University of California Press, 1994.

McSheffrey, Shannon. *Lollards of Conventry, 1486-1522.* Cambridge: Cambridge University Press, 2003.
Memoir of the Life and Ministry of William Bramwell. London: Simpkin, Marshall & Co., 1848.
Miller, Perry. *The Life of the Mind in America.* New York: Brace & World, 1965.
Mitchell, Brian R. *International Historical Statistics: The Americas, 1750-2000.* Basingstoke: Palgrave Macmillan, 2003.
Noll, Mark A. *A History of Christianity in the United States and Canada.* Grand Rapids: Eerdmans, 1996.
———. *The Rise of Evangelicalism: The Age of Edwards, Whitefield, and the Wesleys.* Vol. 1. A History of Evangelicalism: People, Movements and Ideas in the English-Speaking World, Ed. David W. Bebbington and Mark Noll. Downers Grove: IVP Academic, 2003.
Orr, J. Edwin. *Campus Aflame: A History of Evangelical Awakenings in Collegiate Communities.* Wheaton, IL: International Awakening, 1994.
———. *The Eager Feet: Evangelical Awakenings, 1790-1830.* Chicago: Moody, 1975.
———. *The Event of the Century: The 1857-1858 Awakening.* Wheaton, IL: International Awakening, 1989.
———. *The Fervent Prayer: The Worldwide Impact of the Great Awakening of 1858.* Chicago: Moody, 1974.
———. *The Flaming Tongue.* Chicago: Moody, 1973.
———. *Good News in Bad Times.* Grand Rapids: Zondervan, 1953.
———. "Revival and Evangelism." *World Evangelization,* March 1985.
Osborn, Eric. *Tertullian, First Theologian of the West.* Cambridge: Cambridge University Press, 1997.
Osiek, Carolyn, Margaret Y. MacDonald, and Janet H. Tulloch. *A Woman's Place: House Churches In Earliest Christianity.* Minneapolis, MN: Augsburg Fortress, 2006.
Oxford English Dictionary. 2nd ed. 20 vols. Oxford: Oxford University Press, 1989. Continually updated at http://www.oed.com/.
Parham, Sarah E. *The Life of Charles Parham, Founder of the Apostolic Faith Movement.* New York: Garland, 1985.
Phillips, Thomas. *The Welsh Revival: Its Origin and Development.* Edinburgh: Banner of Truth, 1995.
Piper, John. *Desiring God: Meditations of a Christian Hedonist.* Sisters, OR: Multnomah, 2003.
Plass, Ewald M. *What Luther Says: An Anthology.* Vol. 3. St. Louis, MO: Concordia House, 1959.
Plueddemann, Jim, and Carol Plueddemann. *Pilgrims in Progress: Growing through Groups.* Wheaton, IL: Shaw, 1990.
Pollock, John C. *Moody: A Biographical Portrait.* New York: MacMillan, 1963.
Powers, B. H. *The Henrietta Mears Story.* Westwood, NJ: Fleming H. Revell, 1957.
Prime, Samuel I. *Prayer and Its Answer.* New York: Charles Scribner's Sons, 1882. <http://search.ebscohost.com/login.aspx?direct=true&db=H7H&bquery=(HJ+5XKH)&type=1&site=ehost-live>.
Prime, Samuel I., and Luther G. Bingham. *The Power of Prayer, Illustrated in the Wonderful Displays of Divine Grace at the Fulton Street, and Other Meetings in New York, Etc.* New York: Charles Scribner, 1859.

Rack, Henry D. *Reasonable Enthusiasts: John Wesley and the Rise of Methodism.* Philadelphia: Trinity, 1989.

Rasmussen, Cecilia. "Billy Graham's Star Was Born at His 1949 Revival in Los Angeles." *Los Angeles Times.* September 2, 2007. https://www.latimes.com/archives/la-xpm-2007-sep-02-me-then2-story.html.

Rawlyk, George A. *The Canada Fire: Radical Evangelicalism in British North America, 1775-1812.* Montreal: McGill-Queen's University Press, 1994.

Reid, Daniel G., ed. *Dictionary of Christianity in America.* Downers Grove, IL: InterVarsity, 1990.

Rice, Edwin W. *The Sunday School Movement, 1780-1917.* Philadelphia, PA: American Sunday School Union, 1917.

Robertson, Darrell M. *The Chicago Revival, 1876: Society and Revivalism in a Nineteenth-Century City.* London: Scarecrow, 1989.

Rudolph, Frederick. *The American College and University: A History.* New York: Alfred A. Knopf, 1965.

Schaff, Philip. *Fathers of the Third Century: Hippolytus, Cyprian, Caius, Novatian, Appendix.* Vol. 5. Ante-Nicene Fathers. New York: Christian Literature, 1885. http://www.ccel.org/ccel/schaff/anf05.

———, ed. *Latin Christianity: Its Founder, Tertullian.* Vol. 3. Ante-Nicene Fathers. New York: Christian Literature Publishing Co., 1885. http://www.ccel.org/ccel/schaff/anf03.

Scharpff, Paulus. *History of Evangelism.* Translated by Helga R. Henry. Grand Rapids: Eerdmans, 1966.

Scheitle, Christopher P. "From Religious Societies to Public Charities: A Parachurch History." In *In Beyond the Congregation: The World of Christian Nonprofits.* Oxford: Oxford University Press, 2010.

Schneider, Hans. *German Radical Pietism.* Lanham, MD: Scarecrow, 2007.

"Six Megathemes Emerge from Barna Group Research in 2010." *Barna Research Group*, December 13, 2010. https://www.barna.com/research/six-megathemes-emerge-from-barna-group-research-in-2010/.

Smith, Chuck, and Hugh Steven. *The Reproducers: New Life for Thousands.* Glendale, CA: Regal, 1972.

Smith, Frank. *The Life and Work of Sir James Kay Shuttleworth.* London: John Murray, 1923.

Smither, Edward L. *Augustine as Mentor: A Model for Preparing Spiritual Leaders.* Nashville, TN: B & H Academic, 2008.

———. *Mission in the Early Church: Themes and Reflection.* Eugene, OR: Cascade, 2014.

Spener, Philip Jakob. *Pia Desideria.* Philadelphia, PA: Fortress, 1964.

Spring, Gardiner. *Memoir of Samuel J. Mills.* New York: Saxton & Miles, 1842.

Stewart, James A. *Invasion of Wales by the Spirit through Evan Roberts.* Ft. Washington, PA: Christian Literature Crusade, 1970.

Strickland, Arthur B. *The Great American Revival.* Cincinatti: Standard, 1934.

Strobel, Kyle. *Formed for the Glory of God: Learning from the Spiritual Practices of Jonathan Edwards.* Downers Grove, IL: InterVarsity, 2013.

Swearingen, Chet, and Phyllis Swearingen. "1907-1910 Pyongyang Korea Revival." *Beautiful Feet* (blog), nd. https://romans1015.com/1907-pyongyang-revival/.

———. "1967-1972 The Jesus Movement." *Beautiful Feet* (blog). Accessed March 7, 2020. https://romans1015.com/jesus-movement/.

BIBLIOGRAPHY

"The 1904 Welsh Revival." Pisgah Chapel, Brynymor Rd, Loughor, Swansea SA4 6TD, UK. Accessed March 3, 2020. http://www.pisgahchapel.com/wp-content/uploads/2016/05/Flier-The1904WelshRevivalv4.pdf.

Thompson, Charles L. *Times of Refreshing: A History of American Revivals from 1740-1877, with Their Philosophy and Methods*. Hardpress, 2012.

Tiller, J. E. *Puritan, Pietist, Pentecostalist: Three Types of Evangelical Spirituality*. Bramcote, UK: Grove, 1982.

Tocqueville, Alexis de. *Democracy in America*. Translated by Harvey C. Mansfield and Delba Winthrop. Chicago: University of Chicago Press, 2002.

Tourn, Giorgio, Giorgio Bouchard, Roger Geymonat, Giorgio Spini, and Frank G. Gibson. *You Are My Witnesses: The Waldensians across 800 Years*. Torino, Italy: Claudiana, 1989.

Tourn, Giorgio, Camillo P. Merlino, and Charles W. Arbuthnot. *The Waldensians: The First 800 Years, 1174-1974*. Torino, Italy: Claudiana, 1980.

Towns, Elmer L. "Preface, The Bicentennial History of the Sunday School." In *The Holy Bible: Bicentennial Sunday School History, Analytical Study Edition*. Nashville: Regal, 1980.

Towns, Elmer L., and Douglas Porter. *The Ten Greatest Revivals Ever: From Pentecost to the Present*. Virginia Beach, VA: Academx, 2005.

Towns, Elmer L., and Vernon M. Whaley. *Worship through the Ages: How the Great Awakenings Shape Evangelical Worship*. Nashville: Broadman & Holman, 2012.

Vandenakker, John Paul. *Small Christian Communities and the Parish*. Kansas City, MO: Sheed and Ward, 1994.

Watson, David Lowes. *The Early Methodist Class Meeting*. Nashville: Discipleship Resources, 1987.

Waugh, Geoff. "20th Century Revival." *The Revival Library* (blog). Accessed March 7, 2020. http://revival-library.org/index.php/catalogues-menu/20th-century/20th-century-revival.

Weber, Erwin. "Luther the Swan." *The Lutheran Journal* 65, no. 2 (1996).

Weinlick, John R. *Count Zinzendorf*. New York: Abingdon Press, 1956.

Weisberger, Bernard A. *They Gathered at the River: The Story of the Great Revivalists and Their Impact on Religion in America*. Boston: Brown and Company, 1958.

Wesley, John. *The Works of John Wesley: Bicentennial Edition*. Edited by Richard P. Heitzenrater and Frank Baker. Oxford: Oxford University Press and Abingdon, 1975. http://www.ministrymatters.com.ezproxy.liberty.edu/library/#/ 000wjw-new/aaf6fab153518614c7e1b8bda45798bc/journal.html.

White, Charles E., ed. "Concerning Earnest Christians: A Newly Discovered Letter of Martin Luther." *Currents in Theology and Missions* 10, no. 5 (1983): 273–80.

Whitefield, George. *The Journals of George Whitefield*. Shropshire, Eng.: Quinta, 2009. http://quintapress.webmate.me/PDF_Books/Journals_first_edition_v2.pdf.

Whittaker, Colin C. *Great Revivals: God's Men and Their Message*. Basingstoke, UK: Marshalls, 1984.

Wiersbe, Warren, and Lloyd Perry. *The Wycliffe Handbook of Preaching and Preachers*. Chicago: Moody, 1984.

Wilken, Robert L. *The First Thousand Years: A Global History of Christianity*. New Haven, CT: Yale University Press, 2012.

Williams, Don. *Call to the Streets*. Minneapolis, MN: Augsburg, 1972.

Williams, George H., Frank F. Church, and Timothy F. George. *Continuity and Discontinuity in Church History: Essays Presented to George Huntston Williams on the Occasion of His 65th Birthday.* Boston, MA: Brill, 1979.

Wolffe, John. *The Expansion of Evangelicalism: The Age of Wilberforce, More, Chalmers and Finney.* Vol. 2. A History of Evangelicalism: People, Movements and Ideas in the English-Speaking World, Ed. David W. Bebbington and Mark Noll. Downers Grove, IL: IVP Academic, 2007.

Wuthnow, Robert. *Sharing the Journey: Support Groups and America's New Quest for Community.* New York, NY: Simon and Schuster, 1994.

Young, Doyle L. *New Life for Your Church.* Grand Rapids, MI: Baker Book House, 1989.

Zdero, Rad. *The Global House Church Movement.* Pasadena, CA: William Carey Library, 2004. *Time,* February 20, 1950.

www.ingramcontent.com/pod-product-compliance
Lightning Source LLC
Chambersburg PA
CBHW062044220426
43662CB00010B/1643